P9-AZX-413

COMPREHENSIVE
CITY PLANNING
INTRODUCTION
& EXPLANATION

BOOKS BY THE SAME AUTHOR
Federal Aids to Local Planning (Editor), 1941
Urban Planning and Public Opinion, 1942
Aerial Photography in Urban Planning and Research, 1948
The Corporate Planning Process, 1962
Selected References for Corporate Planning, 1966
Planning: Aspects and Applications, 1966
Comprehensive Urban Planning: A Selected Annotated Bibliography
   with Related Materials, 1970
City Planning and Aerial Information, 1971
Urban Air Traffic and City Planning: Case Study of Los Angeles
   County, 1973
Planning Urban Environment, 1974, Russian Edition, 1979
Urban Planning Theory (Editor), 1975
Comparative Urban Design, Rare Engravings, 1830–1843, 1978
Continuous City Planning: Integrating Municipal Management and
   City Planning, 1981
Comprehensive Planning, General Theory and Principles, 1983

COMPREHENSIVE CITY PLANNING
INTRODUCTION & EXPLANATION

MELVILLE C. BRANCH

Planners Press
AMERICAN PLANNING ASSOCIATION
Washington, D.C.; Chicago, Illinois

Copyright 1985 by the American Planning Association
1313 E. 60th St., Chicago, IL 60637
ISBN: 0-918286-41-7
Library of Congress Catalog Number: 85-70970
Printed in the United States of America
All rights reserved.

Branch, Melville Campbell, 1913–
   Comprehensive city planning.

   Bibliography
   Includes index.
   1. City planning—United States.   2. Land use,
Urban—United States.   3. Urban Policy—United
States.
   I. Title.
HT167.B66   1985   307.1′2′0973   85-70970
ISBN 0-918286-41-7

Book and cover design and unattributed illustrations by the author.
Word processing and typesetting by Graphic Typesetting Service, Los Angeles, California.
Printed by BookCrafters, Chelsea, Michigan.
Cover Photograph: Courtesy of MPSI Americas Inc.,
Indianapolis, Indiana, May 1983.

ACKNOWLEDGMENTS

Since this book addresses all of the most important considerations in comprehensive city planning, the author sought substantive review of some of the chapters. Each of the following
individuals reviewed a chapter concerning an area of his special
interest and expert knowledge.

Chapters 10 (Land Use Control) and 11 (Environment):
Donald W. Cunningham of Steven A. Cunningham & Associ-
ates, Land Use Planning & Zoning Consultants; and Lindell L.
Marsh, Adjunct Associate Professor of Law, and a partner in
the law firm Nossaman, Guthner, Knox & Elliott.

Chapter 12 (Redevelopment, Rehabilitation): William C. Baer,
Associate Professor of Urban and Regional Planning.

Chapter 13 (Urban Design): Tridib K. Banerjee, Associate
Professor of Urban and Regional Planning and Associate Dean.

Chapter 15 (Metropolitan Urban Planning): Frank Hotch-
kiss, Director of Comprehensive Planning, Southern California
Area Governments.

Chapter 16 (Professional Practice and Education): John D.
Gerletti and Gilbert Siegel, Professors of Public Administra-
tion; and Alan Kreditor, Associate Professor of Urban and
Regional Planning, and Dean.

Chapter 17 (Related Planning): Robert M. Carter, Professor
of Public Administration and Major General, United States Army
Reserve.

The confirmation and suggestions contributed by these
exceptionally competent acquaintances are greatly appreciated.

The professors in the group are all associated with either the School of Public Administration or the School of Urban and Regional Planning at the University of Southern California.

David Mars read an early draft of the manuscript, suggesting clarifications and improvements based on his broad knowledge as Professor of Public Administration and as Chairman of the City Planning Commission of Torrance, California.

My wife—Hilda S. Rollman-Branch, M.D.—was an early advocate of my writing this book and encouraged me during the period of its preparation. She was the first reader of the manuscript commenting on each chapter as it was written, and reviewed the entire text in its next to final form. Her constructive questions, comments, and suggestions contributed greatly to the quality of the book.

These various contributions are recognized and appreciated. They do not relieve the author of his sole responsibility for the finished product.

PREFACE

This book is intended to serve several needs. It can be used as a textbook or reference for senior level courses in civics or government at preparatory schools, upperclass college and university courses covering city planning, and by various undergraduates whose major or minor concentration includes city planning. It can satisfy the interest of both older and younger people who would like to know what city planning is all about without becoming involved in academic programs.

An introductory book is also needed for students entering graduate programs in urban and regional planning who have not acquired preliminary knowledge of city planning in their undergraduate study or work in an allied field. They need this preliminary understanding before they undertake the specialized courses leading to a professional degree.

This book can provide introductory knowledge of city planning as part of certain undergraduate and graduate courses in public administration, public policy, and public affairs. And there are courses in some business schools that cover management and planning in the public sector, and courses in land use and environmental law in law schools, that require introductory knowledge of city planning as the subject is treated in this book.

This explanatory volume will be useful to city planning commissioners when they are appointed to fill vacancies on the hundreds of city planning commissions in the United States, with five or more citizen members and an average length of service of several years. Because their knowledge of cities and city planning usually is limited, they must acquire this understanding by special study before or while serving on the commission. Certainly their decisions as newly-appointed city planning commissioners are more informed when they have completed a period of preparatory study. In some cities, short courses are organized to provide newly appointed city planning commissioners with sufficient knowledge to perform effectively with minimum delay. This book would be a suitable text for such courses, or for independent reading by new commissioners.

It would also provide introductory information for county and municipal officials who have been delegated to serve on councils of government (COGs) or other coordinative bodies engaged in metropolitan studies and planning. Some of these elected or appointed representatives have not had occasion to become familiar with city planning, which is not only politically and operationally critical in metropolitan studies but replicates the process of fully developed metropolitan planning in all essential respects.

In addition, there are professional people who have frequent business with city planning commissions and departments, and with city councils that receive planning recommendations and make legislative decisions. They include lawyers concerned with land use and environmental matters, engineers and architects working on proposed projects, land developers and others involved in real estate. Those establishing contact with municipal planning for the first time without prior knowledge of the city planning field and process would do well to read this book carefully.

Last but by no means least are concerned and interested

citizens, representatives of citizen associations, and owners of property affected by city planning actions. Certainly, the impact of these individuals or groups at city hall is enhanced if they are informed about the municipal activity they wish to influence. A single book is more likely to be read in preparation than an assortment of materials, some of which are likely to be more detailed than need be because they were written for professional practitioners rather than for introductory use.

The range of intended users includes individuals with very different educational backgrounds, related experience, and willingness to absorb needed knowledge. Some of them have thought about cities and city planning, most have not. These reader characteristics call for the simplest language and clearest statement. Professional jargon and academic elaboration are avoided in favor of essentials and readability. References are kept to a minimum and do not interrupt the text. An effort is made to formulate and present material so that it is interesting and stimulating for potential readers.

The subjects selected from the vast content of city planning for inclusion in this book are the most descriptive that can be covered within space limitations. Because the book is intended to be widely applicable, cities are not referred to by name. To do so would tend to associate the reference with a specific municipality rather than cities in general; but every reference is supported by a known example and every statement of fact is based on established knowledge or experience in real life. Besides portraying city planning as it exists and is developing in the United States, the contents of this book may prove useful to those concerned with communities in other parts of the world.

CONTENTS

ILLUSTRATIONS

COMPREHENSIVE
CITY PLANNING
INTRODUCTION
& EXPLANATION

The appointment of planning commissions is the most recent step in the development of the unit idea in city planning [overall planning for the city as a whole]. In theory, the function of this new agency is to correlate the official plans prepared in the various municipal departments, to pass upon unofficial plans or suggestions for improvement, and to make plans of its own in all cases where no existing agency has jurisdiction.

Flavel Shurtleff, *Carrying Out the City Plan*, The Practical Application of American Law in the Execution of City Plans, 1914.

Local planning should be given or must gain for itself a place in the structure of government, where it will be closer to the local legislative body, the chief executive and the administrative departments.

Report of the Urbanism Committee, National Resources Committee, *Our Cities, Their Role in the National Economy*, June 1937.

In the past, city planning has stressed design and engineering to the exclusion of administrative and social considerations. . . . The city planning department should be a great coordinating agency, intimately contacting every municipal department.

John M. Pfiffner, *Municipal Administration*, 1940.

CHAPTER 1
UNDERLYING ASSUMPTIONS

Urban and regional planning, municipal operating planning, management planning, and public administration planning should be treated as comparable activities.

T HE ADJECTIVE *comprehensive* signifies that this highest, most complex, and most difficult form of city planning encompasses conceptually and analytically the principal elements of the city that determine its current activities and future development. It is planning for the city as a whole, rather than for one or several of its constituent functions such as water supply and distribution, police and fire protection, vehicular and pedestrian traffic, or any one of the many particular activities of local government. Engineers and scientists call it system planning because it is broader and more inclusive than subsystem planning which integrates several municipal functions that are closely interrelated. For example: those that protect persons and property from the different dangers to which they are subjected, dispose of different kinds of liquid and solid waste, or supply the city with energy generated in different ways at separate locations.

Because normally no distinction is made between the terms *city* planning and *urban* planning, either in the literature of planning or in everyday use, they are considered synonymous in this book. Strictly speaking, however, city means a *municipality* legally established in the United States by a state government which designates its spatial jurisdiction and legal powers. "Cities are creatures of the state." In this book cities refer to any settlement of several thousand people or more. Urban refers to areas built up with structures and streets to a density of concentrated settlement requiring more extensive utility and other supportive services than are needed in rural areas.

Metropolitan areas around the world include a number of separate municipalities or districts, each legally, institutionally, culturally, or historically distinct. As cities have grown, extending farther and farther into the surrounding countryside, metropolitan urban areas have been built up that encompass many municipal jurisdictions or distinct districts with boundaries difficult or impossible to discern on the ground. Large metropolises may include 40 or more such communities, making it difficult to achieve the coordination necessary for comprehensive metropolitan planning.

There are basic requirements for the successful management and planning of all urban places. City planning is most similar in communities at comparable stages of development, whether they are primitive settlements or large cities incorporating the latest knowledge and technology. Individual characteristics and important differences between cities, discussed in the next chapter, are identified and taken into account since they shape the precise nature and form of city planning.

This book focuses on city planning in the United States, with emphasis on the California experience. It is the state most active and influential in the practice and procedural advancement of urban planning in the United States. In part this is because the people who have moved to California and made it the most populous state in the union are adventurous, less inhibited in their new home, willing to experiment and innovate. As a consequence, what happens in California often foreshadows what happens elsewhere in the nation. Total treatment of the diversity of city planning experience and practice among the full 50 states would require several lengthy volumes and would likely be more confusing than revealing of fundamental facts and considerations.

Because the concept and practice of city planning in the United States are undergoing fundamental change, more than the presently existing situation must be covered. The administrative, managerial, and physical planning roots of municipal planning are converging. The consequences of their merger should be considered part of the forthcoming substantive content of city planning.

Since earliest times, communities have required the municipal services that make possible these concentrations of people within relatively small areas on the ground. Potable water must be available at the site or imported. Food and supplies produced elsewhere must be brought in and distributed. Sufficient waste disposal and sanitation must be provided to keep sickness, disease, and potential plague within tolerable limits. Police and fire protection must allow the urban activity and intercommunication that make possible the urban concentrations that constitute cities.

Throughout the 7,000 or more years of urban history these essential conditions have been provided by officials designated by the ruling authority. They were the predecessors of the *city managers, public administrators,* and other local government officials who conduct the day-to-day operational affairs of municipalities throughout the world today. The activities of these officials are represented substantively and professionally by the educational fields of public administration, business management, medicine, engineering, law; the many specific programs concerned with public finance and taxation, health and safety, local legislation and regulation, environmental quality; and the almost limitless range of knowledge and activity involved in municipal operations, management, and planning.

The other historical root of city planning as it is practiced today in the United States and parts of Europe and Asia has had to do with the use of land within the municipality, primary transportation routes, and various large-scale projects. From earliest times, the use of land in cities has been restricted by rudimentary forms of zoning separating different classes of people or types of activity. Urban projects were the product of the desires and intervention of the highest authority: tribal chiefs in primitive settlements, legislative bodies in republican Athens and ancient Rome, emperors in imperial Rome and until the present century in imperial China, kings and lesser royalty in Renaissance France, or czars in Russia. Many of their personal projects—palaces with extensive gardens, boulevards and esplanades, temples and churches, parks, city squares, civic centers—took years to complete because of their size, grand design, and cost.

This second type of city planning was conducted by architects, landscape architects, and engineers carrying out the wishes of the ruling authority. They are the predecessors of those engaged in *urban and regional planning* today, many of whom received their advanced education in one of the colleges and universities giving graduate degrees in this field. Others are graduates in disciplines integrally involved in the broadening scope of city planning, such as engineering, one of the social sciences, geography, law. Some come from arts and letters. Most are members of national and international associations of practicing urban and regional planners.

In both of these historical roots of city planning economic and social concerns were unimportant. The populace was subservient to royal or ecclesiastical control. Religious beliefs supported unquestioned acceptance of higher authority. Personal armies not only ensured civil order but could be used to acquire additional wealth by conquering additional territory. Over the years, however, the municipal administrators representing one path of historical development incorporated in their operational planning those socioeconomic considerations that have to be taken into account in providing essential urban services.

Urban and regional planners, representing the second path of historical development, did not follow suit. Only recently have they become concerned with socioeconomic factors. In addition, the limited physical city planning they practice has remained distinct from the continuous operational planning of the regular municipal departments. Separate city planning commissions with part-time citizen members, supported by a planning staff or department, conduct urban and regional planning by recommending to the city council legislative actions concerned mainly with land use.

This separation of planning activities is not present to the same degree in cities abroad. And it will gradually disappear in the United States as it becomes increasingly clear that city planning cannot be effective as long as administrative-operational and land use-project planning are conducted separately. The artificial distinction between the two that has existed since the turn of the century is no longer feasible.

For these reasons urban and regional land use planning, municipal operational planning, management planning, and public administrative planning should be treated as comparable activities. They constitute in fact one combinational endeavor because longer range plans emerge from and affect day-to-day

operations, and an operating need or crisis may require immediate modification or complete revision of longer range plans,
policies, or objectives. This book may be the first treatment of
these different participants as parts of what is in fact a common
endeavor.

> . . . most people do not appreciate just how ill-equipped
> our government is to perform long-range planning. The
> most able officials are constantly involved in the meeting
> of day-to-day crises . . . investigations, budgetary prob-
> lems, and administrative detail, with little time to devote
> to the long-range problems. . . . (Kahn, 1962)

Nor is it widely recognized that legislators avoid longer range
planning because it necessarily involves commitments with
respect to the future that can operate to their disadvantage at
reelection time, when public attitudes and desires may have
changed. It is also a difficult and demanding responsibility. In
large part this is why comprehensive planning has not yet been
achieved at any of the three levels of government in the United
States.

However, certain developments are forcing cities to plan
more effectively if they are to continue to function successfully
and avoid a form of urbanwide managerial "gridlock." These
include rapid growth, higher urban densities, increasing operational complexity, technological advances requiring a high order
of functional planning, and worsening environmental pollution. Comprehensive planning in the future will include a city
planning center containing relevant information, closely integrated planning by all municipal agencies, reflecting continuous concern by legislators with city planning as one of their
primary responsibilities, and their active participation in its
successful effectuation.

Reference materials relevant to comprehensive city planning are associated with public administration, urban and
regional planning, business management, engineering, and most
of the technical and social sciences. Because of this diversity,
explanatory references are most useful for the decision makers
and staff directly responsible for city planning. It would be
impossible for them to read, comprehend, and apply in their
urban analysis corroborative material supporting the multitude

of facts and opinions involved in comprehensive planning. They must rely on others for most specialized knowledge. In keeping with the fundamental nature of the planning process as an inherent aspect of human activity operating continuously over time, useful references may date from any period of time.

The most valuable substantive material relates to those elements and aspects of city planning that are universal in nature rather than immediate and temporary concerns, although the latter may be all-important at times. It is these fundamental concerns and issues underlying transient developments that are of lasting value and continuing relevance as advancements are made.

There can be no doubt that the subject of cities is important. They are, of course, the dwelling and work places for larger and larger percentages of the world population, providing opportunities or hope for personal betterment which have attracted people from the countryside throughout the ages (Wilsher, 1975). Seventy-five percent of the world population may be living in urban communities within the next century. Even if rural migration to cities is reversed at some future time, the societal functions now performed by larger cities will be transferred to smaller but more numerous communities in the countryside (Herbers, 1983). Urban places have always been centers of intellectual, cultural, and commercial activity. Concentrations of people stimulate ideas in art, science, commerce, government, and every other human interest and endeavor. Spatial proximity and easy intercommunication promote creative energy.

Large cities are the most complex of human organisms. The concentration of people and their myriad activities means a multitude of structures, utilities, services, governmental and market mechanisms. Cities are also places where the inevitable problems of society are intensified and most apparent. The stresses and strains inherent in human activities are exacerbated and highlighted in urban environments. The absolute dependence on food, energy, and critical supplies produced elsewhere makes large cities the most sensitive, vulnerable, and volatile units of society—subject to sudden and extensive disruption.

For these reasons, cities could not exist without the planning required for their operational components to function successfully. But municipal management must do much more if it is not only to conduct operations most effectively, but avoid or ameliorate forthcoming problems, meet anticipated needs, and attain longer range objectives. The development and application of this comprehensive managerial capability will represent a significant achievement in itself, and both confirm and exemplify what can and should be accomplished in planning at the state and federal levels of government. Most such advances occur first at the local level, where needs are most immediately felt, problems are most directly apparent, and the complex of components and considerations to be taken into account is most clearly conceptualized. Cities are the best seedbeds for advances in the art, science, and practice of comprehensive planning.

CITATIONS

[1] Herbers, John, "Major Cities Ringed by Suburbs Yielding To Sprawl of Small Metropolitan Areas," *The New York Times*, 8 July 1983, p. 9. [2] Kahn, Herman, *Thinking About the Unthinkable* (Horizon), 1962, p. 32. [3] Wilsher, Peter, "Everyone, Everywhere, Is Moving To the Cities," *The New York Times*, 22 June 1975, p. IX, 3.

SELECTED REFERENCES

[1] Branch, Melville C., *Comprehensive Planning, General Theory and Principles*, Pacific Palisades, CA (Palisades Publishers), 1983, 203 pp. [2] —————————————— , *Continuous City Planning, Integrating Municipal Management and City Planning*, New York (Wiley), 1981, 181 pp. [3] Caiden, Gerald E., *Public Administration*, Pacific Palisades, CA (Palisades Publishers), Second Edition, 1982, 321 pp. [4] George, Claude S. *History of Management Thought*, Englewood Cliffs, NJ (Prentice-Hall), Second Edition, 1972, 223 pp. [5] Hamilton, John J. *Government by Commission, or the Dethronement of the City Boss*, New York (Funk & Wagnalls), 1911, 285 pp. [6] Krueckeberg, Donald A. (Editor), *Introduction to Planning History in the United States*, New Brunswick, NJ (Rutgers University), 1983, 302 pp. [7] Lepawsky, Albert, *Administration, The Art and Science of Organization and Management*, New York (Knopf), 1955, 669 pp. [8] Pfiffner, John M. and Frank P. Sherwood, *Administrative Organization*, Englewood Cliffs, NJ (Prentice-Hall), 1960, 481 pp.

Some 2,500 years ago when Greeks were busy fighting Persians at places like Thermopylae and Marathon, Zapotec Indians across the Atlantic began building a great city, possibly the first in the New World. The job called for reshaping Monte Albán, a 1,500-foot hill overlooking the Valley of Oaxaca in central Mexico. Cutting into the hillsides, workers constructed hundreds of terraces, stepped platforms with retaining walls designed mainly for plain and fancy residences. For the seats of the mighty, the palaces and temples and major administrative centers, they leveled the entire hilltop, creating the main plaza on a 55-acre super-terrace perhaps eight times bigger than St. Peter's Square at the Vatican.

Monte Albán endured for more than a millennium. It housed 20,000 to 30,000 persons at its height, and lost its position as a regional capital some seven to eight centuries before the arrival of invaders from imperial Spain.

John E. Pfeiffer, "The mysterious rise and decline of Monte Albán," *Smithsonian*, February, 1980.

CHAPTER 2
CITIES IN HISTORY

A look back in history confirms the two roots of comprehensive city planning. It also reveals how often history repeats itself, achieving a regulatory advance that is often discarded or forgotten, to be replaced years or centuries later by the same type of restriction.

HUMAN SETTLEMENTS have existed for many thousands of years to provide the greater security of numbers, various forms of group support, and familial relationships that perpetuate the species. In earliest times they were temporary places to live, occupied as long as the surrounding countryside provided water and food. As developments in agricultural production and animal husbandry allowed sedentary life to replace nomadic wandering, permanent communities were established. These increased in number and size with the development of selective agricultural cultivation, a written language, and the specialization of labor and leadership that permitted expanded commercial activity, handicrafts, and fabrication.

Physical-Spatial Design

Even the most primitive settlements displayed forethought in their physical-spatial design, selection of the site, determination of the general layout of the settlement, physical-spatial design, and precise arrangement of structures and open spaces. Sufficient space was provided between the thatched huts not only for people to move about, but also to reduce the likelihood of a cooking fire destroying one flammable hut, spreading quickly to its neighbor, and progressively burning down the entire settlement. The dwelling of the tribal chief, with open space adjacent for communal gatherings, was centrally located so that it was equally accessible to those living in the settlement and most secure from outside attackers. Water supply was within the protective palisade or close by. (Figure 1,a) *primitive settlements* a *Ual-Ual, Abyssinia (Ethiopia), twentieth century.* [A] tribal chief's house, [B] council chamber, [C] dwellings, [D] protective palisade, [E] defensive earthwork embankment, [F] water wells, [G] settlement entrance.

b *Priene, Ionia (Asia Minor) fourth century B.C.* [A] Agora (marketplace), [B] Temple of Pallas Athene, [C] theater, [D] gymnasium, [E] stadium, [F] defensive city wall.

c *Turin, Italy, 1833.* Portion of map-plan showing layout of original Roman city of 72 square city blocks, designated by the surrounding dashed lines.

d *Monpazier, France, founded 1284.* [A] central city square with market hall, [B] cathedral and square, [C] defensive city wall, [D] alley, [E] gardens in back of row houses, [F] city gate.

e *Nördlingen, Germany, ninth century.* [A] central plaza and cathedral, [B] protective moat, [C] defensive city wall, [D] circumferential street where earlier circular city wall was located, [E] plaza and church, [F] original pattern of town houses with garden space inside city block.

f *Washington, D.C.* Major Pierre L'Enfant's plan for Washington in 1791, approved by George Washington and Thomas Jefferson. [A] western end of mall shown in black tone, [B] termination and indicated extension of Renaissance design diagonal avenue, [C] Renaissance design "rond point" or traffic circle.

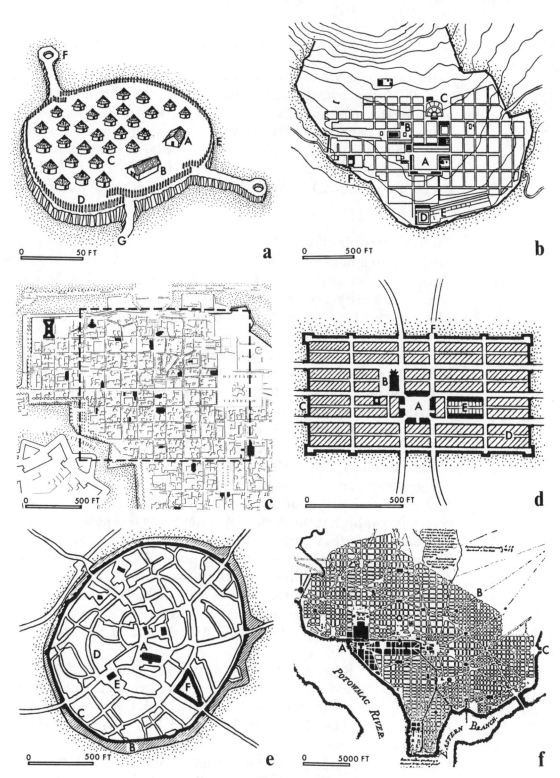

Figure 1
Views of Cities in the Past

11

> [In Lepenski Vir on the Danube River in Yugoslavia] . . .
> 5,000 or more years before the Greeks . . . all the houses
> are neatly arranged in a fan-shaped pattern opening out
> from the riverbank. There was always an empty space
> . . . "market place" . . . in front of the bigger houses. And
> between all the houses narrow alleys run in straight lines
> either to this marketplace or to the river's edge. (Wernick,
> 1975)

Rudimentary planning—the placement of structures and spaces
for the movement of people and vehicles—is found in cities
throughout history. Without it, they could not function. When
ruling authority so desired, complete street systems were
planned and large projects were designed and constructed.

ancient   According to Greek travelers to the Orient, as early as
cities   3000 B.C. cities in India were divided into square blocks with
broad streets oriented to the four cardinal directions. At
approximately the same time in ancient Egypt, new towns for
workers building the pyramids were laid out in a checkerboard
pattern within protective walls. Over 2,000 years later beginning in the sixth century B.C., the Hellenistic colonies founded
around the rim of the eastern Mediterranean were also arranged
in a gridiron pattern of small rectangular city blocks of the same
size, enclosed within an irregular city wall or protected by an
acropolis on high ground nearby. There was a central agora or
marketplace with a surrounding colonnade and small shops.
Temples and theaters were usually located beside small city
squares. Athletic facilities including a stadium occupied considerable space toward the edge of town. The planning underlying such deliberate arrangements is apparent in archaeological reconstructions of Priene in Asia Minor or Selinonte in
Sicily. (Figure 1,b)

When the Roman legion encamped for a single night or a
prolonged period of time, its components were arranged in a
gridiron pattern. They were always placed in the same relative
position, protected by an enclosing ditch, palisade, or wall.
Permanent Roman settlements throughout the empire were
laid out in the same gridiron pattern with a central marketplace. Reflecting Pierre Lavedan's "la loi de la persistance du
plan," these patterns of early settlements can still be clearly

distinguished in aerial photographs of the city centers of Vienna, Bordeaux, Turin, and other European cities. (Figure 1,c)

The checkerboard was also characteristic of the new towns *medieval* called *bastides* founded during medieval times in southern France *towns* to protect the borders of principalities against encroachment or invasion by neighboring states. They were populated by retired soldiers and other citizens attracted by the greater political freedom granted to the inhabitants of these new towns, which were founded and finished in a few years.

Bastides were protected by city walls forming a rectangle. Principal streets connected the city gates, converging at the marketplace or a public square at the center of the city. Rectangular city blocks, bisected by narrow alleys, were divided into lots of the same size. This made it easier for founding fathers to treat all settlers equally, avoiding the dissension that often results when properties of different size, orientation, or other features must be allocated among different individuals. Bastides such as Monpazier, founded in southern France in 1284, were the epitome of geometric planning. (Figure 1,d) The outer walls of bastides were not always rectangles; Sauveterre de Guienne was pear-shaped to fit the topography of the site.

The physical arrangements of primary streets in older, long-established medieval cities were very different from those of the bastides. They were radial-concentric rather than rectangular for two reasons. First, pathways to the surrounding countryside naturally radiated out in four or more directions from the original settlements; as the towns grew, these early paths became permanent radial routes. Second, the radial-concentric pattern fitted the circular outer defenses characteristic of all medieval cities except the rectangular bastides. When young communities needed city walls to protect them against attack, they could enclose a given area with a circular wall shorter in length than the wall required to enclose a rectangular area of the same size. Radial streets connected the city gates with the central square. Circumferential streets extended just inside and along the city walls to permit the rapid deployment of defending troops to the point most threatened by attackers. When the wall and its adjacent circumferential route were relocated farther out to provide space for population growth, the inner circular route was preserved after the old wall was demolished so that its construction materials could be used in building the new defenses. The medieval cities of Nördlingen in Germany, Carcassonne in France, and the street pattern of the old central city of Milan, Italy, are good examples. (Figure 1,e)

Renaissance   During the European Renaissance large formal gardens, designed as part of the palaces of royal and religious rulers, featured long straight pathways radiating from different focal points. This garden design was applied much later to cities. New patterns of primary circulation were created by cutting straight streets and broad landscaped boulevards through the dense areas with narrow crooked streets built up during the Middle Ages, when people crowded within the city walls for protection. More than one-third of the houses in Paris were wholly or partially demolished to make way for construction of new major thoroughfares radiating from city squares created as small parks and traffic circles. The historical central area of Paris is the best known example of Renaissance urban design: with its urbanwide system of primary circulation created by Baron Haussmann for Napoleon III in 1853; the Place d'Etoile with 12 avenues radiating outward like the spokes of a wheel; and the Tuileries Gardens extending westward from the palace which is now the Louvre. This type of physical planning can be seen in sections of many European cities—Rome, Berlin, Bordeaux, St. Petersburg (Leningrad)—and in Washington, D.C. (Figure 1,f)

Most of the thousands of cities in history do not display such clear-cut indications of the physical planning that always exists in some form. Without the instigation of ruling authority through supervising architects, landscape architects, and engineers, urban development followed the day-to-day decisions of local leaders responding to particular problems, requests, or opportunities. This usually resulted in the gradual estab-lishment of either the checkerboard or radial-concentric pat-

basic   tern, the two most basic and widely tested arrangements for
patterns   the movement of people and vehicles and the subdivision of land. In the United States, the cartographic subdivision of the country into mile squares or "sections" favored adoption of the checkerboard pattern for most early American communities unless the site dictated otherwise.

In the largest ancient cities, physical planning was limited usually to the design and construction of large projects: temples, theaters, athletic facilities, and city squares in ancient Athens, aqueducts, public baths, theaters, temples, palaces, and stadia in imperial Rome. These cities became so large, dynamic, and important politically and economically that even absolute rulers could not or chose not to try to impose an overall pattern of physical planning throughout the entire city. It was not until the mid-nineteenth century that Napoleon III achieved this in part with the pattern of boulevards crisscrossing Paris.

Compared with urban places today, cities prior to the nineteenth century were small both in population and size. Even Rome, the largest ancient city never exceeded its population of 650,000 reached in 100 A.D., reduced to 17,000 people in 1377 after well over a thousand years of prolonged decline under a succession of emperors, barbarian rulers, and popes. Its area in the nineteenth century was still only about five square miles. Except for a few such primate cities, historical communities rarely reached 25,000 inhabitants until the explosive urbanization that began in the eighteenth century. But the problems of much smaller historical communities were as critical for them, with their level of knowledge and technology, as present day urban difficulties are for much larger cities today. *size*

After the Industrial Revolution began in England in the late eighteenth century, formal spatial planning of the type attained during the Renaissance is no longer found. Physical planning is limited to what enables the city to function according to its new socioeconomic purpose and condition brought about by technological developments. Industrial manufacturing was introduced. The scope and intensity of commercial activity increased. There were dramatic increases in the urban population as people migrated from the countryside to cities seeking work. Cities spread out over much larger areas. And regal or other central authority gave way to numerous entrepreneurial interests. *Industrial Revolution*

Coincident with the Middle Ages and Renaissance in Europe, many major cities in China were laid out in rectangular form with sections of the cities designated for different classes of people, and special districts for leading families within separate *Asia* sets of walls inside the walled city. In capital cities, the imperial family lived in a fortress-like walled palace comparable to the separately fortified citadels within many medieval cities in Europe which housed the ruling authority. Early Japanese cities followed Chinese precedents in their rectangular form and arrangement. Although technologically less advanced, historical physical planning in Asia was generally comparable to European counterparts built several centuries earlier. Physical planning in the East is not treated at greater length in this brief historical review because the roots of city planning in the United States lie in Western Europe rather than in Asia.

Administrative Laws and Regulations

The placement of huts referred to in the previous section—providing space for circulation and limited fire protection within the primitive community—was a first step in a long history of administrative regulations relating to physical planning.

streets   Encroachment has always been a problem. As early as 350 B.C., Plato speaks of the "astynomi": Athenian officials charged with preventing shopkeepers and homeowners from building balconies or otherwise extending their properties into the adjoining street. Two centuries later the Code of Pergamon, the Hellenistic colony in Asia Minor dating from 300 B.C., added another provision. Any structure designated by the astynomi as obstructing a public way or threatening to collapse into the street had to be torn down. The damages paid by the transgressors and collected in the municipal treasury were used by the astynomi to pay for sweeping and cleaning the streets. In thirteenth century Paris, authorization by an "overseer of streets" was required before a shop window, flight of steps, seats, or sheds could be built in the street right-of-way. A municipal regulation in Amiens, France, imposed at the end of the fifteenth century, protected streets from overhead encroachment by limiting the overhang of abutting structures to one foot for the first floor and another one-half foot for additional floors. This historical progression of rules and regulations has culminated today in the building setback lines in municipal zoning codes in the United States, enforced under the police powers granted the city by the state.

Besides protecting streets from encroachment by abutting buildings, traffic within the streets has also been of regulatory concern throughout history:

One of Julius Caesar's first acts on seizing power was to ban wheeled traffic from the center of Rome during the day, [creating] such a noise at night . . . that the racket tormented sleep. . . . Claudius extended Caesar's prohibitions to the municipalities of Italy; and Marcus Aurelius, still later, applied it without regard to their municipal status to every town in the Empire; while, to complete the picture, Hadrian (A.D. 117-138) limited the number of teams and loads of carts permitted to enter the city—cutting down even the night-time traffic at its source. In a century and a half, traffic congestion had gone from bad to worse. (Mumford, 1961, Harcourt, Brace & World)

traffic

Traffic was so congested in London in the seventeenth century that for a while vehicles were licensed and the width of wheels on carts and drays and the number of horses pulling them were limited, anticipating today's restrictions on the size and weight of trucks using certain streets, and relating horsepower to license fees.

Regulations anticipating modern building codes were imposed some 5,000 years ago in India. The width of footpaths next to a house were to be one-third the width of the house, and all houses were to face on the royal road with narrow lanes at their back. The Code of Pergamon in the third century B.C., besides protecting streets from encroachment, included provisions for the protection of private buildings. For example, owners were required to repair their buildings when needed and prevent dampness from being transmitted between adjacent buildings. If the owners did not comply, municipal magistrates were to perform the work and recover the costs. In Rome during the first century B.C. when space was limited, public laws forbade walls of houses abutting a public street to be more than one and one-half feet thick. Fireproof party walls and roof were required in Lübeck, Germany, in 1276. In 1521, Amsterdam's "building code" required "fireproof" construction with brick and tile instead of wood and thatch, and a short

buildings

time later a 56 percent maximum coverage of sites by buildings and a minimum distance of 160 feet (48.8 meters) between buildings to provide light, air, and space for gardens. In England it was more than a century and a half later, after the Great Fire in London of 1666 destroyed 13,200 houses and many public buildings, that King Charles I issued a proclamation calling for the exteriors of buildings to be constructed of fire-resistant materials. And several catastrophic fires in Copenhagen led to the Building Act of 1856 requiring two staircases as fire escapes in every apartment building.

public
health
Public health codes also have their historical precedents. In ancient Athens, dustmen were required to dispose of waste more than 10 stades (approximately 1,900 meters or 2,060 yards) beyond the city walls, and there was a fine for citizens soiling the streets. It was not until some 1,500 years later that the English Parliament for the first time passed legislation to eliminate dumping of house and workshop waste in city streets. Ternel in Aragon, France, passed a statute in 1176 regulating the use and maintenance of public baths, something one would have expected almost a thousand years earlier in ancient Rome with its public baths of a size and magnificence achieved neither before nor since. But "Rome for all its engineering skill and wealth, failed miserably in the rudiments of municipal hygiene" (Mumford, 1961, Harcourt, Brace & World). In Venice, a permanent health magistry was established in 1485, and in 1556 inspection and enforcement procedures were enacted which for many years served as a model for the rest of Europe. Regulations in Amsterdam in the middle of the sixteenth century dealt with health within the home by requiring a sink with drain and a privy for each plot of land. By the same century:

> In well managed towns that had made provisions for street cleaning, there was also a ban on keeping pigs in any part of town. But in the early days the pig was an active member of the Board of Health. (Mumford, 1961, Penguin)
> An early form of zoning is referred to in one of the hundred Vedic treatises dating before 1000 B.C.
> In Ancient India folkplanning set up an interrelation between the site, the breadth of a street . . . and the rank of the residents of that quarter. The rule worked out in

such a way that the high class people were given premises alongside thoroughfares, while the low class people were relegated to comparatively narrow roads. . . . (Adams, 1935)

The first use of the word "zoning" may have appeared in 593 B.C. in the prophecies of Ezekiel, in which he describes the desirable assignment of uses or zoning of land in Palestine for the city of Jerusalem: one part a sanctuary for the temple, another for the houses and suburbs, and the remainder for the prince. Efforts to control the use of land through zoning have a long history. *use zoning*

One of the oldest and most frequent applications of land use control has been the exclusion of "noxious" or "nuisance" activities from urban areas where they would be incompatible. During the third century B.C., the Code of Pergamon expressly forbade the location and operation of brickfields within the city. Zoning was employed by the Romans to keep industries out of city centers. Venice in 1104 set aside the Arsenal section of the city for industry, the first large area zoned specifically for industry which did not allow the mixed land uses characteristic of the medieval city. And by decree in 1291, the supreme council of Venice removed the glass furnaces at Castello to Murano to free the city from industries considered a nuisance or unhealthy. In the United States, Massachusetts in 1628 passed a law—applying to Boston, Salem, Charlestown, and any other market town in the province—that prohibited certain noxious and nuisance industries from conducting business in any district not specifically designated for such use. And in 1710, the Court or General Sessions was empowered to suppress such industries if they were found to have "become a nuisance because of offensive and ill stenches proceeding from the same, or otherwise hurtful to the neighborhood." This is possibly the first example of "use" zoning in America.

The height of buildings has been regulated since ancient times. Augustus, the first Roman emperor, limited the height of buildings in the capital city to 70 feet (21.3 meters); Nero reduced this limit to 60 feet (18.3 meters); and Trajan established a maximum height of twice the width of the adjoining street. The visual attractiveness of the historical central area of Paris is enhanced by the uniform building height limit set by *height regulation*

Henry IV in the seventeenth century. In the next century, the Dublin Corporation in Ireland, the largest landlord in the city, added an element of what today is called aesthetic zoning: requiring that housing on its leased land be built in a uniform manner, at least three stories high, and every house of equal height. This architectural consistency contributes to the particular aesthetic quality of Renaissance and Georgian design. In Moscow, after three-quarters of the houses were burned by Napoleon in 1812, a commission appointed by the government to supervise reconstruction restricted the architectural elements that could be employed in rebuilding. But enough combinations of elements were allowed to provide both variety and unity in the design of urban dwellings.

There are historical precedents for other aspects of modern zoning practice. Assessments of homeowners for street improvements, reservation of sites for churches and market-places (commercial use), and the power of eminent domain existed in Amsterdam in the sixteenth century. In the same century, England's Queen Elizabeth sought to impose growth control in her famous proclamation, which

> doth charge and strictly command all manner of persons, of what quality soever they be, to desist and forebear from any new buildings of any new house or tenement within three miles of any gate of the City of London.

A law in 1588 imposed "density" zoning by requiring that no cottage be built on less than four acres of ground (except cottages for paupers, built on waste land at roadside).

A look back confirms the historical roots of comprehensive city planning in administrative and physical planning. It also reveals how often history repeats itself, achieving a regulatory advance that is often discarded or forgotten, to be replaced years or centuries later by the same type of restriction. History also confirms the oft-quoted observation of Supreme Court Justice Oliver Wendell Holmes: "The life of the law has not been logic, it has been experience."

CITATIONS
[1] Adams, Thomas, *Outline of Town and City Planning*, New York (Russell Sage), 1935, p. 43. [2] Mumford, Lewis, *The City in History*, New York (Har-

court, Brace & World), 1961, pp. 218, 216. [3] _____, *The City in History*, New York (Penguin), 1961, p. 337. [4] Wernick, Robert, "Danubian minicivilization bloomed before ancient Egypt and China," *Smithsonian*, Vol. 1, No. 12, March 1975, p. 38.

SELECTED REFERENCES

[1] Haverfield, Francis J., *Ancient Town Planning*, Oxford, UK (Oxford University), 1913, 152 pp. [2] Hughes, Thomas H. and E.A.G. Lamborn, *Towns and Town Planning, Ancient and Modern*, Oxford, UK (Oxford University Press), 1923, 156 pp. [3] Mumford, Lewis, *Culture of Cities*, New York (Harcourt, Brace), 1938, 586 pp. [4] Pirenne, Henri, *Medieval Cities*, Their Origins and the Revival of Trade, Garden City, NY (Doubleday), 1956, 185 pp. [5] Reiner, Thomas A., *The Place of the Ideal Community in Urban Planning*, Philadelphia, PA (University of Pennsylvania), 1963, 194 pp., [6] Spreiregen, Paul D., *Urban Design: The Architecture of Towns and Cities*, New York (McGraw-Hill), 1965, pp. 1-48. [7] Wycherly, R.E., *How the Greeks Built Cities*, Garden City, NY (Doubleday), 1969, 251 pp.

The urbanizing trend which has produced vast settlements of human beings and reduced the agricultural population to a shadow of its former self shows no sign of abating. Cities continue to break out of their old bounds and invade the "open country" in their quest for *lebensraum*. Ring upon ring of suburbs continue to be added to what were once single and relatively compact communities. Census figures on population, density, and territorial area . . . present a picture of massive change and astonishing growth.

John C. Bollens and Henry J. Schmandt, *The Metropolis*, 1965.

CHAPTER 3
URBAN GROWTH AND ITS CONSEQUENCES

Urbanized societies, in which a majority of people live crowded together in towns and cities, represent a new and fundamental step in man's social evolution.

UNTIL ABOUT the tenth century *world population growth* was slow and gradual because of the extreme rigors of simply surviving. The more rapid increase that began thereafter was possible because of advances in agricultural practices and the development of mechanical power such as the water wheel. The Black Death, which decimated one-fourth of Europe's 25 million people in the fourteenth century, interrupted but did not stop the increase. The general pattern of cumulative growth is indicated by the following estimate for 1845, approximate figures for 1929, 1960, and 1980, and a projection for the year 2000. Even approximate data are not available for world population prior to the nineteenth century.

population growth

	Population (Billions)	Average Annual Increase (%)
1845	1.0	—
1929	1.9	1.1
1960	3.1	3.0
1980	4.4	2.1
2000	6.2	2.0

The national problems associated with this growth are well known: feeding, housing, educating, and providing needed services for more people; crowding and congestion; increased environmental pollution and societal stress; depletion of petroleum, timber, and water resources; and probable reduction in the average standard of living in the future.

urbanization   *Urbanization* was a corollary development. Thousands of years elapsed between the appearance of smaller cities and the emergence of urban societies. Until the eve of the Industrial Revolution Europe was overwhelmingly agrarian, although it was also the most urbanized region in the world with some 2,500 towns founded between the fourteenth and eighteenth centuries by the German colonization movement alone. Only 1.6 percent of Europe's estimated population lived in cities of more than 100,000 people in 1600, 1.7 percent in 1700, and 2.2 percent in 1800. However, in England where the Industrial Revolution began, nearly one-tenth of the population lived in cities over 100,000 in 1801; this proportion doubled in the next 40 years, and doubled again in the following 60.

The urban explosion was underway, at first largely because of the migration of people from rural areas to cities seeking work in new factories. This urbanization occurred in almost direct proportion to industrialization (Mumford, 1938). By 1950 all industrial nations were highly urbanized.

The typical medieval town ranged in size from several thousand people to 40,000, the size of London in the fourteenth century.

> After the sixteenth century. . . . About a dozen towns quickly reached a size not attained in the Middle Ages even by a bare handful: in a little while London had 250,000 inhabitants, Naples 240,000, Milan over 200,000, Palermo and Rome, 100,000, Lisbon, a port of a great monarch, over 100,000; similarly Seville, Antwerp, and Amsterdam; while Paris in 1594 had 180,000. (Mumford, 1961)

By the middle of the 1850s, London reached a population of two million, Naples increased to 345,000, Rome to 164,000, Lisbon to 292,000, Amsterdam to 207,000, and Paris to just over one million. During the next 100 years, cities with more than 100,000 population increased 600 percent as a group, from slightly more than 50 million people to about 300 million, while the total world population increased by only 67 percent from approximately 1.5 billion to 2.5 billion. If the rate of increase that occurred between 1950 and 1960 were to continue, more than one-half of the people on the globe would be living in cities of more than 100,000 in 1990. Most of the forthcoming increase in the total world population over the next several decades will take place in the developing countries, which will find that the problems this creates will be most difficult to resolve economically, socially, and politically.

The greatest urbanization—as well as the greatest growth in total world population—is occurring in developing countries. According to a United Nations forecast, nine out to ten of the largest urban areas in the year 2000 will be in Asia, South America, and Latin America (Figure 2). A disproportionately large number of cities smaller than these largest agglomerations, but with more than a million population, will also be found in developing countries.

Increases in *urban density*—population per unit of area— *urban* accompany urban growth and city size. The highest density in *density* the United States is in the Upper East Side of Manhattan in New York City, with 130,000 persons per square mile in 1984. In the same year, Cairo's densest neighborhood housed 250,000, and an apartment area in Hong Kong east of the Kai Tak airport 350,000. There are sections in the Kowloon district of Hong Kong, less than a mile square, that reach an equivalent density of 430,000 persons per square mile. In the area north of Bom-

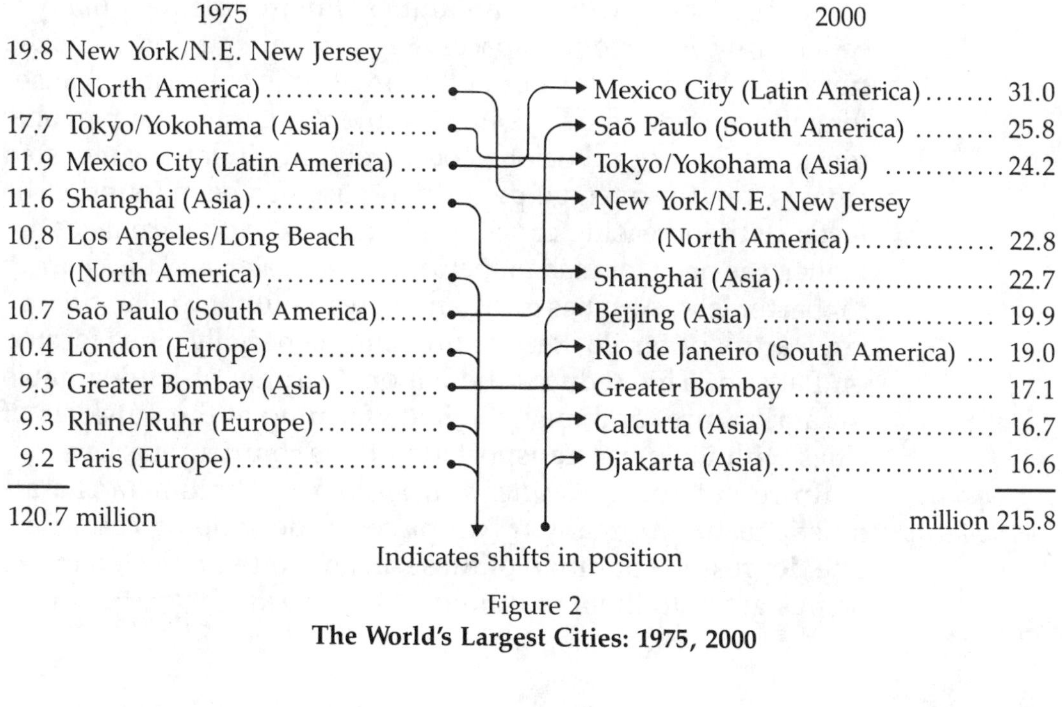

	1975	2000	
19.8	New York/N.E. New Jersey (North America)	Mexico City (Latin America)	31.0
17.7	Tokyo/Yokohama (Asia)	Saõ Paulo (South America)	25.8
11.9	Mexico City (Latin America)	Tokyo/Yokohama (Asia)	24.2
11.6	Shanghai (Asia)	New York/N.E. New Jersey (North America)	22.8
10.8	Los Angeles/Long Beach (North America)	Shanghai (Asia)	22.7
10.7	Saõ Paulo (South America)	Beijing (Asia)	19.9
10.4	London (Europe)	Rio de Janeiro (South America)	19.0
9.3	Greater Bombay (Asia)	Greater Bombay	17.1
9.3	Rhine/Ruhr (Europe)	Calcutta (Asia)	16.7
9.2	Paris (Europe)	Djakarta (Asia)	16.6
120.7 million		million	215.8

Indicates shifts in position

Figure 2
The World's Largest Cities: 1975, 2000

bay's commercial district, census takers measured 453,000 people per square mile in 1984 (708 persons per acre, 287 per hectare). (Patera, 1984)

"Urbanized societies, in which a majority of people live crowded together in towns and cities, represent a new and fundamental step in man's social evolution" (Davis, 1965). The expanding size and higher densities of cities create or intensify a whole set of urban problems. Day-to-day municipal management is more complicated, with most of the effort devoted to catching up with the provision of essential city services for a rapidly increasing population. Some of these, such as water supply and waste disposal, become progressively more difficult with increasing city size. The larger the city, the more people are affected immediately when these services are curtailed or fail completely; the effects are particularly disruptive in dense, often overcrowded, and usually low-income areas. Crime rates on the average are higher in the larger cities. And the gap between the living standards of the rich and the poor is likely to be more conspicuous and involve the perceptions and reactions of more people as cities increase in size.

Great concentrations of people and structures are quantitatively more vulnerable to natural catastrophes and civil disturbances than smaller communities. Environmental quality is reduced by fewer open spaces, higher ambient and localized noise levels, air and water pollution. Traffic congestion causes longer waiting and delays in movement, aggravating personal tensions. So far gridlock has occurred only in large congested cities. Even the average pedestrian pace has been found to be faster with increasing city size. Living costs and local taxes are higher, the need for cash money or credit greater, and the chances for barter less. As cities grow and spread out they often occupy large areas of fertile agricultural land, especially cities located on flatland. This reduces the national supply of land suitable for agriculture, and may eliminate farming at the outskirts of cities with its lower transportation costs to urban markets.

squatter settlements   In recent years, *squatter settlements* have become a characteristic feature of many urban places in developing countries. The depressed condition of these areas is often reflected in the names given to them in different countries.

bandas de miseria (Argentina)	gecekondu (Turkey)
barranca (Chile)	jhuggi jhompri (India)
barrios, pueblos jovenes (Mexico)	pan-ja-chor (Korea)
bidonvilles (France, Algeria)	kampongs (Malaysia)
favelas (Portugal, Brazil)	ranchos barriada (Peru)

shanty towns, squatter settlements (United States)

No one knows how many people live in these distressed settlements, but it has been estimated that it is more than one-
fourth of the population in South America. Besides the economic and social problems represented by the very existence
of squatter settlements, the usual randomness of their layout
presents a persistent problem with respect to the future street
pattern of the city, as irregular lot lines become fixed on the
ground and these property boundaries are legalized eventually.

Rapid urbanization can also create regional and national
problems, particularly in developing countries. For example,
to the extent that the migration of people from rural areas to
cities reduces the capacity of a nation to feed itself at a subsistence level, the money required to make up the deficit by buying agricultural products abroad is not available for investment
toward other national objectives.

Whether the recent reduction in the rate of increase of the
world's population will continue remains to be seen. In large
part it will depend on national efforts to reduce population
growth in China, India, the Soviet Union, and Indonesia which—
together with the United States—account for more than one-
half of the world's population.

> By the end of the century the pace of population growth
> is expected to fall by 20 percent, to 16 births per thousand
> a year, compared with 20 per thousand now. This will still
> mean a rise in the world population of from 4.4 billion to
> 6.2 billion, causing "explosive growth" in the already-over-
> crowded cities of the third world. (Nossiter, 1980)

Even when population eventually levels off, as projected in the
"S-curve" pattern of growth that applies to so many societal
activities, and extensive urban decentralization is promoted and
achieved, the more numerous and larger communities created
in the countryside will need comprehensive city planning.

CITATIONS

[1] Davis, Kingsley, "The Urbanization of the Human Population," *Scientific American*, September 1965, p. 41. [2] Nossiter, Bernard D. "World Population Explosion Is Slowing, U.N. Finds," *The New York Times*, 15 June 1980, p. 10. [3] Patera, Alan, "A Perspective on Population Densities," *The Wall Street Journal*, 1 May 1984, p. 33. [4] McDowell, Bart, "Mexico City: An Alarming Giant," *National Geographic*, August 1984, pp. 138-185. [5] Mumford, Lewis, *The City in History*, New York (Harcourt, Brace, & World), 1961, p. 33. [6] _____ , *Culture of Cities*, New York (Harcourt, Brace), 1938, p. 59.

SELECTED REFERENCE

[1] Jones, Emrys, *Towns and Cities*, London (Oxford), 1966, 152 pp.

The city differs from a beehive or a termite mound; it is not a habitat harmoniously adapted to the organic drives and reflexes of the species, but rather an alien environment precariously rigged so as to avoid disastrous consequences that would otherwise occur.

Kingsley Davis, *Cities: Their Origin, Growth and Human Impact*, 1973.

CHAPTER 4
CIRCUMSTANCES AFFECTING URBAN DEVELOPMENT

Significant differences between cities must be taken into account. But there are also basic mechanisms or "common denominators" of munic-ipal management and planning that maintain regardless of differences in circumstance.

THE GREAT variety of cities throughout the world is self-evident: small, middle sized, and large; old and new; growing and declining; crowded and sparsely occupied; often operating under very different economic, political, social, religious, and cultural conditions. Many exist in very different physical environments. Any one or more of many circum-stances may dominate a city at some point in time, but certain situations and conditions are of underlying importance at all times in comprehensive city planning.

The geographical *situation* of a city is not only an essential consideration in its initial location but affects its subsequent functioning and shapes its physical form. If the founding fathers had a maritime purpose for their settlement, as a place for the transfer of goods between land and sea, it was located at the coastline or along the banks of a river providing access for oceangoing vessels. If the purpose of a town was to house workers for some extractive enterprise in the mountains, it was established near enough to the mining operation to keep "com-muting" time and cost within bounds. A town intended as a commercial shopping and service center for a flat agricultural region would often be located at one of several places near its center, where well water was available, at an existing cross-road, or where urban routes could fan out in four cardinal directions leading to and from the surrounding farmland. Unlike communities in the United States that were founded on flatland

situation

29

whenever possible, many European towns were located on hillsides adjacent to agricultural flatlands in order to preserve the highly fertile topsoil built up by centuries of erosion from the surrounding hills.

In each of these illustrative cases, the physical form and arrangement of the community was different. The town at the coastline necessarily developed within the available semicircle of land. The mountain settlement was tucked along the lower slope of a hill or along the bottom of a valley on land not threatened with frequent flooding. Most likely its layout was linear, if not at first, then as it grew. The town on flatland had the greatest freedom of spatial development. It could expand more or less equally on all sides, unless growth in one direction was impeded by some physical feature or local governmental policy.

site   The *site* is the second critical consideration in urban location. Existing slopes determine the pattern of drainage and possible flooding. When slopes are steeper than a percentage grade designated by the municipality, one set of streets is usually laid out along the contours to provide greater comfort of walking and safety of driving along relatively low grades, and to reduce the velocity of storm drainage in the gutters of these streets. Geological conditions at the site may require the extra expense of heavier or specially engineered foundations.

function   The *function* the city performs—its reason for existence—is its most basic feature affecting every aspect of its operations and development. It may be a place to manufacture or transship goods, or serve as a regional shopping, service, educational, or research center. It may be a national or state capital, a recreational, religious, military, or retirement community. The different functions performed separately or in combination by human settlements are legion. The initial purpose of the city may have changed. How a community is affected by its basic functions depends on their nature and number.

The viability of a single-purpose town—what some call its economic health—requires the successful functioning of this primary productive activity. A city depending on a single enterprise for local employment, the so-called "company town," is the classic example. Furthermore, in today's world tied together by an increasing number of national and international interconnections, the successful operation of the basic economic activity may relate to a product price or wage rate hundreds or thousands of miles away. In one city product success may depend on labor intensive operations; in another the same objective may require extensive automation and robotics. Some cities serve unique purposes shared by few others, such as a world financial center or place of international religious pilgrimage. The squatter settlements referred to in the previous chapter perform a special function of providing dwelling places at a minimum subsistence level for rural migrants illegally occupying public or private property.

Normally, the city with multiple functions is stronger economically and less vulnerable because the depressive consequences of unfavorable developments in one of these functions are less severe if the other economic activities are unaffected. This is why most cities seek to diversify their economic base. Whereas the effects of an unfavorable event far away on one of a number of productive activities are not as economically damaging as for a single-function city, multiple functions are exposed collectively to more numerous potential impacts.

Inevitably, the basic function of cities is reflected in their economic and sociopolitical life, in their physical features, and spatial arrangement. The single-enterprise town signifies this interrelationship by its support of the productive activity on which its economic health depends. This may involve reduced municipal taxes, a zone change, new or improved street access, water supply or waste disposal by the city, or any one of many helpful actions. For the most part, the social environment and political actions of the community with a dominant business enterprise are determined by the people it employs, its corporate views and public relations activities, and to a lesser extent by those whose livelihood depends on providing it with supportive services. As would be expected, corresponding activities and attitudes in multi-function cities are more varied, representing the diverse preferences and behavior of different types of employees and the broader range of backgrounds represented in the urban population as a whole.

The economic base of cities is also reflected in their physical facilities and form. For example, a well-planned retirement community provides places and spaces for the numerous social and recreational activities and health services needed by its primary population. The capital city of a state or nation incorporates some form of spatial monumentality that symbolizes its governmental importance: a mall, an impressive arrangement of public buildings, or a special structure designed for the purpose. The city located on a coast or river attempts to make the most of this prospect, providing space and access for industrial and commercial enterprises that must be placed along the waterfront, but also creating esplanades and other spaces that provide a view over the water for as many people as possible. The multi-function city exhibits greater physical and spatial variety with no single predominant feature or overriding visual character.

history
culture
  History and *culture* also affect both the physical character and societal characteristics of cities. Most societies permanently preserve certain historical sites and protect them from encroachment by incompatible land development. Important temples, churches, mosques, and other religious shrines have been preserved throughout history. Cemeteries and tombs are considered by city planners as the most inviolable of urban land uses because of ancestral and religious attachments established over many centuries. As archaeological science has advanced and interest in cultural precedents has grown, many cities require preservation of important archaeological sites or a period of delay for their excavation before any construction can begin. Almost all cities have some places treated in accordance with their historical or cultural significance.

  The beliefs and attitudes of people are deeply rooted in the distant past. The influence of cultural threads extending far back in history is seen in the number and quality of urban activities and facilities serving intellectual interests, art, music, theater, and dance. Religion has played an important part in urban development in the past and continues to do so for most of the people in the world today. At times religion has been the predominant force controlling and directing cities in some countries. A mixture of inhabitants with different ethnological histories and cultural backgrounds produces a corresponding mix of urban effects to be taken into account in comprehensive city planning.

As active organisms, cities have *stages of development*: birth, *stage of* infancy, youth, maturity, old age, senility, and finally death in *development* the case of abandoned communities, known today through their ruins or as "ghost towns." The stage of development of a city represents its economic, social, organizational, and technological state at a particular time during its evolution. It signifies what the city can expect to accomplish at that time and condition. Urban places appear to progress through successive stages of growth and development defined in different ways by different scholars. Certain of these stages seem to be widely characteristic, although this is not obvious when the transition from one stage to the next is prolonged in one case and very brief in another. There are also exceptions when an unforeseen event of great magnitude disrupts or terminates the usual development: a natural catastrophe such as a flood or earthquake, or social upheaval by prolonged revolution or great changes in the composition of the population.

One "theory about economic growth and a more general, if still highly partial, theory about history as a whole" identifies six stages of economic development: traditional society (pre-Newtonian), preconditions of take-off (process of transition), take-off (period of growth), drive to maturity (sustained progress), age of high mass consumption, and beyond consumption (Rostow, 1971). Another formulation, describing the development of larger cities, identifies an initial stage lasting until a second stage when advances in agricultural knowledge and practice and the division of labor into different trades and professions produces a variety of goods and services that are bought and sold. In the third stage, the production of material goods is replaced by the provision of particular services and increasingly specialized knowledge. In the fourth stage, sophisticated automation and robotics leave most people in the city with self-advancement through adult education and self-satisfaction through entertainment as their main endeavors. The final stage would be when most inhabitants leave big cities and move to smaller towns dispersed throughout the countryside.

Cities are recent and relatively untried societal organisms. It is not surprising therefore that they have been less permanent in the past than they are likely to be in the future. Unless there is a nuclear, pestilential, or contaminatory catastrophe on a global scale, the life span of most cities should be extended by technological and socioeconomic advancements that increase their stability, and by large capital investments at the site that favor permanence.

basic
mechanisms

Significant differences between cities must be taken into account in the most effective city planning. But there are also *basic mechanisms* or "common denominators" of municipal management and planning that maintain regardless of differences in circumstance: such as a form of government and administrative organization; a system of economic production, taxes, and financial management; budgets; transportation networks; provision of water, energy, social and other services; uses of land; treatment of the city center and subcenters; density distribution; building coverage and height. It is the task of comprehensive planning to adjust municipal policies and objectives to fit the basic circumstances of the city, and determine how common mechanisms of planning are best applied.

CITATION
[1] Rostow, W.W., *The Stages of Economic Growth* A Non-Communist Manifesto, Cambridge, UK (Cambridge University), Second Edition, 1971, 253 pp.

CHAPTER 5
WHAT IS A CITY?

When the different physical and socioeconomic views of the city are combined with the multiple interconnections between them, the operational and analytical complexity of cities is apparent.

IF VIEWED one element at a time, cities do not seem so complicated. But there are a multitude of elements ranging from tangible components such as housing and public utilities to the intangible political and legal powers that shape and constrain municipal activities. In addition, the multitude of interactions between the many elements of different kinds are as essential to the functioning of a city as the elements themselves. When elements and interrelationships are viewed together, the sizable city emerges as probably the most complex organism created by human beings. Comprehensive city planning seeks to understand this complex sufficiently to enable staff personnel to recommend constructive actions by the powers that direct the development of the municipality, and to enable these powers to take such actions on their own initiative.

One way of comprehending the complexity of a city is to view it briefly through the eyes of people in different fields who have either direct contact with city planning or an indirect impact on urban activities. The vignettes that follow are in no priority order. Any one of the many substantive fields and professions affecting cities could be most important at a particular place and a particular time.

Geographers focus on the physical features of the city and surrounding urban region: situation, site, terrain, climate, vegetation, pathways. They explore the interrelationships between these features and the form and functioning of the city. Their viewpoint varies depending on their particular emphasis within the broad scope of geography. The "physical" geographer considers how spatial features affect the disposition and functioning of the different components of the city. The "economic" geographer is concerned with the interrelationships between

geographer

the spatial characteristics of the urban area and the existence and operation of industrial, commercial, service, and other economic activities of the city. The "social" geographer studies the effects of the spatial environment on the composition, distribution, attitudes, and behavior of the urban inhabitants. Each of these viewpoints contributes to further understanding of the city and more effective city planning.

geologist   The *geologist* looks at the surface and subsurface of the terrain: the topsoils and upper levels of earth that affect drainage and waste disposal, the stability of the surface terrain and the use of land; or subterranean formations that affect construction above and below ground and the extraction of underground resources. Municipal regulations may require a licensed geologist's report before building and subdivision plans are approved.

economist   The productive functions of the city are the concern of the *economist*: the profitable manufacture of goods and provision of services, available investment and financing, the tax base, export/import balance of urban trade, or local dependence on income from higher levels of government. Also of continuing concern are interest rates, the rating of the city's bonds by investment services, the prices of goods and services the city must purchase, and actions, rules and regulations beyond its boundaries that impose costs on the municipality it cannot control. The consequences of localities becoming more closely connected with national and international conditions and events must be taken into account in any analysis of the economic health of a city.

political scientist   The *political scientist* addresses fundamental questions of governance. How does the form of the municipal government relate to city planning? What organizations and individuals hold the reins of power? Are there private institutions or individuals who in fact exercise more control over the current activities and future development of the city than the political and bureaucratic organizations the general public assumes are most influential? How do the political realities affect people's voting on different issues, their attitudes, and even their behavior? How is comprehensive city planning best conducted, considering all relevant political factors?

sociologist   Classification of the urban population is a foremost concern of the *sociologist*: by age, sex, marital status, educational level, ethnic background, and other categorizations compiled by various censuses and surveys. When population characteristics are associated with particular areas of the city, organizational affiliation, or behavior as revealed by crime rates or delinquency, statistical correlations are developed to confirm certain municipal policies and programs, or to reveal the need for their revision or replacement. In recent years greatly increased immigration has added a new set of sociological concerns resulting from language difficulties, differences in ethnological and cultural background, value systems, and living habits.

As noted in an earlier chapter, modern municipal health codes are the result of centuries of development. Until relatively recently, unsanitary conditions, environmental pollution, and the absence of preventive medicine and effective treatment often led to widespread sickness, early death, and occasionally devastating epidemics. Today, the *public health physician* applies medical knowledge to the formulation of municipal standards for a potable water supply, public and private sanitation, minimum residential space, light, and air, general and emergency hospital facilities, or paramedical services. Professionally, the public health physician sees the city as a place presenting many problems for community medicine, involving people individually and collectively, the physical environment, many urban activities, and the enforcement of health regulations under the police power. *physician*

Lawyers draft the many municipal ordinances and regulations that relate to city planning. Every zone change is effectuated by a separate ordinance of the city council. Lawyers are involved in appeals from these laws and regulations, representing the municipality on one side and the litigant challenging their legal validity or procedural application on the other. City attorneys draw up the local legislation that supports the master planning process. State legislators, their staffs, and state attorneys draft the state laws that define the police powers delegated to the municipality, and the state enabling acts that prescribe local master planning activities and procedures in increasing detail. The legal specialties of land use, master planning, and environmental law are now recognized. *lawyer*

Most municipal actions and activities relate to some physical structure in space. Even policies, ordinances, and regulations that are intangible in themselves almost always affect the design, *engineer*   construction, or maintenance of some structure, system, or physical object through a conceptual requirement or regulatory restraint. As a consequence, *engineers* have participated in town planning since earliest times, witness the remarkable Roman aqueducts and roads, some of which still exist. Today, engineers are active in the design and construction of the urban transportation and utility systems, buildings, and other structures of many kinds that constitute the major part of the anatomy of the city. Civil, structural, and electrical engineers are most often engaged but any one of the many engineering specialties may be needed in connection with some physical structure, law, or regulation requiring particular technical expertise. As engineers look about a city just about everything they see above ground has had their input, together with the multitude of underground utilities and other installations unseen except in the mind's eye.

architect   *Architects* view the city in much the same way as engineers. They are concerned with the architectural aspects of individual buildings and groups of buildings, the open spaces within and around them, and the laws and regulations relating to their design and construction. They are also concerned with the "urban design" of streets and other urban spaces, and the aesthetics of the city in general. In times past, architects were often responsible for the design of the city as a whole.

> Hippodamus of Miletus who was born about 480 B.C. . . .was one of the earliest Greek architects to practice the planning of cities. Aristotle says that he introduced the principle of right-angled, wide streets in Greece, and was the first architect to provide for the grouping of dwelling houses, as well as the combining of different parts of the town centered round the marketplace into a harmonious whole. (Adams, 1935)

Architects have continued this active role in citywide planning whenever opportunities arise, since "every architect dreams of designing a city" (Johnson, 1979). This has been less frequent in recent years, especially in the United States where urban planning has become a separate field of education and professional practice. The architect continues his contributions in urban design as indicated in Chapter 13, planning and designing individual buildings, groups of buildings, and large physical projects.

Landscape architects focus on the vegetative elements of the *landscape* city such as parks, playgrounds, and other open areas, street *architect* trees, or parkway and freeway landscaping. In recent years, their role has expanded to include the selection of vegetative cover to reduce erosion, resist brush fires, and discourage insect pests. Some cities in the United States incorporate these selections as part of their municipal code regulating private building design and construction, or as specifications for public projects.

Urban activities are so numerous and diverse that a long list of professions may be associated with city planning at one time or another. Scholars and experts in almost any field can find an aspect of city planning relating to their work. The purpose here is to note a number of these associations to illustrate the complexities of cities and comprehensive planning. Smaller communities are less complicated and it is not necessary, cost effective, or budgetarily possible for them to engage in the level of city planning that is needed in larger cities and possible with their greater resources.

Besides the professions active in city planning, there are many more people who regard the urban community from the viewpoint of a profession, occupation, or activity that is involved with the life of the city rather than its planning.

Artists, for example, look to cities for personal stimulation, *urban* education, and professional opportunity. There are museums *opportunity* displaying works of art and schools of painting, sculpture, music, dance, and other artistic endeavors that are found only in larger cities. The latest developments in art can be expressed and exhibited in cities, relatively free from the restraining conservatism characteristic of most smaller communities, and with a much larger number of potential viewers. These urban viewers constitute the largest market for the purchase and sale of art objects. For most artists with professional aspirations a time in the city is essential.

People engaged in all sorts of activities see cities as places of employment or occupational opportunity: providing patients for medical specialists, construction jobs for contractors and workers in the building trades, clients for a host of special services, or customers for the many commercial enterprises. Among this group are the rural dwellers who in recent years have been flocking to cities around the world. For those who find it difficult or impossible to survive in the countryside, cities offer hope of a job, educational opportunity, and a supportive reception by relatives or friends living in the community. However unrealistic these hopes may be, they motivate millions of people to migrate to cities in many parts of the world.

Cities are places seen and experienced from many different viewpoints, signifying their activeness, diversity, and complexity.

Analytical comprehension of communities is facilitated by examining them from two points of view: the physical city, and the socioeconomic city. In reality, these two aspects constitute one totality. For example, economic conditions determine what buildings and structures in a city are built and well maintained. Physical features in turn affect social satisfactions and the attractiveness of the community for productive enterprise and economic investment. Awareness of the primary components and considerations in each of these two major subdivisions is a useful first step toward a more complete urban comprehension.

The Physical City

The physical community is the contiguous built-up urban area extending outward from its center into the surrounding countryside. In smaller towns the radius of this urban development may be half a mile or less. In large metropolitan areas it can extend many miles encompassing an area containing as many as 30 or more municipalities. But in the overall view of the city, the jurisdictional boundaries of these separate municipalities are usually indistinguishable.

The physical city exists at three levels: buildings and operations on or close to the ground, underground installations, and activities in "empty" space overhead. Until the last several centuries, socioeconomic considerations were relatively unimportant since the ruling authority provided the labor force and money, and elicited whatever social responses were required to initiate and complete the desired projects.

overall form   At the broadest scale, the *overall form* of the city reflects its geographical location and its particular site. Generalized forms of urbanwide development on flatland are portrayed schematically in Figure 3.

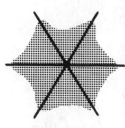
radial
continuous

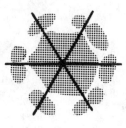
radial
discontinuous

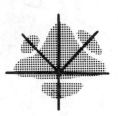
radial
discontinuous

— BASIC STREET SYSTEM   ▦ URBANIZED AREA

gridiron
continuous

radial-concentric
continuous

linear
continuous

Figure 3
Generalized Forms of Overall Urban Development

In the city conceptualized in Figure 4A, growth has been much greater on the side of the river where the original settlement occurred. In most such site situations, the "opposite" side of the river develops more slowly, largely because of the cost of bridging the river and the corollary ease of extending the original built-up area outward without having to surmount the physical obstruction represented by the river.

The *topography* of the site affects elements within the city. *topography* Normally, primary roads extend out in roughly four compass directions along favorable grades. Railroads require very low grades of 2 percent or less. In cities located on rivers, railroads are usually routed along the riverbank where grades are lowest. Storm drainage, water supply pipelines, and sewer systems are designed to take advantage of gravity flow. In general, structures avoid physical conditions that increase costs of construction, such as unstable geological conditions, wetlands, or areas subject to regular and severe flooding. Mechanized man-

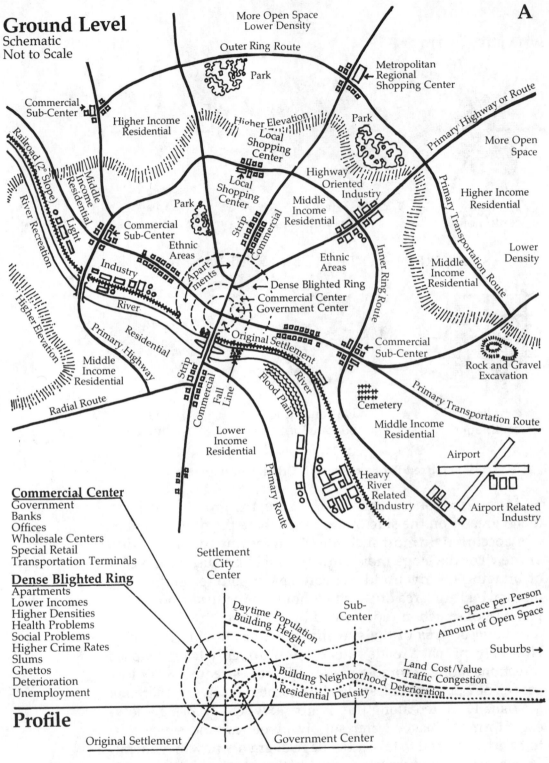

Ground Level
Schematic
Not to Scale

A

More Open Space
Lower Density

Outer Ring Route

Park

Metropolitan
Regional
Shopping Center

Commercial
Sub-Center

Higher Income
Residential

Higher Elevation
Local
Shopping
Center

Park

Primary Highway or Route

More Open
Space

Railroad (2° Slope)

Middle Income Residential

Light

Highway
Oriented
Industry

Higher Income
Residential

River Recreation

Higher Elevation

Commercial
Sub-Center

Park

Strip Commercial

Local
Shopping
Center

Middle
Income
Residential

Primary Transportation Route

Lower
Density

Ethnic
Areas

Apartments

Ethnic
Areas

Middle
Income
Residential

Industry

River

Dense Blighted Ring

Commercial Center

Government Center

Inner Ring Route

Residential

Original Settlement

River

Commercial
Sub-Center

Rock and Gravel
Excavation

Primary Highway

Strip

Commercial

Fall
Line

Flood Plain

Cemetery

Primary Transportation Route

Middle
Income
Residential

Radial Route

Middle
Income
Residential

Lower
Income
Residential

Airport

Heavy
River
Related
Industry

Airport Related
Industry

Primary Route

Commercial Center
Government
Banks
Offices
Wholesale Centers
Special Retail
Transportation Terminals

Dense Blighted Ring
Apartments
Lower Incomes
Higher Densities
Health Problems
Social Problems
Higher Crime Rates
Slums
Ghettos
Deterioration
Unemployment

Profile

Settlement
City
Center

Sub-
Center

Space per Person

Daytime Population
Building Height

Amount of Open Space

Suburbs →

Building Neighborhood Deterioration

Land Cost/Value
Traffic Congestion

Residential Density

Original Settlement

Government Center

Figure 4A
Schematic View of Medium Size Physical City
Ground Level

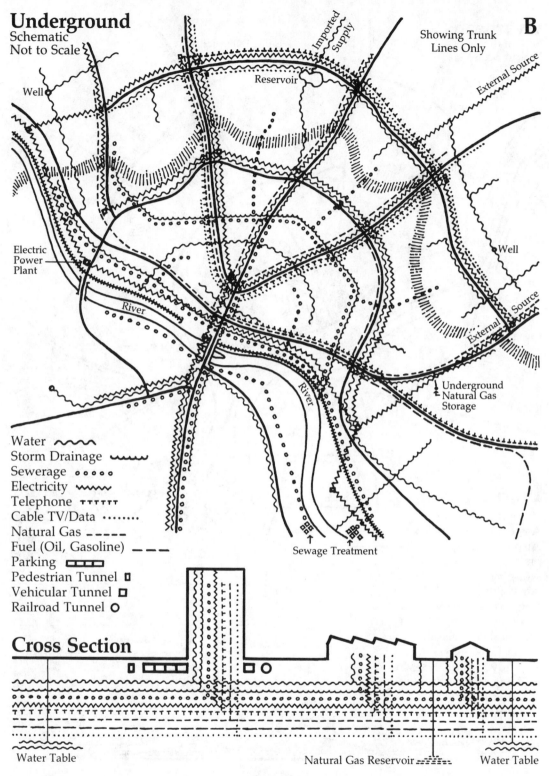

Underground

Schematic
Not to Scale

B

Showing Trunk
Lines Only

Imported Supply

Reservoir

External Source

Well

Well

Electric
Power
Plant

River

External Source

River

Underground
Natural Gas
Storage

Water ~~~~
Storm Drainage ﹋
Sewerage ∘∘∘∘∘
Electricity ⌁⌁⌁
Telephone ⊤⊤⊤⊤⊤⊤
Cable TV/Data ⋯⋯⋯⋯
Natural Gas _ _ _ _
Fuel (Oil, Gasoline) _ _ _
Parking ▭▭▭▭
Pedestrian Tunnel ▯
Vehicular Tunnel ▭
Railroad Tunnel ○

Sewage Treatment

Cross Section

Water Table

Natural Gas Reservoir

Water Table

Figure 4B
Schematic View of Medium Size Physical City
Underground

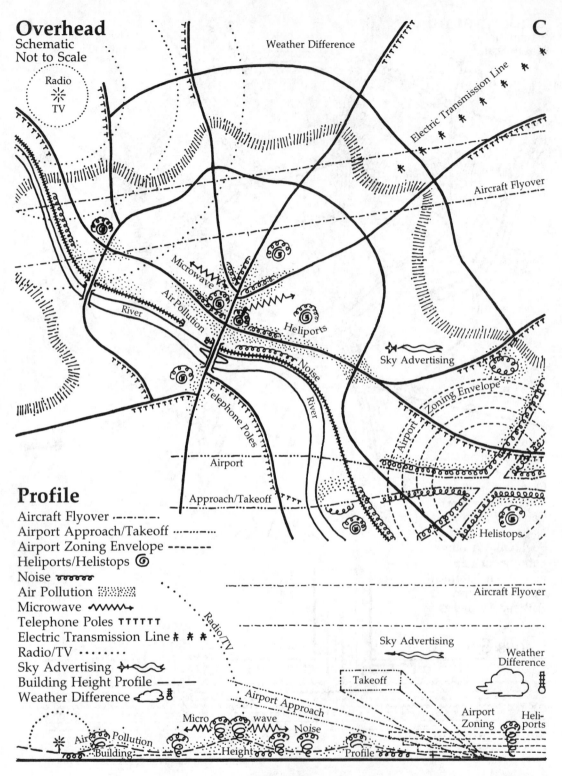

Overhead

Schematic
Not to Scale

Radio
TV

Weather Difference

C

Electric Transmission Line

Aircraft Flyover

Microwave

Air Pollution

River

Heliports

Noise

Sky Advertising

River

Telephone Poles

Zoning Envelope

Airport

Airport

Approach/Takeoff

Helistops

Profile

Aircraft Flyover ·—·—·—·
Airport Approach/Takeoff ·———·——·
Airport Zoning Envelope - - - - - -
Heliports/Helistops ⑤
Noise ᵥᵥᵥᵥᵥ
Air Pollution ▒▒▒▒
Microwave ᴧᴧᴧᴧ➤
Telephone Poles ⊤⊤⊤⊤⊤⊤
Electric Transmission Line ⚹ ⚹ ⚹
Radio/TV ·······
Sky Advertising ➤~~
Building Height Profile - - -
Weather Difference ☁🌡

Aircraft Flyover

Radio/TV

Sky Advertising

Weather
Difference

Takeoff

Airport
Zoning

Heli-
ports

Airport Approach

Micro   wave
Air Pollution
Building

Noise

Height

Profile

Figure 4C
Schematic View of Medium Size Physical City
Overhead

44

ufacturing seeks flatland where single-story plants can be built with surrounding open space for vehicular access, employee parking, outdoor storage, and other use. This is not always the case. When urban space is limited, land costs are high, and labor costs are low, multistoried buildings may be used for small-scale manufacturing. Throughout history, many of the well-to-do have favored higher ground for detached houses in a visually attractive area toward the urban periphery. In general, hilly terrain develops more slowly than flatland in cities in the United States because of higher construction costs for both buildings and utility services.

In some parts of the world, earthquake fault lines, alluvial flatlands sensitive to seismological tremor, or other geologically unstable conditions exist beneath the physical city. They present urban development with the choice of prohibiting building at these places, paying the higher cost of structures specially designed to reduce potential damage, or accepting the risk with no related provisions.

Because *buildings* provide the shelter necessary for human survival, they are the first element constructed in the city after water and food are available. Initially, their placement determines the circulation pattern of the locality or they are arranged with relation to a proposed street pattern. Sooner or later they are connected with municipal utilities when these exist or as they are installed. The uses of buildings are as varied as the tremendous range of human activities they contain. The major categories of their use—residential, commercial, industrial, governmental, transportation—establish the "land use" pattern of the city.

buildings

Dwelling units constitute the largest number of urban buildings: detached single-family units, row houses, apartment buildings, or the many other types and arrangements of residential quarters that exist around the world. They vary tremendously in size, character, and cost, from the mud hut or "squatter settlement" shack to large palatial residences. Commercial and industrial buildings range from tiny enclosed work spaces to large stores and single-story factories covering acres of ground under one roof. Some are permanent, intended to last indefinitely; others are temporary, anticipating early replacement or moving to another site. On the average they cover a smaller percentage of the land, are lower in height, and therefore not a dense land use—particularly toward the periphery of cities.

Buildings are certainly the most apparent of urban elements, in view at all times everywhere in the city. Whether made of adobe or steel and glass, they exhibit great diversity of construction materials and methods and quality of design. In the United States it has been estimated that fewer than 20 percent of buildings are designed by architects; in Europe this percentage is much higher. In many parts of the world people cannot afford such professional service; designs and construction methods are traditional or follow immediate precedents with minor modification. Available building materials, the cost and time required for construction, and cultural influences combine to encourage uniformities of design and methods of construction.

structures   The physical city is also filled with *structures* that are not buildings: bridges, culverts, irrigation and flood channels, municipal utility lines, electric transformer substations, sewage treatment plants, reservoirs, oil refineries and other open-air industrial operations, and many other installations that are not commonly called buildings because they do not enclose space in the same way. Structures are as important to the functioning of cities as buildings. In industrialized countries engineers are involved in the design and construction of almost all structures. But the skills needed for the simple structures that suffice in many parts of the world are commonplace, handed down from generation to generation.

transportation   The location of transportation routes and municipal utilities shapes the use of land in cities. Since the earliest communities, business has sought locations along primary trafficways and wherever else potential customers are concentrated. *Transportation* and land use are often referred to by city planners as "two sides of the same coin," since some form of transportation ingress and egress is required for the productive use of any land, and a trafficway performs no useful purpose unless it serves some existing or proposed activity at both ends.

The extent to which successive additions and superpositions of transportation systems have affected the pattern of cities in the United States and Europe is rarely recognized. Some additions, like the streetcar and the bus, imposed further loads on streets for which they were not designed. Other systems formed separate barriers at ground level, often cutting across the pattern of streets and property lines established in the past. (Figure 5)

It is the automobile which has had and will continue to have the most pervasive physical impact on cities in industrialized countries. This is also the case in developing nations as their communities grow in size and rising personal incomes allow more extensive private ownership of automobiles. The impact of the automobile is everywhere: in the pattern and detailed design of streets, parking provisions, traffic control, congestion, air pollution, accidents, personal mobility, construction costs, transportation expenses, image and prestige, and—most recently—increased vulnerability to fuel prices. No single improvement can resolve the problems created in cities by the automobile. A comprehensive approach is required, which on

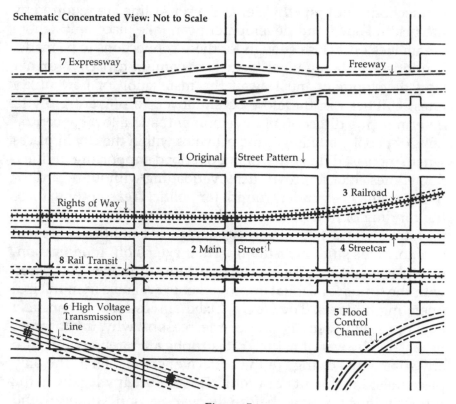

Figure 5
Transportation and Surface Utility Systems and the Urban Street Pattern

the "demand" side involves a set of interrelated actions to reduce the daytime use of downtown streets where the greatest congestion is caused by privately owned automobiles carrying only the driver. These actions could include increased private automobile sales taxes and registration fees, a user or road tax, increased parking fees, and area licensing allowing a certain number of private cars with passengers to enter the downtown area. On the "supply" side, public transportation systems are required that efficiently meet the demand, with routes and schedules closely correlated with where people live, work, shop, recreate, and visit.

utilities   Most inhabitants of modern industrialized cities are unaware of the networks of *utilities* that exist beneath their feet. When mapped in their entirety, they constitute a maze of underground pipelines and conduits ending in individual buildings and structures, portrayed schematically in Figure 4B. Utilities affect or determine land use in several ways. When connections with piped water and a sewer line are required by the health code, land development can take place only where the utilities exist close enough for these connections to be made. If utilities are being used to their maximum capacity, further land development must await the installation of new utility lines. Utilities can therefore be employed to prevent growth, determine the direction of development, and allow concentrations of people, buildings, and activities within the city in places where increased density will not overload supporting utilities. Sometimes cities approve such overloading without regard for the consequences underground, for political reasons or to force the funding of new or larger utility systems.

Literally and figuratively, underground utilities represent an enormous sunk investment. Their extension, modification, or replacement involves very large sums of money compared with the funds for capital improvements available in municipal operating budgets. They are a "fixed" investment, financially and physically. This is one of the reasons why urban areas devastated by war or natural catastrophe are rarely rebuilt with any substantial change in the pattern of streets. First, the only place most inhabitants can return to and occupy legally is the property they occupied before the war. Second, underground utilities are seldom damaged to the same extent as structures above ground; they remain serviceable for the most part or can be repaired quickly and at far less cost and time than would be required for a revised pattern of streets and the utilities that normally run beneath them. In some countries underground shelters to protect inhabitants against attack from the air are an important part of city planning, providing subterranean dwelling places and supporting services.

Open space in the physical city is determined by how build-   *open space*
ings and structures are developed on the land. This development is a product of urban economics and building code regulations formulated to carry out local government policies. Open space is more than parks, playgrounds, and other recreational areas. There are the setbacks for buildings required by most municipal codes in the United States: front, back, and side yards, and lines setting back structures from the boundaries of public rights-of-way. There are also open spaces over flood control channels, rivers and surface streams, railroads except when they pass through tunnels, underneath overhead high voltage transmission lines, and above or beneath other utilities requiring unobstructed corridors. There are also sizable land uses open to the sky, such as cemeteries, airports, and farmland that add considerably to urban open space.

Usually the percentage of open land increases toward the periphery of the city, as indicated diagrammatically in the profile section of Figure 4A. In part this is the result of geometry: the disproportionate increase in the ground area within city limits as these boundaries are extended outward. In both circular and square areas, doubling the radius of the circle and doubling the distance from the center of the square to the midpoint of its sides quadruples the area enclosed. When the medieval city moved its encircling wall outward by only an additional one-half the distance from the central town square to its previous location, the area within the city wall was more than doubled to accommodate a growing population and reduce overall urban density—usually temporarily until garden spaces were filled with buildings. When the city wall was moved outward twice as far from the center, the enclosed area of the city was increased four times.

As shown in Figure 3C, human activities and their effects occurring in the open space overhead are part of the physical city. Air pollution or noticeable degradation of air quality is present in most large communities around the world. Aircraft movements in, out of, and within urban areas require air traffic control and contribute to noise pollution. Electronic communication has introduced microwaves into the urban atmospheric environment.

density   Urban *density* depends on three conditions: the percentage of parcels of land that are covered with buildings without open areas on the property, the height of buildings, and the amount of permanent open space provided throughout the city. Since densities and land values decrease toward the periphery of cities—except for localized increases at any decentralized sub-centers—the opportunity exists in the suburbs for more of the open space that most people desire as part of their dwelling place. There are also a larger number of public and private open spaces away from the central city, such as parks and recreational areas, airports, and institutions requiring large properties. The higher densities characteristic of central areas are a response to their location being equally accessible from all parts of the city, the need for certain business and governmental activities to be close to one another, and often a municipal policy of deliberate concentration to preserve existing investments downtown. Urban density signifies a spatial concentration of buildings and consequent activity that is productive until it so far exceeds transportation access that destructive congestion sets in.

climate   The pervasive effects of local *climate* are reflected in the physical city. Average rainfall relates to the need for storm drainage, to street and building design, to the type and extent of urban vegetation, to the balance between indoor and outdoor activities. Temperature is not only related to rainfall but to many units of the physical city directly through air conditioning and heating requirements. Insolation, which varies greatly from place to place, affects the need for protective arcades along major streets, the amount of uncovered open space, and the feasibility of solar heating. In turn, the local climate is affected by the city:

> . . . the presence of the city exerts a pronounced influence on storm activity downwind. . . . Because the city is warmer than the surrounding territory, the air over it rises. The

resulting atmospheric instability may cause storm clouds to form. On the other hand, the urban air is dry as well as warm; because storms require moisture to sustain themselves, storms passing over the city may absorb the dry air, begin to dissipate, and drop their water load downwind. Air turbulence generated by city buildings may also lead to atmospheric instability, again resulting in increased cloud formation and rainfall. (Ferrell, Adams, 1977)

On a much smaller scale, localized wind turbulence can rattle buildings and cause windows to shatter under the worst conditions. It can render certain streets uncomfortable for pedestrians and prevent their safe use by vehicles as well as people. Some shopping centers have had to close after completion for modification to reduce air turbulence that turned potential shoppers away and threatened the financial success of the center. It is not unusual for scale models of groups of buildings or "walled streets" to be tested in a wind tunnel for *microclimatic* effects that would impair their immediate environment and possibly jeopardize their success. *microclimate*

Vegetation is another significant element of the physical city. It makes it more attractive and helps clean the air. It can reduce soil erosion, the danger of landslides, and noise pollution. It can act as a windbreak. Certain vegetation reduces the danger of brush fires, repels some insects, is more tolerant of air pollution. Most important, vegetation satisfies the inherent human desire for some close association with nature, a desire represented around the world by the almost universal tending of potted plants on balconies, window ledges, or whatever place open to the sun is available in the dwelling or office. *vegetation*

Vegetation may exist in many places and in different forms throughout the city: along streets, major thoroughfares, flood control channels, railroads and other rights-of-way; in parks, playgrounds, recreational and agricultural areas, cemeteries, and other open areas. It is also manifest in the treatment of private open spaces, whether owned or leased: atriums, ground areas around dwellings and places of business, golf courses, country clubs, and the hundreds of spaces maintained by private individuals and institutions. Naturally, the type and extent of vegetative treatment in the physical city differs drastically among geographic regions, for example between communities in arctic and desert areas and those in the tropics and temperate latitudes. In general, as cities grow and density increases, the amount of vegetation within the city decreases.

aesthetic quality   Although personal and cultural concepts of beauty vary widely, most people agree that there are certain features of the physical city that contribute to its *aesthetic quality*. The first of these is urban cleanliness. Despite the human capability of blocking out from continuous awareness unpleasant conditions that can neither be changed nor avoided, a clean well-kept city is certainly more attractive to the eye and nose than one littered with dust and refuse. The second feature contributing to urban attractiveness is the absence of "excess outdoor advertising." There are those who find unlimited signs and billboards interesting because of their diverse content. A few people maintain that all outdoor advertising is aesthetically acceptable because they believe it correctly expresses the culture that produces it. But most people find a large number of billboards unattractive because of their calculated intrusion upon the visual senses, sometimes hiding but always diverting awareness and appreciation of the structures that compose the habitable environment. Buildings comprise the third most important aesthetic element because they are so completely visible throughout the city. When well designed individually and compatible collectively they contribute significantly to urban beauty. Open space is a fourth aesthetic element providing relief from the walled-in feeling that is present in dense concentrations of big buildings that block out most of the view of the sky above. Another aesthetic element is vegetation. People who appreciate contact with nature find expanses of building and pavement surfaces more attractive and livable when they are interrupted by trees and plants.

urban design   Last, there is *urban design*, which enhances the aesthetic quality of the city by applying a high level of design to as many of its physical elements as feasible. These include major streets and boulevards, esplanades, and other monumental public spaces; small parks, gardens, museums, exhibits, and other places intended for visual pleasure as well as spatial enjoyment; "street furniture" such as street and traffic lights, park and bus benches, trash receptacles, and vending machines. Urban design is discussed at greater length in Chapter 13.

The physical city is far less fixed and permanent than its   *change*
solid form might suggest. In the United States, most cities are
in process of continuous *change*. New structures and installations of many kinds are built to provide more inhabitants with
places to live, work, and play. Old buildings are remodeled to
accommodate changes in use or are torn down to make way
for new buildings that usually are larger and more costly than
those they replace. Small "temporary taxpayer" buildings may
be erected to provide sufficient income to cover taxes while
waiting for land value and market demand to increase and
justify selling the property or replacing the taxpaying structure
with a much larger building. Zone changes permitting a "higher
and best use" on one parcel of property often trigger similar
changes on adjacent properties, because city councils cannot
identify a stopping point for successive zone changes that they
can defend logically and politically against accusation of "une-
qual treatment under the law."

The life of different urban facilities varies widely. Utility
trunk lines, major highways, historic churches and palaces may
exist for many years or centuries. The famous Cloaca Maxima,
the central sewer of ancient Rome constructed in the sixth century B.C., was used for more than 2,500 years. Some buildings
and structures have much shorter lives: for example, inexpen-
sive single-family homes in areas prone to more intensive
development, industrial buildings subject to technological
obsolescence, or temporary structures such as the prefabri-
cated offices used at different construction sites.

"Nothing is permanent but change" applies to the physical
city as well as everything else. When city planning is applied
consistently, major changes can be affected in the overall form
of the physical city in a much less time than the hard materials
of its buildings, structures, and paved surfaces suggest to most
people.

The Social City
People are both the reason for and the purpose of communities, which were created originally to increase human productivity through the concentration and specialization of labor
and provide the diversity of intellectual, cultural, and recreational activity possible in cities.

population   Every aspect of a city is affected by the *size of its population.*
size The number and capabilities of its work force determine what
productive enterprises are feasible within the city without
importing labor. The size of the police, fire, and other municipal services required "to protect persons and property" relates
to the number and kinds of inhabitants. Utilities are scaled to
the size and distribution within the city of its projected population 15 to 20 years in the future, and to the expected residential, commercial, industrial, and agricultural demand for
water, sewers, electricity, natural gas, telephone, and cable television. Each of these utilities and most municipal services
present "the problem of the peak load." Shall sufficient capacity
be provided to meet the greatest demand during 95 percent or
more of the time, with no additional capacity for the maximum
peak load that occurs occasionally for short periods of time?
The cost of meeting maximum peak load is high. And some
people maintain that there is almost no limit to the maximum
capacity of a utility system since the peak load provision will
be used regularly, not because it is needed, but because it is
available.

composition   The *composition of the population* focuses the need for particular municipal activities and services. For example, many
working mothers increase the need for nurseries to care for
their young children during working hours. The number of
elementary and high schools is determined by the size of the
age group that uses these facilities. In periods of lower birth
rates, some schools may be abandoned or used for different
purposes. An increase in the divorce rate leads to a corresponding increase in the number of dwelling units required to house
two people in separate abodes.

the elderly   The *"elderly"* exemplify the multiple interrelationships that
exist between a particular age group and the municipality. Medical advances have lengthened the life expectancy and there
are now over 25 million people 65 and older in the United
States. Most large cities and many small communities have
substantial numbers of "senior citizens." Fewer and fewer parents live with or are supported by their children, as is the case
in most countries where such support is a firm tradition or
legal obligation. Those parents who can afford it, live in homes

for the aged, retirement communities, or in their own houses or apartments with hired help. But a great many must fend for themselves as best they can on social security.

> The aged poor drift to the inner cities. . . . They come by
> necessity not by choice; only in neighborhoods like these
> can they find low rents and easily available shopping and
> services important to people for whom even a few blocks
> may be too far to walk and for whom 25 cents for the bus
> is an expenditure to be carefully weighed. (Isenberg, 1972)

Most of these aged poor live alone, many without friends or relatives, afraid to go out because of the high crime rate in the neighborhood and fearful the rent will be raised if they ask the landlord to make necessary repairs. Such conditions present the city with a set of aggravated problems and responsibilities involving safe and sanitary living quarters, affordable bus transportation, sufficient police protection, and home care and services when necessary.

Each population category has its particular needs. Those of *minorities* minority groups concerning housing, employment, municipal *and the young* services, and socioeconomic acceptance throughout the city are well known. Also recognized are the special needs of disadvantaged children faced with abandonment, malnutrition, physical and psychological neglect and abuse, unhealthy neighborhood conditions, and limited educational opportunities. Adolescents, the age group most vulnerable to serious delinquencies with lifelong impact, need recreational outlets and supportive services suited to their characteristics and behavior as teenagers. Yet few cities have amusement parks, dancing pavilions, or hillside motorcycle tracks where teenagers can "let off steam."

The size and composition of urban populations are subject *change* to *change*. Calculating this change must take into account births and deaths, people leaving the city, people moving to the city from surrounding rural areas or other parts of the nation, and immigrants from other countries. As a consequence, the composition of the population and the relative proportion of different age groups may be altered. New ethnic minorities may create a different set of cultural, religious, and educational requirements. Change is inherent in the population of most cities in the United States because people move their place of residence every five years or so on the average. However, many of these moves are within the same city, and the population of many smaller communities remains relatively stable for years.

spatial location
The social city can also be viewed *spatially*, seen from above as shown schematically in Figure 4A. Around the governmental and commercial center there is usually a ring of old, deteriorated apartment buildings housing a large percentage of the poor, low income, elderly, and minority populations. The most extensive blighted areas and worst slums are likely to be in this section of the municipality; if there is a "skid row" it will be here. Crime rates are higher. In larger cities, distinct ethnic neighborhoods or "ghettos" are found around the central city where new arrivals from abroad can find cheaper housing among compatriots whose comparable cultural backgrounds, common language, and similar problems give rise to greater community cohesion and mutual support than is normally found elsewhere in the city. In the biggest cities, these ethnic neighborhoods have played an important role in the acculturation of immigrants: receiving and accommodating the first generation, and transforming the second generation sufficiently to make possible their moving out and establishing themselves in other parts of the community and nation, better able to cope with the new or even alien features of their adopted land.

The squatter settlements of poor migrants from the rural countryside comprise a significant percentage of the population in many cities in developing countries. They are found on open land at the urban periphery and within the city wherever illegal occupation is possible: along the borders of highway, railroad, and utility rights-of-way, on steep hillsides and industrial, waste, and other land not yet developed. As time passes, these settlements acquire water and electric connections and progressively improve residential and commercial shacks constructed initially with discarded, purloined, or the cheapest materials available. Some squatters become landlords and rent rather than occupy their units in the settlement. Squatter settlements have existed off and on during the brief history of the United States, most notably during the Great Depression in the early 1930s. They may come again if the present situation of more and more immigration and less and less affordable housing continues.

The large expanse surrounding the central areas of cities, composed mainly of commercial and apartment buildings, is occupied for the most part by the middle-income majority of the municipal population, with occasional pockets of low- and high-income housing. Well-to-do people tend to locate in the suburbs where urban density is low and the most desirable building sites are found. In most cities in the United States there are large areas with the same use and development of the land, occupied for the most part by the same socioeconomic category of people, a consequence of "area classification" or "use" zoning and federal home mortgage policies. This has produced sections of cities devoted to "single land uses" such as low, medium, or high priced homes, apartment buildings in different price ranges, large or small commercial structures, and light or heavy industry. "Mixed land uses" within the same immediate neighborhood, with the more heterogeneous population that accompanies such development, are common in most communities around the world. In the United States they are found mainly in the largest cities.

Since there are exceptions to almost every generalization, the spatial disposition of land uses and population may be different when there are particular site conditions, unusual population characteristics, or exceptional economic circumstances. Whatever the precise spatial disposition of people and land uses, identification and analysis of its socioeconomic implications are an important part of successful city planning.

In general, some of the basic social problems confronting society are most apparent and accentuated when people are concentrated in cities: the quest for reasonable environmental safety and security, affordable shelter, adequate education for average and gifted children, special care for children subject to harmful conditions, recreational opportunities for all age groups, support services for the poor and the destitute, the physically and mentally handicapped, the delinquent and released criminal. Such fundamental social problems have existed since earliest times. Progress has been made, but complete solution is a goal to be sought, recognizing that it is unlikely to be achieved.

The Economic City

The basic function of a city is to generate enough income from the production of goods and services to support its inhabitants and perpetuate itself. The urban economy may be viewed in three parts. The public economy includes the operations of the municipal government as shown in the revenues and expenditures of the regular operating departments, the school district, and special districts established for particular purposes. The private economy is composed of the many different activities conducted by private enterprises, ranging from large industrial and commercial establishments to the independent business or professional person providing a service. The special economy consists of the many nonprofit, volunteer, tax-exempt organizations that are neither governmental bodies nor strictly private profit-oriented enterprises.

A healthy urban economy provides for the urban growth normally necessary to accommodate new developments brought about by technological advances and changing conditions. For a city with a diversified economic base, a static or declining urban economy usually means losing out in time to a competing city that is successful in absorbing internal growth and attracting new business from outside. A few communities supported by a relatively unchanging and permanent source of revenue may continue for many years in a stable economic condition.

competition   The extent to which economic *competition* is inherent among cities is demonstrated in the United States by the strenuous efforts of many local governments to attract new industry. They may reduce the local taxes assessed the new industry for a period of time, assist in training potential employees in the skills that are needed, and provide entirely at municipal expense special physical facilities or support services benefitting the industry. History records many cities that have declined in vitality and size and eventually disappeared because of adverse economic circumstances.

From a peak of 250,000 in the 1950s, the city is down to 156,000 people. Moreover, its economic base has disappeared. Once a major textile city, its biggest business today is jewelry. It also has little to offer new industry, particu-

larly as its tax rate rises. [It] relies heavily on property taxes
for revenue, but 30 percent of its real estate is tax exempt. . . .
Moody's Investor Services Inc. has reduced the city bond
rating . . . to . . . the lowest grade at which a municipality
can enter the bond market. (Lynch, 1981)

The *public economy* of a city consists of three parts: the   *public*
municipal budget, special districts, and the local educational   *economy*
system, as shown graphically in Figures 6A, 6B, and 6C on the
following pages. Special districts are being used increasingly.
Each is devoted to a particular governmental activity paid for
by the recipients of the service. Special districts may be favored
because they avoid the angry reaction of taxpayers who are
more likely to take issue with increases in the municipal budget
than with special charges for services provided by special districts. As shown in Figure 6C, states are providing an increasing share of funds for public education.

The operational well-being of a city depends on the revenues or income it collects from property taxes, licenses, permits, fees, and other sources. This income is larger when the
local economy is strong. If municipalities in the United States
relied on local taxes alone the level of governmental services
and public activities would be severely curtailed. Part of the
federal and state income taxes paid by urban inhabitants is
remitted to the city where the taxpayer resides, by revenue
sharing or grants-in-aid of many kinds reflecting the willingness of Congress and the state legislature to respond to particular needs. This direct assistance, together with the economic
support provided by federal activities and regional offices, is
noteworthy for its range and variety. Figure 7 illustrates *federal*   *federal*
support during a single year for a county almost conterminous   *support*
with a metropolitan city of a million people. (Yao, 1981)

Federal aid accounted for 7.8 percent of [city] revenues
while state aid was more than double that at 16.2 percent. . . For the cities with more than 250,000 people, federal aid in 1982 accounted for 12.4 percent and state aid
accounted for 17.4 percent. . . . The fiscal year 1982 was
the first to show a sharp drop for federal aid for cities'
operating expenses. That decline was greatest for those
cities . . . with populations over 250,000. (Herbers, 1982)

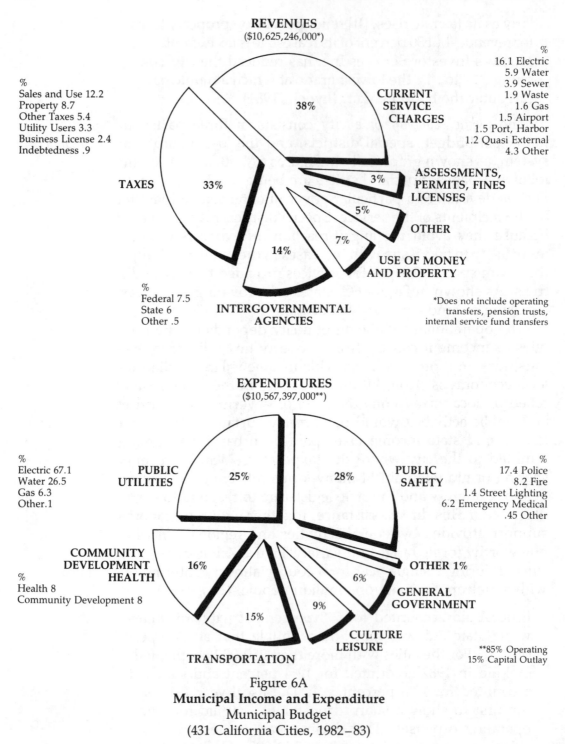

REVENUES
($10,625,246,000*)

%
16.1 Electric
5.9 Water
3.9 Sewer
1.9 Waste
1.6 Gas
1.5 Airport
1.5 Port, Harbor
1.2 Quasi External
4.3 Other

%
Sales and Use 12.2
Property 8.7
Other Taxes 5.4
Utility Users 3.3
Business License 2.4
Indebtedness .9

**CURRENT
SERVICE
CHARGES**

38%

TAXES   33%

**ASSESSMENTS,
PERMITS, FINES
LICENSES**   3%

OTHER   5%

7%

**USE OF MONEY
AND PROPERTY**

14%

%
Federal 7.5
State 6
Other .5

**INTERGOVERNMENTAL
AGENCIES**

*Does not include operating
transfers, pension trusts,
internal service fund transfers

EXPENDITURES
($10,567,397,000**)

%
Electric 67.1
Water 26.5
Gas 6.3
Other .1

**PUBLIC
UTILITIES**   25%

28%   **PUBLIC
SAFETY**

%
17.4 Police
8.2 Fire
1.4 Street Lighting
6.2 Emergency Medical
.45 Other

**COMMUNITY
DEVELOPMENT
HEALTH**   16%

%
Health 8
Community Development 8

OTHER 1%

6%

**GENERAL
GOVERNMENT**

9%

15%

**CULTURE
LEISURE**

TRANSPORTATION

**85% Operating
15% Capital Outlay

Figure 6A
Municipal Income and Expenditure
Municipal Budget
(431 California Cities, 1982–83)

GOVERNING BODY AND TYPE
(Revenues/Proceeds $8,152,076,000*)

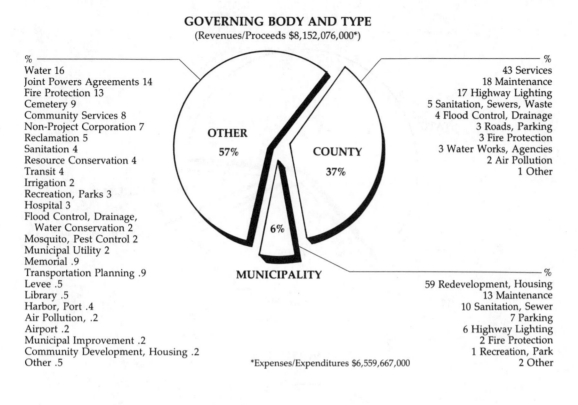

%
Water 16
Joint Powers Agreements 14
Fire Protection 13
Cemetery 9
Community Services 8
Non-Project Corporation 7
Reclamation 5
Sanitation 4
Resource Conservation 4
Transit 4
Irrigation 2
Recreation, Parks 3
Hospital 3
Flood Control, Drainage,
    Water Conservation 2
Mosquito, Pest Control 2
Municipal Utility 2
Memorial .9
Transportation Planning .9
Levee .5
Library .5
Harbor, Port .4
Air Pollution, .2
Airport .2
Municipal Improvement .2
Community Development, Housing .2
Other .5

OTHER
57%

COUNTY
37%

6%

MUNICIPALITY

%
43 Services
18 Maintenance
17 Highway Lighting
5 Sanitation, Sewers, Waste
4 Flood Control, Drainage
3 Roads, Parking
3 Fire Protection
3 Water Works, Agencies
2 Air Pollution
1 Other

%
59 Redevelopment, Housing
13 Maintenance
10 Sanitation, Sewer
7 Parking
6 Highway Lighting
2 Fire Protection
1 Recreation, Park
2 Other

*Expenses/Expenditures $6,559,667,000

Note

Special Districts serving an area within city boundaries and governed by City Councils constitute the 6% shown above for Municipality. Most of the County and Other Districts serve several or many cities that are part of the larger area they cover. Similarly, most School Districts, Community Colleges, and Regional Occupational Centers (Figure 6C) serve a number of urban communities.

Data for the revenues and expenditures for these two important elements of the municipal governmental economy are not available for cities separately, preventing direct comparison with Municipal Budget (Figure 6A).

However, since it is reasonable to assume that Special Districts and three categories of education institutions involve municipalities in the same ratio as urban (91%) to rural (9%) population in the state, the total revenues and expenditures shown above and in Figure 6C represent 91% of the total for the state.

The pie charts representing the three categories of direct financial activity by municipal government are sized to reflect the total dollar involvement of each. (Sources: Cory, Kenneth, Annual Report 1982–83, *Financial Transactions Concerning Cities of California*, Sacramento, Ca. (Controller), 1984, pp. ix, xvii... *Special Districts of California*, p. I–32; 1980 Census of Population, *General Population Characteristics, California*, Part 6, Washington, D.C. (U.S. Census Bureau), July 1982, Table 14, p. 6–7.

Figure 6B
Municipal Income and Expenditure
Special Districts
(5217 California Districts, 1982–83)

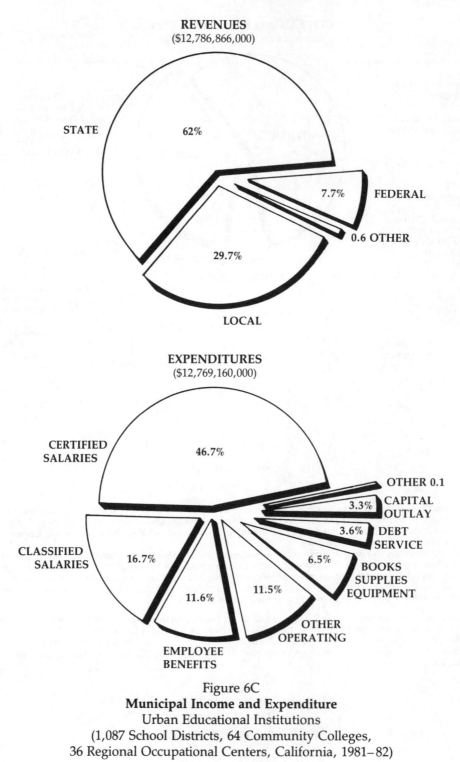

Figure 6C
Municipal Income and Expenditure
Urban Educational Institutions
(1,087 School Districts, 64 Community Colleges,
36 Regional Occupational Centers, California, 1981–82)

The impact of federal tax law on the local economy is illustrated by the effect of tax-reform proposals on the construction of large-scale incinerators, which are needed to replace landfills that have reached capacity. New landfill sites that are environmentally acceptable are so far away that few cities can afford the cost of transporting the huge amounts of refuse they generate every day to these distant places.

Under the Treasury blueprint companies that build and operate these trash-to-energy incinerators in partnership with local governments would lose . . . investment tax credits and five-year straight-line depreciation on most equipment plus accelerated depreciation on energy-generating gear. More important, the Treasury's desire to curtail the tax-free status of industrial development bonds would sharply raise the cost of borrowing money to build these multimillion dollar garbage-disposal projects. It's a

Airport development (22)	Rapid transit, renovation (400)
Child day care (3.7)	Rapid transit, opertions (16.5)
Child placement, homes (6)	Recreation center, elderly
Hospitals (91)	Regional offices, federal
Housing grants/subsidies/ insurance (113.3)	Research center, aerospace (120)
Housing rent subsidies*	Schools (85.4)
Industry, defense (1,300)	lunches
Legal aid society (1.8)	medical (37.9)
Museum, art (.33)	public (47.5)
Orchestra, municipal (.33)	Sewer, district (400)
Pensions (1,366.5)	Small business, loans (13.4)
civil service retirement/ disability (66.1)	Students, grants/loans
coal miners disability (21.6)	Television, station
railroad retirement/disability (3.8)	Theater, reconstruction (3.1)
social security (1,200)	Training, employment
veterans (75)	Training, vocational
	Welfare (192)

*Amount of federal support not known for items without quantities shown in parentheses.

Figure 7
Illustrative Federal Support of a Local Economy
(Numbers in parentheses are thousands of dollars. Total: $4.135 million)

prospect to make local government officials, industry executives and bond lawyers blanch. "It will certainly make
financing very difficult. . . ."(Carlson, 1985)

When authorized by their state government some municipalities collect income taxes from residents and those who work
in the city but live in another jurisdiction. Some levy a city
sales tax. The unreimbursed costs of servicing tax-free institutions can seriously affect a city's operating budget, as indicated by the experience of the economically depressed city
referred to on p. 58. Federal and state agencies acknowledge no
legal obligation to pay local taxes, although some may agree to
make annual payments "in lieu" of taxes. Nonresident employees of these agencies, and students who reside elsewhere but
attend a tax-free educational institution located within the city,
contribute to municipal income through the sales tax on pur-
chases they make within the city and their patronage of business enterprises taxed by the municipality.

public
education

"*Public education* is the largest operation of local governments, viewed in terms of capital investments, current operating expenditures, and the number of employees" (Blair, 1981).
Traditionally, school districts have been financed from local taxes,
mainly the property tax. To equalize expenditures per pupil
among communities with very different property evaluations
and tax rates, states are increasing their direct support. Recently,
for the first time, the states as a whole paid more than one-half
of local education costs. (Figure 6C)

The expenditures of local governments have increased from
$1 billion at the turn of the century to some $175 billion today.

> Cities are the largest spending units for libraries, high-
> ways, airports, parking facilities, water transport and ter-
> minals, police protection, fire protection, protective
> inspection and regulation, sewage, other sanitation, parks
> and recreation, and housing and urban renewal. (Blair,
> 1981)

Some public facilities and general services used by a city may
be shared with or administered by the county, usually because
its larger area permits more efficient operations or more nearly
encompasses the area of need.

Special districts are employed to finance and administer a *special* wide range of local services. In number and variety they exceed *districts* all other units of government. They are employed by some communities to provide certain basic municipal services most cities normally incorporate in the general operating budget, such as fire protection, water supply, housing, drainage, or sewerage. Some urban problems, such as air pollution and solid waste disposal can rarely be resolved by the actions of a single municipality. They require a special organizational entity that covers the large geographical territory involved or required for an effective solution. At the small end of the scale, special districts make it possible for people who are willing to be assessed an annual charge to obtain an installation or service, such as street lighting or a neighborhood park, that benefits them almost exclusively and cannot therefore be properly charged to the municipal public as a whole. (Figure 6B)

Municipalities at the center of metropolitan areas are con- *metropolitan* fronted with a special tax problem. As noted in a previous chap- *centers* ter, these extensive urbanized areas are composed of many municipalities once separated spatially as well as legally. As they grew, they coalesced into one large metropolitan expanse. Industry and the well-to-do moved to the outskirts to obtain more space and to escape the deteriorating physical and social environment at the metropolitan center. They took their tax payments with them to suburban municipalities. This reduced the operating income in precisely those places where municipal needs are greatest and costs are higher than anywhere else in the metropolitan region. For it is in the central cities that the preponderance of blighted and older housing exists, where minorities, the elderly poor, and other disadvantaged people are likely to be found. One medium size central city in the United States reports that it houses

> . . . more than 90 percent of the poor in the region because there was no place else for them to go. . . . Many cities consider themselves in [the same] position: Middle class residents, along with much business and industry, have left city centers for the suburbs, and pay their taxes there. With steadily shrinking tax bases, the cities find they must cope with deteriorating housing and increasing costs. (*The New York Times*, 1976)

To date, depressed central cities have depended on federal and state aid to help them bear the financial burdens imposed on them by the flight of business, industry, and high-income people to the metropolitan suburbs. One solution that is being tried is a sharing of the local taxes collected by municipalities at the periphery where businesses have relocated, with the central city from which they came.

financial rating

A healthy municipal economy enhances the general reputation of the city, favors industrial growth and modernization, tends to attract new business, encourages population growth, reduces unemployment, and improves the *rating* of the municipality by financial institutions. Without a good bond rating, a city must pay higher interest to borrow the money it needs for new construction, to make needed improvements in existing facilities, or even to meet current expenses until it is time for the next tax collection. Without a viable economy, police and fire protection, municipal utilities, public health and other services cannot be maintained much less improved, and are likely to deteriorate.

Unlike many communities in other parts of the world, cities in the United States have left the direct profits of new urban projects to the private land developer. Traditionally, cities have limited their land development activities to transportation facilities, utilities, and other projects long accepted as "public works." The remaining construction in the city is produced by private enterprise with an average expectation of at least doubling the money invested by the time the project is completed. Both categories of projects are built by private construction companies.

Greatly increased fiscal difficulties are changing municipal attitudes and introducing a new element into the economic city. More municipalities maintain that economic markets are created and land development projects are made possible by concentrations of people dependent on utilities and services provided by the city. Access to and from urban projects is on streets and highways built by, maintained, and policed by the municipality or another public body.

In return for aiding developers . . ., cities are demanding a slice of the action. And they are getting it in the form of percentages of rents and growth in the project's values.

This signals a shift in cities' attitudes. Not long ago, most cities were content to reap the extra property tax and greater employment as their reward for making redevelopment happen. . . . The relationship between cities and developers now is more of a *partnership venture*. (Guenther, 1982)

In the United States, more than anywhere else, private enterprise is the primary force in the urban economy. It conducts almost all industrial and commercial activity. It provides the biggest share of local employment, wages and salaries, and pensions for many retired workers. Directly or indirectly it accounts for most of municipal tax revenue. The recreational activities sponsored within business and industry are extensive and a more important part of urban recreation than most people realize. Educational and cultural contributions are considerable: gifts of equipment and scholarships to universities and schools; grants to symphony orchestras, theater and public television programs; supporting charitable enterprises. Private investment is a vital element in the urban economy; it is the sole source of financial support for new and high-risk endeavors. Private enterprise accounts for almost all land development within the city, apart from areas devoted to public transportation, parks and recreation, and other publicly owned land. Collectively, these activities constitute the *private economy*. *private economy*

In large part, the private economy determines the overall economic health of the community, what facilities and services it can afford, how attractive it is to business expansion and consequent urban growth. Business and industry are interested in all municipal activities and intentions that affect their profitability and survival. They exert their influence through chambers of commerce and other business organizations, executive contacts, and political contributions. Physical planning of the city involves a continual adjustment between some public purpose of the municipality, the spatial needs of business and industrial enterprises, and the judgments of land developers concerning the market for different land uses.

The industries most beneficial to a municipality are those that add the greatest value to products by processing raw materials or converting partially finished goods into a finished product or higher level of completion. Similarly, commercial and service activities are most successful if they produce an added value of product availability, procurement convenience, expert knowledge, or some other marketing or helpful attribute. These economic activities are better protected against the risks that confront every enterprise if they serve a demand beyond the city boundaries, as well as the local market created by the municipal population itself. Conversely, too much reliance on external demand increases the exposure of business to unfavorable conditions or harmful events occurring without warning far away. "The economics of the large urban area rests more on intra-urban analysis, quite distinct from the inter-urban economics of the smaller place" (Thompson, 1967).

diversification   The greater the *diversification* of the products and services, the less vulnerable the local economy to adverse developments in one sector of business endeavor or demand. On the average, it will suffer less in recessions than an economy that is less diversified. Some communities can diversify only to a limited extent. The town in the mountains or at the seashore whose economy is dependent on seasonal recreation can usually do little more than try to develop other activities that will attract different people during the "off season." A town located at the site of a natural resource extracted or processed by an industry that supports the community economically, finds it difficult or impossible to attract a different industry to reduce its economic dependence on the fortunes of a single business.

financing   The availability of *financing* is essential to all economic activity. If an enterprise has not accumulated the funds it needs to modernize or grow, it must borrow from financial institutions, wealthy investors, or from the public at large through the sale of securities. The availability of risk capital is crucial for new enterprises venturing in new directions with the possibility of achieving significant advances and large profits. All successful economic activities went through a pioneering period in the past.

economic environment   The urban economy does not exist in a vacuum. It functions within an *economic environment* which influences local conditions increasingly as economic developments at different levels and at different places become more interdependent. A depressed national economy reduces the effective demand for goods and services, increases unemployment and related governmental costs. If interest rates rise, construction falls off and business in general finds the higher cost of borrowing money makes it difficult to finance expansion and modernization. Also the sale of municipal bonds to pay for capital improvements and other needs is more costly for the city.

Nonprofit, volunteer, tax-exempt organizations constitute the *special economy* or "independent sector" of cities. They are also an important element of the social city discussed earlier in this chapter, providing charitable help, various forms of assistance, and an array of services not supplied by government or by private enterprise for profit. The special economy is larger and more diverse than most people realize. It includes educational institutions ranging from large universities to special programs small in size, church and religious activities of many kinds, many types of charities, foundations, fraternal, professional, and veterans organizations, social and recreational clubs, labor, agricultural, and advocacy groups, nonprofit businesses, and many others.

special economy

> There may be as many as six million voluntary organizations in the United States alone and nonprofit organizations employ one out of six professional workers and they own one-ninth of all property. (Commission, 1975) Voluntary services and amenities are key components of the urban economy, since they provide jobs and income that stimulate growth, they increase the productivity potential of the urban labor force, and they create conditions essential for urban development. (Wolch, 1983)

The average employment in the special economy of cities is probably between 10 and 15 percent of the total municipal work force. The economic significance of this employment is augmented by the multiplier effect of the goods and services purchased by the wages and salaries involved.

There are more than 750,000 *tax-exempt nonprofit organizations* in the United States. They eliminate a substantial portion of municipal revenue. On the other hand, some of them reduce the costs of certain social services that would otherwise be provided by the municipality. Others, as reported above, contribute indirectly to the economic health of the community.

The social and economic views of the city noted in this chapter indicate the kinds of forces and considerations involved in comprehensive city planning. When these two views are combined with their multiple interconnections, the operational and analytical complexity of the socioeconomic city is apparent. When the socioeconomic city is conceptually combined with the physical city and with the multiple interrelationships that exist between them, comprehensive understanding of the city is advanced.

CITATIONS

[1] Blair, George S., *Government at the Grass Roots*, Pacific Palisades, CA (Palisades Publishers), 1981, pp. 270, 268-269. [2] Carlson, Eugene, "Treasury's Proposal Threatens Cities' Garbage-Disposal Plans," *The Wall Street Journal*, 8 January 1985, p. 35. [3] Commission on Private Philanthropy and Public Needs, *Giving in America: Toward a Stronger Voluntary Sector*, New York, 1975, p. 11. [4] Ferrell, Tom and Virginia Adams, "Downwind from St. Louis," *The New York Times*, 20 March 1977, p. 6. [5] Guenther, Robert, "Cities Getting Part of Profits For Giving Aid to Developers," *The Wall Street Journal*, 29 September 1982, p. 29. [6] Herbers, John, "Congress Survey Finds Cities Using Property Tax to Absorb Losses in Aid," *The New York Times*, 17 October 1982, p. 124. [7] Isenberg, Barbara, "To Be Old and Poor Is to Be Alone, Afraid, Ill-Fed and Unknown," *The Wall Street Journal*, 15 November 1972, pp. 1, 16. [8] Lynch, Mitchell C., "Smaller Cities Aren't Immune to Fiscal Ills: Just Ask the Mayor of Providence, R.I.," *The Wall Street Journal*, 10 April 1981, p. 27. [9] *The New York Times*, "Hartford Suburbs Must Obey Rules to Get U.S. Aid," 1 February 1976, p. IV, 4. [10] Thompson, Wilbur R., "Urban Economics," in: Wentworth, Eldridge (Editor), *Taming Megalopolis*, Garden City, NJ (Anchor-Doubleday), 1967, Vol. 1, pp. 156-190. [11] Wolch, Jennifer R., "The Voluntary Sector in Urban Communities," *Environment and Planning D: Society and Space*, 1983, pp. 181-190. [12] Yao, Margaret, "Federal Money Flows in Wide, Deep Stream Across American Life," *The Wall Street Journal*, 9 April 1981, pp. 1, 16.

SELECTED REFERENCES

[1] Banerjee, Tridib and William C. Baer, *Beyond the Neighborhood Unit*, Residential Environments and Public Policy, New York (Plenum), 1984, 153 pp. [2] Butler, Edgar W., *The Urban Crisis: Problems & Prospects in America*, Santa Monica, CA (Goodyear), 1977, 240 pp. [3] Freeman, T.W., *Geography and Planning*, London (Hutchinson), Fourth Edition, 1974, 200 pp. [4] Hodgkinson, Virginia Ann and Murray S. Weitzman, *Dimensions of the Independent Sector, A Statistical Profile*, Washington, DC (Independent Sector), 1984, 69

pp. [5] Jacobs, Jane, *The Economy of Cities*, New York (Random House), 1969, 286 pp. [6] Owen, Wilfred, *The Accessible City*, Washington, DC (Brookings), 1972, 150 pp. [7] Raban, Jonathan, *Soft City*, Douglas, Isle of Man (Fontana/ Collins), 1975, 253 pp. [8] Schreiber, Arthur F.; Paul K. Gatons; Richard B. Clemmer, *Economics of Urban Problems*, An Introduction, New York (Houghton Mifflin), 1971, 153 pp. [9] Shannon, Thomas R., *Urban Problems in Sociological Perspective*, New York (Random House), 1983, 289 pp. [10] Urozsky, Melvin I. (Editor), *Perspectives on Urban America*, Garden City, NY (Anchor-Doubleday), 1973, 307 pp. [11] Weber, Max, *The City*, New York (Free Press), 1958, 242 pp.

What the government wants to do, and has the power to do, it will generally try to do—law, ethics, and common sense frequently notwithstanding. Officials may pause at the outset of an undertaking for a nominal weighing of the pros and cons. This can involve elaborate cost-benefit analyses, hearing records, legal briefs, committee reports, environmental-impact statements, and the like. Still, it will be the enthusiasm of the proponents and their political power, rather than the merits of the case, that usually prove decisive. Once a major project is begun, moreover, it will grow and create a life of its own. If its rationale is disproven or forgotten, if it produces unwanted side effects, or even if it fails utterly, the momentum it achieves—its ineradicable, weedlike vitality—will often be enough to sustain the program long past the point at which it should be curtailed or abandoned. Curiously, the more that is at stake the more this appears likely to be the case.

Daniel Ford, "The Cult of the Atom—II," *The New Yorker*, 1 November 1982.

CHAPTER 6
WHO PLANS THE CITY?

City planning cannot be effective unless it identifies, understands, and utilizes the governmental and non-governmental power structure.

A S WOULD be expected, who plans the city differs among countries, cultures, and political systems. In decentralized governmental systems, local communities enjoy different degrees of autonomy depending on the policies and strength of higher levels of government and the political and economic situation of the municipality. In highly centralized societies, basic policies and operating directives are made for subordinate units of government by the national authority: political, military, or religious, acting separately or in combination. Cities in democratic societies may be planned by a loose-knit power structure composed of the most influential forces in the community, by a single business in a "company town," by a local leader in a small village, or by any one or several of many actors and organizations. They may be directly active or indirectly manipulative, well known or unrecognized behind the scenes. In all of these situations planning is woven into the directive fabric of society.

Truly comprehensive planning cannot be conducted by a single individual or several people, although they may greatly influence the process. Even in the smallest and simplest communities planning involves many actions, participants, fields of knowledge, and levels of decision and implementation. It is impossible for any one person to comprehend analytically the network of major elements and interactions that are involved in comprehensive planning for a modern industrialized city, much less to direct its primary operating components personally. It is a collective process with varying degrees of individual understanding and participation.

73

In the United States city planning is the product of two groups of forces: government and non-government. *Government* is the official organizational structure of representation and administration established under law to govern and operate the city. *Non-government* comprises those forces that are not part of official government but nonetheless influence or determine the planning of the city. The relative power of these two forces to shape municipal planning varies greatly among societies, political systems, and historical times. But usually city planning is the product of the activities of many organizations and individuals both within and outside government.

Government

City planning by larger municipalities in the United States is performed by city councils and their staff offices, operating departments, city planning departments and commissions, and other local agencies.

city *council* The elected *city council* or an equivalent governing body with a different name is the ultimate decision making authority in the municipality. It bears final responsibility for the scope and effectiveness of city planning within its jurisdiction. It effects its collective will by formulating and enacting legislation concerning a host of municipal matters, establishing policies, controlling the collection and allocation of municipal taxes and other money channeled through the city government, exercising its power of investigation, and generally overseeing the performance of staff offices and operating departments. Some city councils appoint a number of the administrative officials and supervise certain areas of managerial activity. In small communities council members may be directly responsible for municipal activities that are performed by large operating departments in big cities. If overall municipal management does not incorporate sufficient planning, public utilities and services will not function properly and in free societies the public will be heard from quickly and in no uncertain terms.

> [Council members] are reluctant to support comprehensive planning for the organism as a whole when it does not conform to the precise concerns and expressed wishes of their electoral district. They resist the commitments nec-

essary for long range planning because they fear that voter attitudes in the future on the issues involved may haunt them at reelection time. (Branch, 1983)

Council members tend, therefore, to limit their activities relating to longer range city planning to general policies and land use legislation that is as uncontroversial as possible, required by state enabling acts, or recommended by the city planning commission and department.

But developments are forcing a higher level of planning. As the various systems of providing public utilities and services become more complex technically and managerially, superior planning is required. The installation, modernization, and maintenance of most large municipal projects must be planned years ahead. "Lead times" are from five to ten years between the decision to proceed and completion of the project. Municipal systems are also becoming more closely interrelated. For example, petroleum price increases and the recent world shortage have forced many municipalities to consider coal and other alternate sources, as well as energy conservation. As nearby waste disposal sites are filled to capacity, cities are considering building plants that burn waste and produce energy. There is no simple solution to urban traffic congestion in large industrial cities. The different transportation subsystems are closely interrelated. Improvement in one of them does not suffice; they must be planned and operated as a total urban transportation system. As the management of cities becomes more complicated, elected officials are finding that they must devote more time and attention to comprehensive planning to perform well enough to be reelected or attain higher office.

The role and authority of *mayors* depends on the form of *mayor* the municipal government. In strong-mayor municipal governments, the mayor is the administrative head of the city, appoints department directors, can veto council actions subject to an overriding council vote, proposes the municipal budget, and shares policy-making and political leadership with the city council. In weak-mayor municipal governments, these powers and prerogatives do not exist or may be severely curtailed in favor of the city council, the elective term of office of the mayor is usually shorter, and in some communities the mayor is a

administrative designated member of the city council. Either strong- or weak-
officials mayor governments may provide for a *city manager* or *chief administrative officer* appointed by the council to manage the operating departments of the municipality.

Whether weak or strong, the political prestige of the mayorality can be applied favorably or unfavorably to city planning. The extent of the mayor's managerial control over the operating departments and how this is applied is one of the determinants *central* of successful city planning. *Central staffs* may be part of the *staffs* office of the mayor, the city manager, or a member of the city council or one of its working committees. These staffs affect the efficiency of the municipal planning process by proposing procedures, rules and regulations to be followed by municipal departments in making their budget requests, handling their personnel, and purchasing supplies and equipment.

operating Each *operating department* prepares the designs, plans, and
departments programs required to perform the service for which it is responsible in accordance with its own policies and any constraints imposed by a higher level of government. One such restriction with far-reaching consequences for the operating department is the annual budget indicating the funds available to the city as a whole and to each of its parts. In a large municipality operational units are concerned with a wide range of activities which could include:

Airport	Fire protection	Public works
Animal regulation	Harbor	Purchasing
Art	Library	Recreation
Attorney	Museum	Sanitation
Building	Parks	Social services
Controller	Pensions	Transportation
Data services	Personnel	Treasurer
Engineering	Police	Water supply
Health	Power plant	

These kinds of municipal activities enable a sizable city to exist and function successfully. They reflect and shape both the "physical city" and the "socioeconomic city" discussed in the previous chapter. In smaller communities several of these functions are combined in a few departments; some may receive no municipal attention at all. As fiscal situations change, some operations may be transferred to a higher level of government, others to neighborhood groups or to private contractors. The city charter may establish a strong or weak administrative government, which may or may not employ a city manager or chief administrative officer who is responsible for the efficient operation of the municipal departments, reporting to the mayor or to the city council.

Besides the regular operating departments there is the *school district* with its separate budget supported by local taxpayers, state tax rebates, and various forms of federal aid. As shown in Figure 6C, it is the largest public expenditure in urban areas. *school district*

Municipalities depend on *special* or *functional districts* when they cannot supply their own potable water, discharge their effluents, dispose of solid wastes, or control flood waters and air pollution within their own city limits. Special districts combining the financial resources of several or many cities are often needed to finance the capital expenditures required to supply the water they need. Air pollution control and toxic waste disposal usually involve geographical areas much larger than the jurisdiction of any one municipality. Each special district plans and implements its functional responsibility. Ordinarily they are headed by directors or administrators, in a few cities by commissions. In small communities, district functions may be managed by members or committees of the city council or board of trustees, supervisors, or select persons in townships. *special districts*

Among those who plan cities are *city planning commissions and departments*. They have no citywide operating responsibilities. As discussed at greater length in the next chapter, they are an advisory staff making recommendations to the city council and chief municipal official concerning the master planning of land use and certain physical facilities, the subdivision of property, and sometimes capital project improvement programs. As indicated in Chapter 13, when an *urban redevelopment agency* exists it is usually established as a separate body since its activities are operational rather than advisory. There may also be a municipal *housing authority* formed years ago to build and manage lower-income housing financed in substantial part by the federal government. *city planning* *urban redevelopment* *public housing*

Agencies at other levels of government also affect planning a city. The placement of a segment of a transportation route in

other
municipalities

one city may be determined by the location of the route with which it should connect in *another municipality.* Development of a large commercial center master planned for the future at a location near the city boundary is no longer economically feasible if the adjacent city builds a similar center a short distance away within its own jurisdiction, thereby preempting the trade area and local taxes of the center proposed in its neighbor's master plan. Actions by municipalities some distance away may affect planning with respect to air pollution, flood control, and other environmental conditions involving areas or regions much larger than a single municipality.

county

Many of the transportation and utility systems of a city extend into the surrounding territory controlled by the next higher level of government: the *county* in the United States. In most places, part of the working population of the city resides in the county, which often contains competing commercial and industrial work places. Some functional activities—such as those relating to air pollution, drainage, and waste disposal noted in a previous connection—involve a geographical area larger than the area within the city limits. As a consequence, a number of cities in recent years have shared some functional operations with the county.

> Few if any domestic problems—human services, resources, conservation, transportation, what have you—can be solved by the solitary efforts of any one sphere [of government]. (Snelling, 1984)

Some people believe that a wave of the future in city planning is the gradual assumption by county governments of the responsibility for planning the major urban systems that extend throughout its much larger area, now planned separately with limited coordination among the principal municipalities within the county. The difficulties of attaining this larger scale planning are indicated in Chapter 15 on Metropolitan Urban Planning.

state
government

Actions by *state and federal governments* affect municipal planning in many ways, illustrated by the following few of many possible examples. Since municipalities are "creatures of the state," city planning is legalized and prescribed in most states by state enabling acts. State policies and programs may determine what is possible or feasible in city planning with respect to waterways, highways, railroads, parks and recreational areas, airports, communication systems, taxation, social services, or any one of a long list of plans and activities in which the state may be actively engaged or concerned. And as states provide more money supporting local education and other municipal operations, their influence on city planning with respect to these activities can be expected to increase.

The *federal government* has for more than half a century promoted the establishment of city planning commissions and departments in communities throughout the United States, by making grants-in-aid to city planning departments and by requiring proper project planning as a condition for its financial assistance. In recent years, Washington has gone further by defining the more comprehensive kind of city planning the community must undertake to receive federal help, or more specifically the degree of citizen participation that must be encouraged and obtained as part of the process of planning. In the number and range of the direct grants and indirect subsidies it has provided, and the conditional requirements it has imposed over the years, the federal government has profoundly influenced municipal operations and planning, as shown in Figure 7, (page 63).

federal government

City planning must conform with *legislation* affecting urban areas and regions that relates to "public health, safety, and welfare," land use, subdivision, and environmental quality. These laws may be enacted by the municipality itself, the county in which it is located, the state, or the federal government. There are also *court decisions* rendered on appeal that define constitutional requirements and limitations, and legally permissible actions. To the list of laws and court decisions relating to land use referred to in Chapters 10 and 11, must be added those concerning the activities of municipal departments. This considerable collection of laws, regulations, and court decisions establishes the legal boundaries within which those who plan cities must function.

legislation

court decisions

Figure 8 illustrates diagrammatically the range of governmental influences on urban planning in a large city. Although they are indeed numerous and complicated, they must nonetheless be taken into account in realistic planning.

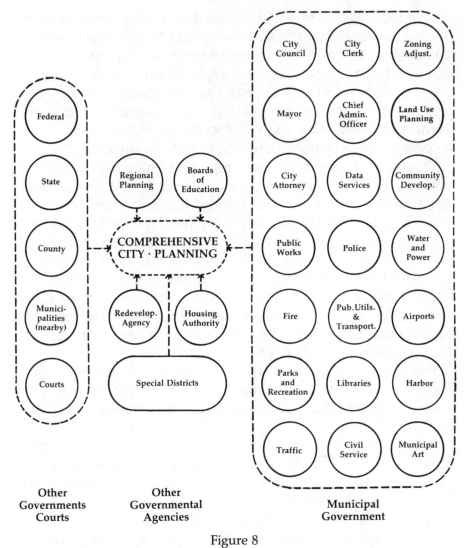

Figure 8
Governmental Participants in Planning a Large City

Non-Government

Because city planning involves such a spectrum of people, organizations, and activities, those who are not part of official government will always have an impact in one or more of the ways discussed in this section. Their influence will vary with the political system and situation. But even in nations highly controlled by their governments there are always people and organizations outside of government which will influence its policies and actions in some way. When non-government forces are dominant, as happens at times, they will shape city planning more than the official government.

Those concerned with the future development of a community identify its *non-governmental power structure* and determine in what ways it will direct the choice of policies and feasible actions in city planning. It may range from a single individual in small communities—or even in larger communities under special circumstances—to a shifting balance among many organizations with decidedly different responsibilities and views. Any reasonable municipal action is feasible if it has the backing of the city government, the leading business enterprises including financial institutions, and those associations that are most representative of the municipal population as a whole or its most influential groups of people. But each of these interests has its own distinct objectives. A coalition requires that those participating avoid seeking to maximize their respective positions in favor of moderation benefitting their mutual self-interest or the general public interest of the community. *power structure*

As the almost universal means of instant communication, television is the most powerful non-governmental force in the United States and increasingly throughout the rest of the world. It is generally agreed that a person cannot be elected to a noteworthy public office in the United States without television and newspaper exposure. If and when this exposure expands in the future to include continuous dissemination of news, comment, and information to electronic terminals in the home, the influence of the *mass media of communication* will be even greater. At present, only those city planning matters that are highly controversial or otherwise "newsworthy" are covered on television, radio, or in the newspapers. There is no regular time and place where the actions of municipal government affecting the city's population are reported regularly and made available to the general public and many special interests. Besides their direct impact on elections and the information the public receives, the mass media influence the policies and activities of financial, political, religious, and citizens' organizations which in turn affect city planning. The pervasive effects of the mass media *mass media* on every aspect of modern industrialized society can hardly be exaggerated.

politics   Although *politics* in one form or another is ever-present in human affairs, it varies as a force in city planning. Political parties are all powerful in some countries where they are the core of government. In some of these there is highly centralized planning implemented by national plans covering five-year periods or longer. In the United States where political parties are not an official part of government, their involvement and strength varies greatly between different sections of the country and different communities. There are cities where a political party dominates municipal policies and actions through elected representatives and appointed government officials. In other places, political parties are not determinative in the election process but influence public or private organizations that are involved with city planning.

Politics is not limited, of course, to political parties. It exists among officials striving to outperform each other, and between different units within the same organization seeking some advantage. Bureaucratic politics can have negative consequences when municipal departments concerned with city planning needlessly compete with each other rather than cooperate constructively. In unusual situations, personal politics between individuals within municipal departments can determine whether city planning is successful for as long as these competing individuals are active. Politics broadly defined is to be expected in most occupational situations involving people: in one form or another, to a greater or lesser degree, with positive or negative results. It is an essential ingredient of human existence.

religion   As noted in a previous chapter, *religion* has played a vital role in urban development throughout history. At times it has been synonymous with government in countries where a strong ecclesiastical tradition exists or a surge of religious zeal has occurred. In some nations the official government is in fact a religious government. In the United States where there is a constitutional separation of church and state, the influence of religion and ecclesiastical organizations differs among cities. It may be exerted directly on members of the city council with respect to general municipal policies and actions, or indirectly through other non-governmental organizations. Usually the direct influence of religion on city planning is concentrated on sites for churches and other ecclesiastical activities, the "land use" or type of activity permitted on church properties, and their exemption from local taxes.

In the past, the national exchequer was controlled by a king, emperor, or another royal personage, but there were always non-governmental sources of funds to support projects undertaken by the ruling authority. In a few countries all economic resources are owned by the government and there are no non-governmental financial institutions. And in most countries today governments play a larger role in their economies than in the United States, where private enterprises account for a greater share of the national economy than anywhere else in the world. *Financial institutions* underwrite private land development projects and make construction and mortgage loans for a substantial part of the physical city which is built for the most part by non-governmental enterprises. Another share of the economy of the city is underwritten by institutions, small investors, and wealthy individuals who invest in municipal bonds and in commerce and industry to start new enterprises and modernize and expand existing businesses. Few democratic governments dare use taxpayers' money for the risk capital needed to fuel pioneering business endeavors and those with a low probability of success and profit.

financial institutions

Private organizations publish *ratings* of the investment quality of the municipal bonds that are sold to finance major revenue-producing or tax-supported public projects. The amount of interest which must be paid and the cost to the city for the loan depends on these ratings. If they are too low, the municipal bonds cannot be sold on the open investment market. The rates charged by private insurance companies also relate to the situation and performance of a city, to its fire department and building code regulations for fire insurance, to its police department for burglary coverage. Some areas of a city that are subject to exceptional hazard are charged higher rates or private insurance may not be available, as is the case for dwellings located in flood plains subject to repeated inundation. Insur-

rating

ance rates constitute a cost of doing business and maintaining most homes, and they are an element in the community's attractiveness to new enterprise and its economic health.

The different responsibilities that exist and the different interests that can develop between governmental and non-governmental forces in city planning are illustrated by the reluctance of private financial institutions to make home mortgage and business loans in the depressed areas of cities most in need of economic revitalization. These financial institutions determine in large part the development of land in cities in the United States, the type and amount of new building construction, the extent of home ownership, and the economic image of the municipality. Each of these has a great deal to do with planning the city.

associations   The United States appears to have more non-governmental *associations* than any other nation, literally hundreds of thousands of organizations, clubs, and groups large and small devoted to many different purposes and kinds of activities. Some of these regularly observe the activities of cities and recommend ways of improving municipal performance. There are leagues of cities and leagues of women voters, neighborhood groups, and the numerous non-governmental associations of professional people concerned with cities: including urban and regional planners, city managers, municipal finance officers, civil engineers, and real estate developers. Many citizens' organizations in the United States are formed on short notice to favor or oppose a proposed municipal action. This is the case in city planning when changes in the permitted use of residential property are proposed that would immediately affect the value of nearby homes, which are zealously protected by their owners because they are the largest investment for the average American family. After the land use decision is made, single-purpose citizen groups usually disband. Labor unions are among the large associations that can have a significant impact on municipal decisions in the United States.

individual   The lone *individual* mounting a strategic and persistent campaign of advocacy or opposition to a municipal proposal concerning city planning can exert an influence far greater than might be expected. Sometimes a person not connected with any governmental organization is in fact the primary city planner through political or business connections, respected professional competence, great wealth, or personal charisma. Naturally, this is most likely to occur in smaller places where the impact of one person is proportionately greater and wide exposure to the local public is possible. Collectively, as members of the political majority or of a sufficiently powerful special interest group to affect the outcome, private citizens are the power behind municipal decisions in democratic societies— provided they are motivated to act, can make themselves heard, and are seriously considered in the political process.

Many governmental and non-governmental forces are involved in planning cities. At any one time and place the decision making combination may be different than in the same city at another time, and probably very different from the decision making forces in other cities. Only a few of the possible actors determine the outcome in any given situation and at any particular time, and a combination of a few powerful forces may be mainly responsible for planning a city during a period of many years. City planning cannot be effective unless it identifies, understands, and utilizes the governmental and non-governmental *power structure* that directly or indirectly plans the city by determining what can and cannot be undertaken and accomplished.

> If you are not willing to learn what the system is, and understand it, then you cannot possibly expect to cope, and you deserve everything it does to you. (Chase, Reveal, 1983)

CITATIONS

[1] Branch, Melville C., *Comprehensive Planning, General Theory and Principles*, Pacific Palisades, CA (Palisades Publishers), 1983, pp. 194–195. [2] Chase, Gordon and Elizabeth C. Reveal, *How To Manage in the Public Sector*, Reading, MA (Addison-Wesley), 1983, p. 79. [3] Snelling, Richard A., Governor (Vermont), quoted in: John Herbers, "City Services Assumed by Bigger Governments," *The New York Times*, 20 February 1984, p. 15.

SELECTED REFERENCES

[1] Adrian, Charles R. and Charles Press, *Governing Urban America*, New York (McGraw-Hill), Fifth Edition, 1977, 401 pp. [2] Banfield, Edward C. and James Q. Wilson, *City Politics*, New York (Vintage), 1963, 362 pp. [3] Harrigan, John J., *Political Change in the Metropolis*, Boston, MA (Little, Brown),

Second Edition, 1981, 462 pp. [4] Hunter, Floyd, *Community Power Structure, A Study of Decision-Makers*, Chapel Hill, NC (University of North Carolina), 1953, 297 pp. [5] Lowry, Richie P., *Who's Running This Tour?*, Community Leadership and Social Change, New York (Harper & Row), 1965, 250 pp. [6] Rabinovitz, Francine F., *City Politics and Planning*, New York (Atherton), 1969, 192 pp. [7] Woll, Peter and Robert H. Binstock, *America's Political System, Urban, State, and Local*, New York (Random House), Second Edition, 1975, 127 pp. [8] Yates, Douglas, The Ungovernable City: *The Politics of Urban Problems and Policy Making*, Cambridge, MA (M.I.T.), 1978, 219 pp.

Continuous planning is needed for the conservation and wise development of our natural resources—both natural and human. With new inventions, new ideals, and new discoveries, no fixed plan or policy will suffice; for any rigid mould or blueprint plan, if strictly adhered to, may restrict our freedom rather than enlarge it. . . . we must constantly make new plans to meet new conditions.

U.S. National Resources Committee, *Planning Our Resources*, 1938.

CHAPTER 7
PROCEDURE

City planning in the United States as presently practiced combines planning by the operating municipal departments and planning by city planning commissions and departments acting as staff to the chief executive official and the city council.

T HE PROCESS of city planning involves a *procedure* for gathering information, making recommendations, and taking action. It also involves a system of analysis, of studying the situation and reaching rational conclusions concerning municipal needs, objectives, and the best courses of directive action. The procedural part of the process is discussed in this chapter, the analytical part in the next.

Procedures for city planning differ between countries, reflecting the political, cultural, and historical situation. In those with a single or dominant political party, local plans are dictated in large part by the national government. Non-governmental input is extensive in some countries, nonexistent in others. Direct citizen participation as practiced in the United States is rare. When financial support of the city planning effort is strong, certain procedures are practical that are impossible when operating funds are minimal.

In the United States, comprehensive city planning conforms to the general requirements and constraints established by the Constitution and interpretive law relating to the powers and prerogatives of the city council, appointed officials, and municipal agencies, and the rights of petitioners and citizens to be heard by their government and to appeal to higher authority. Generally the legislative procedure incorporates the normal sequence of consideration by a committee of the city council or the council as a whole, floor debate, concurrence or rejection by the chief elected official, final debate, formulation of an ordinance implementing the city planning decision, and its adoption into law. Usually the time and place for each of

constitutional conformity

these procedural steps are announced in advance, and the public can attend and be heard at some stage of the procedure. Individuals and organizations are free to communicate in writing with their elected representatives and appointed officials at any time, with reasonable assurance that these expressions will become part of the written record. In some states legislative actions *in camera* are specifically prohibited except for personnel matters requiring confidentiality to protect those involved. While it is easy to assume and appreciate these basic steps incorporated in local legislative procedures in the United States when one is accustomed to them, their significance in free societies cannot be overemphasized.

operational planning   At the present time, city planning in the United States consists of planning by the operating municipal departments and planning by city planning commissions and departments acting as staffs to the chief executive official and the city council. *Operating departments* formulate plans for their own activities and submit them through the chief executive of the municipality to the city council, as part of the department's annual budget request or in connection with some special proposal or response. Regular provisions are made by many municipal departments for petitioners and public to make contact; further access must be made through the director or when the department is appearing before the city council in public session. Direct citizen participation occurs when a controversial issue is raised or a large project is proposed. Arrangements are made at either the departmental or council level for special sessions when citizen support and opposition are heard. The opportunities provided for petitioner and public contact are also avenues for special interest groups that regularly follow the activities of municipal departments to express their opinions and seek to influence decisions and actions. Limited public comment is normally allowed when city councils, city commissions, municipal departments, or departmental commissions conduct their business in open session as is the usual practice or required by law in some states.

land use planning   Staff planning by *city planning commissions and departments* is a more formal and open procedure. Figure 9 depicts the procedure in a large American municipality with a departmental commission form of government and a well-developed pro-

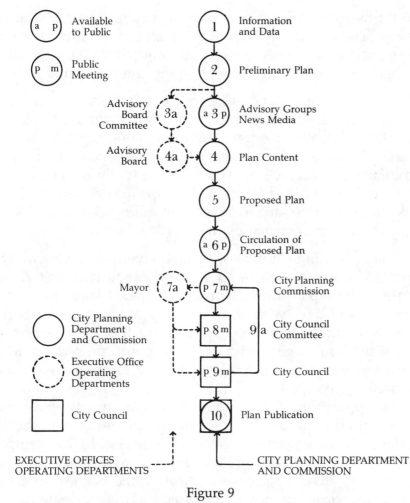

Figure 9
Procedure for Traditional City Planning in a Large Municipality

gram of traditional land use planning. The director of the department is responsible for Steps 1 through 6, with the advice of an advisory board composed of representatives from a number of the operating departments of the city (3a through 4a). The proposed plan is submitted to the city planning commission and the mayor or city manager at the same time (7), with the chief executive official registering his or her reactions with the planning committee of the city council (8) and later with the full council (9) when it considers and acts on the proposed land use plan. Since this example is drawn from a weak-mayor government, the mayor's veto over council actions requiring a

two-thirds vote to override is his main means of administrative
dissent. The city council can require modification or revision
as the final decision making body adopting or rejecting the land
use plan proposed by the city planning commission (9a).

> While the influence and power of commissions varies from
> place to place, the planning commission continues to play
> a role in virtually all organized [urban and regional] plan-
> ning programs…. The primary function of most planning
> commissions continues to be zoning and subdivision review,
> although most of the planning directors questioned would
> like their commissions to devote more time to policy mak-
> ing and comprehensive planning. (Browne, 1980)

Most city planning commissions have seven or nine members
appointed for from four to six years, meeting once or twice a
month without pay. Most members are male Caucasians, over
forty years of age, with the following occupations or backgrounds in the order of occurrence: business and services,
architecture and engineering, real estate and contracting, education and government. Retired people and homemakers are
also well represented.

The opportunity for non-governmental organizations and
individual citizens to participate in city planning is probably
greater in the United States than anywhere else. In the example
shown in Figure 9, both preliminary and proposed plans are
circulated to advisory groups and interested parties for comment (a3p, a6p). The public can attend and participate to the
extent practicable at the three steps conducted as public meetings (p7m, p8m, p9m).

The final product of this procedure is a plan in the form of
a printed publication limited to land use. The combined plans
of the operating units of the city are not included, although
they cover a much larger number and range of municipal activities. Since the land use plan is in the form of a printed publication it cannot be revised quickly or modified repeatedly
because of the considerable time required and cost of reprinting. It has been proposed that requests for changes in land use
be received and considered only every several years or once a
year during a designated period. This proposal is not feasible
even for a traditional land use plan because of developments

that require immediate action. It is all the more unrealistic and impossible for a comprehensive city plan that integrates the policies, objectives, and plans for the ongoing activities of municipal operating departments and agencies. Figure 9 depicts a superior procedure for conducting land use planning, but its failure to include the activities and plans of the municipal operating departments signifies the inadequacy of comprehensive city planning in the United States today.

In smaller communities, the procedures of traditional land use planning are simpler and less specifically programmed, but the essential steps to meet the requirements of "due process" are provided and the public is given an opportunity to be heard. In strong-mayor municipal governments, the mayor may be influential in the formulation of the land use plan. The precise procedure of conducting city planning also depends on the type and placement of the planning unit in the organizational structure of the government.

Three *organizational locations* are illustrated in Figure 10 (Goodman, Freund, 1968). The first of these, the independent planning commission and department (1) is the most frequent form introduced around the turn of the century by well-meaning proponents of good government as a way of surmounting the political corruption disclosed at the time. In each case, the planning commission and department are staff units reporting to the city council. Often they forward their recommendations to the mayor or city manager at the same time. The four illustrative operating departments of the municipality (d) have a line "command and control" relationship with the executive (ex) and legislature (le) as indicated in Figure 10.1. The content, formulation, and implementation of their plans are separate from the land use plans of the city planning commission and department.

The only difference between the planning department (2) and the independent planning commission (1) are the organizational connections to the planning department (pd). Rather than reporting to the commission, the planning department reports to the executive, mayor or city manager; the planning commission continues to report to the legislature, in an advisory capacity as an independent unit. Not only do these two units prepare different plans for different people, but one is

organizational location

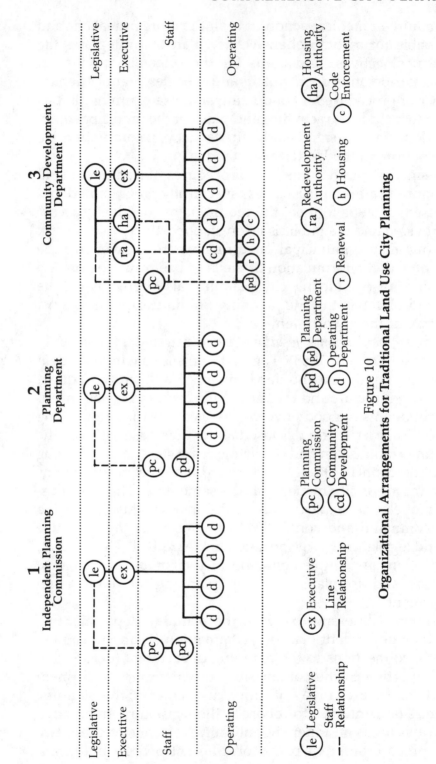

Figure 10

Organizational Arrangements for Traditional Land Use City Planning

advisory only and the other is part of the chain of directive control. This presents a potentially disruptive conflict inherent in the organizational arrangement.

The third form of municipal organization, the community development department (3), incorporates two additional operating units reporting directly to the city council (le): the redevelopment authority (ra) and the housing authority (ha). These are not included in the previous two organizational arrangements because they are considered operating rather than staff agencies, since they involve financing, market analysis, contracting, project design and management, and other activities not normally the responsibility or particular competence of a city planning staff. The community development department (cd) is designed to plan and manage all four of the municipal activities traditionally related to physical planning: community land use planning, renewal of deteriorated sections of the city, provision of lower cost housing, and the enforcement of construction and operating codes required for public health and safety in buildings and structures. Under this arrangement, the planning department (pd) is under the community development department. It would appear from the organizational arrangement that the planning department supports the planning commission (pc) in the formulation of land use plans recommended to the city council (le); at the same time it must perform some operational activities for the community development department under which it is placed. Considerable staff contact is shown in Figure 10.3 between the redevelopment and housing authorities (ra and ha) and the city planning commission at the staff level.

Comprehensive planning of all municipal activities collectively would also be a staff activity. It could be attached to one of three alternate decision making levels of municipal government, depending on the extent to which the higher levels are willing to participate directly in the comprehensive planning process, rather than simply selecting policy objectives and modifying or revising draft plans submitted to them for approval. There is no independent planning commission because comprehensive planning is integrated into the regular operations of the city as the primary instrument of overall municipal management. Land use is not a separate end in itself but part of

comprehensive planning

the much broader content of the comprehensive city plan. With appropriate procedures, the comprehensive planning staff could function at any one of the three alternative organizational locations shown in Figure 11 (alt.1, alt.2, or alt.3).

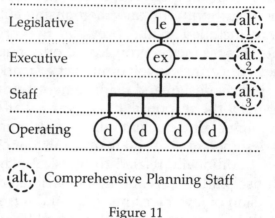

(alt.) Comprehensive Planning Staff

Figure 11
Organizational Locations for a Comprehensive City Planning Staff

CITATIONS

[1] Browne, Carolyn, "The Planning Commission: Its Composition and Function, 1979," Planning Advisory Service Report No. 348, Chicago, IL (American Planning Association), 1980, 11 pp. [2] Goodman, William I. and Eric C. Freund, *Principles and Practice of Urban Planning*, Washington, DC (International City Management Association), Fourth Edition, 1968, pp. 528-530.

SELECTED REFERENCE

[1] Vranicar, John, Welford Sanders, David Mosena, *Streamlining Land Use Regulation*, A Guidebook for Local Governments, Washington, DC (Government Printing Office), November 1980, 74 pp.

CHAPTER 8
ANALYSIS

Unless the functioning of the city can be expressed in some usefully descriptive or analytically representative way, sound city planning is severely limited.

A NALYSIS IS the heart and brain of the city planning process. It is essential to the primary purpose of applying reason in the conduct of municipal affairs. It is the means of evaluating the condition of the community, simulating its functioning, projecting important developments within the city and its external environment, reaching conclusions concerning what can and should be done, and determining how this should be accomplished. Because there are many occasions when purely political considerations, self-interest, irrational opinion, prejudice, emotional overreaction, or best guess determine particular actions, the best comprehensive planning analysis includes these forces in the range of factors it considers in reaching conclusions and taking action.

Since many different elements and aspects of the city are taken into account in comprehensive planning, many forms of analysis are relevant. Each of these forms of analysis has been developed over time by the academic discipline most closely associated with it intellectually. Together they constitute the analytical resources available for municipal management and planning. In recent years the emphasis on computers has tended to obscure other means of analysis of equal or greater importance that are used regularly in planning. Some of these are age-old, others are relatively new.

Observations are the most basic and universal method of analysis, whether obtained directly through one's own senses or indirectly from data representing the reaction of others. Their accumulation over time constitutes an invaluable inventory of awareness, experience, and conclusion within each person's mind. It is certainly the least costly means of analysis. In city

observation

planning, the community itself is the principal source of relevant "facts and figures," observed every day by keeping one's eyes and ears open. It provides an ever-present backdrop for evaluating the validity and pertinence of general theories and specific proposals. It emphasizes reality over wishful thinking. But sensory perceptions are reliable only when they are realistic, accurate, and revealing, unaffected by overreactions, personal prejudices, or fanatical beliefs.

logic   Since *logic* underlies inductive and deductive thinking by interrelating different elements of information and thought in a valid relationship, it is the foundation of analysis. It is the basis for determining what must be considered and in what order so that the inferences drawn are accurate and the conclusions reached are sequentially correct. This may be done intuitively, by conscious manipulation in the mind, or by mathematical methods. Elementary principles of logic are employed continually in formulating the consistent thought required to reach sound conclusions on almost all subjects.

judgment   Personal *judgment* is ingrained in some way in all analysis. It is recognized as the primary basis for evaluating socioeconomic, political, cultural, legal, and other situations involving a multitude of elements many of which cannot be quantified and measured scientifically. Personal judgments can be elicited anonymously, "cross-analyzed," and progressively reiterated and processed to yield *collective judgments*. Even in processes as seemingly predetermined and automatic as computer operations, judgment is applied not only in programming, but in selecting among several alternative "next steps" during computer runs, deciding the number of confirming calculations or checks to be made, and judging the "ball park" accuracy of results at successive stages in the calculations.

Since logic and individual judgment are based on information derived from the external environment and accumulated experience recorded, stored, and processed within the nonconscious mind, the emotional state of the individual sensory system and the cognitive capability of the conscious mind are crucial. Judgments derived from this personal analytical system are impaired when unrecognized internal bias distorts sensory inputs and their processing within the nonconscious and conscious components of the mind. The individual may recognize his personal bias, but if other people are not aware of it, they cannot reject his judgment or compensate for his predilections.

The *spatial arrangement* of elements is a form of analysis occurring in almost all human activities. Everyone arranges the contents of the home. The organization of space within a single building or the location of separate structures within a project area are the province of architecture. The same kind of spatial analysis is applied in many ways in city planning: for example, in the layout of streets and city blocks, the arrangement of structures and open spaces in sections of the city developed as a unit, and establishing minimum open space requirements around buildings for access, health, safety, convenience, or appearance. One of the most complicated calculations of precise spatial arrangement is required when solar zoning of apartment buildings prohibits one dwelling unit casting a shadow on the solar panels of another unit for more than a certain number of hours each day. Spatial arrangement of an entirely different kind expresses the managerial relationships depicted in Figures 9 and 10 (Chapter 7, pages 89 and 92).

spatial arrangement

By placing the three organizational charts in Figure 10 side by side, each divided vertically into legislative, executive, staff, and operating levels of activity, their comparison is made much easier and more meaningful. *Juxtaposition* is such a universal and automatic method of analytical comparison that it is often discounted. Probably its most widespread use is explanation of "before" and "after" performance, prospects, proposals, or situations. Without juxtaposition, analysis would be impossible or severely limited. In comprehensive city planning as in other endeavors, this simple but basic element of analytical thinking is used extensively in evaluating alternative objectives, proposed projects, transportation systems, policies, budgets, political strategies, and other analytical comparisons that are made regularly.

juxtaposition

Superposition of transparent overlays permits more precise visual comparison of several analytical elements than when they are placed side by side. When several conceptualizations are examined one next to another, their mental correlation requires retaining the separate images in the mind's eye. This correlation is attained without memorization by superposing

superposition

transparencies, permitting direct, less effortful, more accurate, and detailed visual comparison. Since most overlays are drawings or other graphical expressions, they are especially revealing of relationships in two- and three-dimensional space.

One of the first uses of graphical superposition in city planning in the United States many years ago was to portray the relationship between physically deteriorated urban neighborhoods and certain socioeconomic conditions. Transparent spot maps were placed on top of color-coded property maps at the same scale showing the physical condition of buildings. Each spot map portrayed different information: the location of the homes of low-income families, crimes, fires, public health hazards, and other indicators of social deterioration believed to increase the costs of providing municipal services. The correlations revealed by looking through a number of transparent spot maps simultaneously were immediate and unmistakable. These correlations could have been made and expressed mathematically, but they would have been understood by and impressed themselves upon far fewer people. Graphical juxtaposition has been applied recently to compare physiographical conditions and environmental impacts in selecting highway routes.

design   Most people are familiar with the word *design* in connection with a building, automobile, or the fashion of the clothes they wear. To an architect, design means arranging the spaces in a building or group of buildings, producing plans, specifications, and cost estimates based on thorough analysis of the many elements and considerations involved. In much the same way the engineer designs bridges, aircraft, municipal utilities, and most of the products and technical systems we use or which affect us. Managerial endeavors are designed, such as policies favoring the production of low-income housing, industrial development strategies, or programs for conducting political campaigns. Some form of design occurs in almost every kind of activity.

In traditional city planning, design is part of the initiation and approval of transportation and communication systems, determination of land use, and means and methods of effectuation. Discussion of the design process in the subdivision of land is included in Chapter 10 (page 171), and Chapter 13 is devoted to what is now known as urban design. A few people define design so broadly that it becomes synonymous with the comprehensive planning process of correlating components, analytically structuring their functioning, and developing a master plan for the city as a whole.

As the freest form of analytical statement, *graphical abstractions* employ whatever notation best expresses the concept in mind. Usually they incorporate familiar notations, such as numbers to indicate relative magnitude or sequence, plus or minus for addition and subtraction, or words for identification. But they are by no means limited to the traditional terms established for different intellectual disciplines. They are likely to include symbols that do not belong to any one field but are more general in nature or more freely and personally expressive: an arrow for direction or force, a zigzag line for resistance or irregularity, a circle or square for containment or enclosure, a dot for a pause or point of activity, an asterisk for emphasis or identification, perspective for three-dimensional differentiation, or any other of such universal indications.

graphical abstraction

Graphical explanations are the only way of expressing certain complicated interrelationships so that most people understand them. It is doubtful if the information reproduced in Figure 12 could be expressed as clearly and comprehended as completely in any other way. In mathematical form it would be understood by very few people. It is probably impossible to express in words.

Graphical abstractions are means of exploring and explaining situations, relationships, or thoughts as they are conceived for the first time, formulated, and developed, either as a working clarification for the creator or as an exposition for others. They are executed in a flexible medium permitting immediate change, repeated modification, and rapid reformulation. The means may be chalk, eraser, and blackboard, pencil and pad, light pencil and computer screen, even a stick and smooth beach sand for the spur of the moment—whatever method allows immediate change with the least effort. In their spontaneity, informality and flexibility, graphical abstractions are very different from the familiar "bar" and "pie" charts and linear projections that are often employed to display statistical data so that they are more widely understood and remembered.

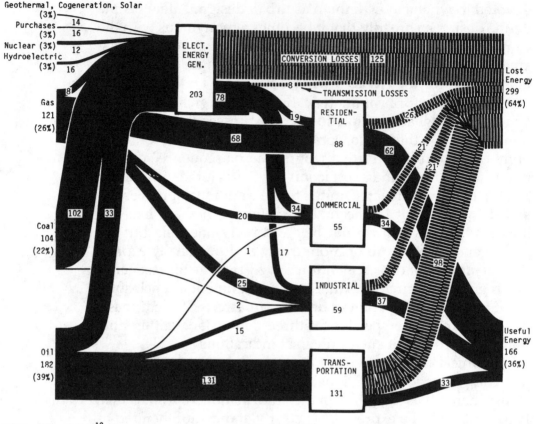

Figure 12
Graphical Exposition
(*The Energy/LA Action Plan*, July 1981, p. 26)

Abstract expressions are well suited to exploratory thinking, brainstorming, research, and development. They are probably most widely employed in science and engineering. They are particularly relevant to comprehensive planning analysis because the diverse elements and interrelationships that must always be taken into account cannot be expressed by the symbology of any one discipline. In city planning, graphical expressions are a way of conceptualizing and working out at the outset the probable content and form of the more organized and thorough urban analysis to follow. They are also used to formulate and resolve some matters to the point that further analysis is concerned only with details; examples are the procedural diagram in Figure 9 (Chapter 7, page 89) and the organization charts in Figures 10 and 11 (Chapter 7, pages 92 and 94). Many organizational variations can be explored with chalk and black-board almost as rapidly as they can be formulated mentally, using freehand solid and broken lines, small circles, arrow-heads, and a few abbreviated labels. This abstract analysis can be carried to the point that it portrays the best resolution in all essential respects. All that remains to be done is to produce the finished drawing for public announcement and publica-tion.

In recent years photographic and other electromagnetic methods of recording information from aircraft and satellites have greatly expanded community analysis. More information concerning natural features, man-made installations, and activ-ities on the ground can be gathered by this *remote sensing* than by any other means—within a short time and at less cost than other methods of collecting the same information. It is the only way of seeing the physical city as a whole, except in the case of the smallest communities. For cities in developing countries and some communities in the United States that do not have sufficient information for comprehensive planning, aerial ster-eophotographs provide enough analytical data concerning land use, circulation systems, open spaces, housing, industrial and commercial activity, environmental conditions, and other physical facilities and services to inaugurate effective city plan-ning. Estimates of population densities and the general income of some areas can be made from the overhead view, but accu-rate population counts and most socioeconomic and cultural data require censuses or sample surveys taken on the ground.

remote sensing

In effect, remote sensing extends personal observation by providing an overhead view covering large areas and recording a multitude of features, activities, and relationships on the ground that cannot be visualized from the ground. Objects on the ground a foot or less in size are shown clearly by the proper combi-nation of flight altitude and camera focal length. Remote sen-sing can also provide specialized information for planning cer-tain municipal operations such as checking the adequacy and condition of the surface marking on streets, disclosing unex-plained or illegal outdoor storage of waste, spotting diseased vegetation, tracing geological faults, recording damage caused by natural catastrophes, and disclosing buildings constructed without permit to escape real property taxes. The cost of the first aerial survey is usually repaid by the number of taxable properties discovered and subsequently listed in the tax assessor's records.

Optimum use of remote sensing requires becoming familiar with the overhead prospect, mentally translating it into the perspective views on the ground most familiar to people, developing the ability to read relative heights from aerial stereophotos, and learning to interpret the wealth of information produced by the different forms of remote sensing. These capabilities can be acquired with study and practice.

surveys

Surveys have long provided an analytical base for the categories of information they measure and the characteristics they reveal. The use in city planning of census counts taken by enumerators is limited by their high cost. Remote sensing can be used for certain surveys. Scientific sample surveys provide statistical data sufficiently reliable for many city planning purposes, and they are the best way of gauging opinions and attitudes that are not expressed in numbers. "Windshield" surveys taken from a slowly moving automobile following a prescribed route are used in urban, regional, and project planning when land use data are not available but are needed immediately; they may be used whenever visual surveys produce worthwhile analytical information without the time delay and higher costs of more exact methods. Small-scale, logically structured inquiries can gauge attitudes too indefinite to be measured by scientific sample survey, such as the political consensus in the city council on a particular subject, or the effect of municipal rules, regulations, and requirements on the loan policies of private financial institutions.

statistics

It would be difficult to find an important analytical or decision making problem in the industrialized world today without some relevant *statistical data* that could be used in its resolution; and the electronic computer is making it possible to record, store, and manipulate more and more such data at decreasing unit cost. Statistics are crucial in many aspects of city planning if it is to be based on more than personal and collective judgment without supporting "facts and figures." No better example exists than data concerning the number and composition of the population of a city: used by every municipal department, commercial and industrial enterprises, and county, state, and federal governments. Nowadays, this population count must include the best information available on undocumented immigrants.

Theoretically, an almost limitless supply of statistics could be justified in city planning if they would improve analytical conclusions and decisions sufficiently to warrant the cost.

> . . . A statistical review of prison suicides . . . revealed that these tragedies occur most commonly during the first ten days of confinement: this led to a new preventive program aimed at new inmates. . . .A look at disease patterns in the city showed that public health programs were making headway in treating one type of VD [venereal disease] but losing on another, which led to redirection of effort. . . . Analytical techniques have a role to play in dealing with street-level problems. (Dickson, 1975)

In most cities in the United States the task today is to make constructive use of existing data rather than wish and wait for more. What precisely do available data measure and disclose? What are their limits of accuracy? Are there key data that are not available but should be obtained, even if some existing data must be discontinued? Answers to such questions are essential for optimal or even valid use of statistics. Only so much of the money budgeted for city planning can be spent on gathering and processing quantitative data without impairing other parts of the procedure.

Mathematics underlies rational thinking employing num- *mathematics* bers, most scientific method, and the use of computers for the analysis and storage of information. It is the accepted language of numeration and quantitative interrelationships and the foundation of statistics. Because it is a language comprehended by relatively few of those engaged in municipal planning, it illustrates a basic problem in comprehensive planning analysis. As knowledge becomes more specialized, no one person can comprehend the technical and other specialized aspects of the different elements that must be taken into account. Yet, municipal legislators and officials are confronted continually with situations requiring decisions on their part based on data or special knowledge they do not understand and cannot confirm. Nor is there any one unit of measure that can be used in city planning to quantify and integrate mathematically relevant information developed by others that may involve operating data, technical specifications, policy questions, personnel matters, public and intergovernmental relations, or legal problems and implications.

In such situations, decision makers can evaluate the information and analyses presented to them only for those subjects they know themselves. They must depend on others for that which they cannot corroborate. They can acquire enough understanding to ask intelligent questions that force those responsible for the information they must depend on to explain their methods of inquiry in ordinary language, and justify their conclusions. But to a great extent, decision makers must rely on their intuition, judgment, and ability to evaluate information analytically rather than accept it on faith, to decide which elements are most important, to integrate them, and reach a conclusion.

simulation   An essential part of the city planning process is some form of *simulation* that represents the structure and functioning of the community. This permits examination of the interrelationships between the most significant elements of the city. It can be used to gauge the effects of an unexpected development or intended change in one element on the other elements. Unless the functioning of the city can be expressed in some usefully descriptive or analytically representative way, sound city planning is severely limited.

Simulation takes many forms. Familiar examples are the scale models showing how buildings, bridges, oil refineries, and other proposed projects will look when completed. These are not intended to allow modifications which would require rebuilding the model, nor do they incorporate the socioeconomic information that is part of the project. Examples of working models that simulate a range of conditions for testing purposes are aircraft flight simulators, wind tunnels, and scale models of bodies of water with mechanically activated wave action used in planning and designing harbor installations. The financial functioning of small businesses can be represented by a mathematical model programmed for the computer that incorporates four basic spread sheets of business: operating and profit-and-loss statements, the balance sheet, cash flow. It portrays the existing financial situation represented in these accounts, and it can track the effect of a change in one item in one account on the others.

Analytical representation of a city is far more complex than for even the largest technical project or the biggest business, because it involves almost every kind of activity and aspect of human existence. It is impossible today to express analytically and integrate mathematically the large number and diversity of components that together simulate the functioning of a city for comprehensive planning. Mathematical models can be formulated that simulate a number of the elements and aspects of a city that can be measured accurately with numbers. But most intangible components require some form of nonnumerical expression, and their integration with other elements of the city is best accomplished by individual and collective judgment applied through the special form of analytical representation described in the next chapter on page 113.

CITATION
[1] Dickson, Paul, "Think tank brings systems analysis to the city streets," *Smithsonian*, March 1975, pp. 45, 46, 48.

SELECTED REFERENCES
[1] Branch, Melville C., *City Planning and Aerial Information*, Cambridge, MA (Harvard University), 1971, 283 pp. [2] Bross, Irwin D. J., *Design for Decision*, New York (Macmillan), 1953, 276 pp. [3] Cantril, Hadley, *Gauging Public Opinion*, Princeton, NJ (Princeton University), 1944, 318 pp. [4] Dornbusch, Sanford M. and Calvin F. Schmid, *A Primer of Social Statistics*, New York (McGraw-Hill), 1955, 251 pp. [5] Enrich, Norbert Lloyd, *Management Operations Research*, New York (Holt, Rinehart, & Winston), 1965, 320 pp. [6] Kraemer, Kenneth L., *Policy Analysis in Local Government*, Washington, DC (International City Management Association), 1973, 165 pp. [7] Krueckeberg, Donald A. and Arthur L. Silvers, *Urban Planning Analysis: Methods and Models*, New York (Wiley), 1974, 486 pp. [8] Lapatra, Jack W., *Applying the Systems Approach to Urban Development*, Stroudsburg, PA (Dowden, Hutchison, & Ross), 1973, 296 pp. [9] Lyden, Fremont J. and Ernest G. Miller (Editors), *Planning Programming, Budgeting: A Systems Approach to Management*, Chicago, IL (Markham), 1967, 443 pp. [10] Rosenbloom, Richard S. and John R. Russell, *New Tools for Urban Management*, Studies in Systems and Organizational Analysis, Boston, MA (Harvard University Press), 1971, 298 pp. [11] Tufte, Edward R., *The Visual Display of Quantitative Information*, Cheshire, CO (Graphics Press), 1984, 197 pp.

Every city administration is concerned with current operations of line departments, auxiliary service functions to support the line services, and overall management. . . . A continuous effort must be made to keep the city on an efficient operational basis. . . . Planning for the future is equally essential to avoid waste of public funds through lack of research, imagination, and foresight. . . . No city administration is complete without personnel engaged in research and planning for the future. . . . If it is to be functional and practical in nature, planning must consider the needs of the line departments and the realities of municipal finance.

Arthur W. Bromage, *Introduction to Municipal Government and Administration*, 1957.

CHAPTER 9
EFFECTUATION

A process as basic to a city as its planning is effective only to the extent it is incorporated in the structure of its government and regular municipal management.

C ITY PLANNING in the United States is realized through the activities of municipal operating departments and agencies, and the land use planning activities of city planning commissions and their staffs.

The plans of *operating departments* are incorporated in the municipal utility system or service each provides. Separately and together these systems and services have a profound effect on the spatial form, physical characteristics, and socioeconomic condition of cities. For example, fire and police departments effectuate their plans for improving the "protection of persons and property" through the guardian services they provide. These can affect the sense of security of the citizenry, the specific protection and treatment afforded different segments of the population, insurance costs, or the general attractiveness of the community to new and expanded private enterprise. Health departments implement the plans implicit in the standards they establish for water purity, eating places, certain consumer products, and various services affecting the health of people. Departments of water and power make urban growth possible by providing more people and their increasing per capita use with these essential public utilities. And by extending the distribution lines required for water and power connections to new housing in undeveloped areas, these departments determine the direction of growth at the city's periphery. Departments of public works, by their selection and scheduling of the construction and maintenance of streets and highways, bridges, culverts, and various physical installations, are responsible in large part for the operation and efficiency of the urban circulation system, the location and condition of numerous physical facilities, even the general appearance of the community. And

operating departments

certainly the legislature and executive offices of the municipality play a decisive role in a city's present and future: determining basic policies, formulating and enacting legislation,
arranging financing, approving the budget, directing management methods, and a host of other vital matters.

independent   The operations and plans of *independent municipal agencies*
agencies   are also part of city planning and its effectuation. Local housing
authorities and urban redevelopment agencies perform oper-
ating functions that are closely allied but managerially different
from the staff activities of city planning commissions and
districts   departments. School *districts* and the many other independent
districts created for a particular purpose carry out their responsibilities in much the same way as regular municipal departments, except that special districts are concerned with a single
activity applied to different areas depending on the function
involved. In the aggregate, special districts are an important
force in the effectuation of city planning in many communities.

In these and other ways noted in this book, municipal operating departments and agencies plan the city by carrying out
their respective plans for the systems and services they provide. In so doing they shape the city and its future in as many
different ways as their activities bring about.

budget   *Budgets* are one of the most important mechanisms for
effectuating comprehensive city planning. They symbolize the
most basic function of planning: the allocation of available
resources among competing needs and demands. They represent the conclusion of the body politic or other decision
making authority concerning the relative importance of expenditures for different activities. They provide a measure of performance. With a "line" budget, spending more or less than
the funds allocated for different categories of personnel, equipment, and supplies is apparent at the end of the year. But
whether these categorical expenditures achieved the intended
purpose is not revealed. Performance, project, or program
budgets, on the other hand, permit evaluating whether the
activities or installations they list have been completed.

Most programs of municipal activity and expenditure extend
over several years or longer. Therefore the commitments represented in the budget for the current year in fact establish
requirements that continue into the following year and, to a

lesser extent, subsequent years. Few budgetary expenditures are completed and terminated at the end of the year. Therefore, by allocating the funds available among different endeavors, the budget determines not only the monetary commitment but the implementing operations that are conducted over a period of several years as a consequence of each expenditure.

Until now in the United States, sufficient coordination of the activities of separate municipal departments and agencies has been brought about by circumstance, political pressure, professional cooperation, and the economic marketplace to avoid economic collapse and severe social conflict. But urban growth, technological development, environmental dangers, and the increasing complexity of life in general in industrialized societies require the greater integration provided by comprehensive city planning and management, if urban crises are to be prevented in the future.

Another means of effectuating city plans in the United States is *land use planning* by city planning commissions and departments. As illustrated in Figures 9 and 10 (Chapter 7, pages 89 and 92), it is a process that has been developed over many years and is now well established in law and widespread practice. But it has three basic limitations which should be borne in mind when evaluating the land use planning process. First, land use planning is not directly concerned with municipal financing and the budget. Second, it does not cover the planning activities of the operating departments, which are the main stem of municipal management and planning. Third, it is not a mandated part of municipal government except in several states, and even when it is required there are ways of avoiding, postponing, or rendering apparent compliance innocuous. A process as basic to a city as its planning is effective only to the extent that it is incorporated in the structure of its government and regular municipal management.

The "master city plan" is the main means of implementing land use planning. It may be divided into district plans. It is produced by the city planning commission and department during a period of study normally lasting several years. Since it is formulated and issued as a printed publication, it is revised infrequently because of the time required for reformulation as a publication and the considerable cost of reprinting the large

land use planning

number of copies needed. Nor can such an important public document be made available for sale only, unless its price is within the means of most people. The average interval between revisions is about 10 years. The state planning enabling act may require that the master city plan treat a prescribed list of urban elements. In small communities without a city planning staff, the city planning commission may contract with a private consulting firm to prepare the master city plan it submits to the city council.

The council may choose to formally adopt, approve but not adopt, revise, table, or ignore the proposed plan, except when adoption is mandated by state legislation. If a city plan is not adopted, municipal operating departments are not obligated to follow its land use recommendations. But with rare exceptions, the city planning commission and department continue to use the master plan they submitted to the city council for approval or adoption as the primary reference for their own actions and continuing recommendations to the council. In some situations, it may be apparent to the city council and the city planning commission that adoption of parts of the master plan over an extended period of time may be more feasible politically and more effective in the aggregate than if the entire master plan were submitted and rejected at one time.

zoning   Since the early 1900s, *zoning* has been the chief instrument of effectuating land use planning in the United States. The most widely used type establishes the "land use" or activities permitted on a parcel of property. Different specific uses are designated within the general categories of agricultural, residential, commercial, and industrial. Sometimes additional categories are zoned, most often transportation and government. Normally each designation includes restrictions and requirements applying to any building constructed on the parcel of property: maximum permitted height; minimum front, side and back yards; minimum width, depth, and area of lots; the volume of building permitted on the lot; required parking spaces. Other kinds of zoning developed over the years are noted in the next chapter on Land Use Control. Every parcel of land in the municipality is zoned; in the largest cities in the United States it is estimated that the number of parcels varies between 500,000 and more than a million. Requests for changes in zone are addressed to the city planning commission which transmits its recommendation to the city council for action. Every change in zone is effected by a separate ordinance.

Project plans or *planned unit developments* relieve the city planning commission from having to consider separately each of several closely interrelated zone change requests that are part of a single project proposal which incorporates several land uses, a number of different buildings, access streets, and other features of a large project designed as a unit. When an extensive area is proposed for development as one entity, an *area plan* may be required showing the proposed circulation system, land uses, buildings, parking provisions, open spaces, and landscaping. In some states, both project and area development proposals are submitted as *specific plans,* and the city planning commission may formulate such plans itself as part of the master city plan. Since specific plans may include an almost limitless range of particular provisions and commitments, they are becoming a means for city planning commissions and departments to impose an increasingly broad and detailed list of requirements on proposed projects and substantial portions of master city plans. For example, they have included provisions restricting the density of development within the project at any given time to the capacity of surrounding streets to accommodate the incoming and outgoing traffic it generates.

Subdivision control is another means of implementing portions of a land use plan. City planning commissions and departments must approve dividing a parcel of undeveloped property into smaller parcels intended for a different land use. The street pattern, uses of land, size and disposition of properties, buildings, open spaces, landscaping, and other elements of the proposed design must meet requirements established for the "health, safety, welfare, and convenience" of the future inhabitants of the subdivision. The proposed subdivision must also fit with the transportation and utility systems and other facilities existing in surrounding areas and the city as a whole. *Official maps* are another means of effectuating certain elements of a master city plan. These are explained and subdivision is treated at greater length in the next chapter.

project plan

planned unit development

area plan

specific plan

subdivision control

official map

capital improvement plan

Municipal *capital improvement programs* were introduced almost 50 years ago as a sensible method of planning new and improved physical facilities: streets and highways, public utilities, flood control installations, municipal buildings and structures of various kinds—the more permanent physical elements that represent "additions or betterments" to the capital stock of the community. There is a best sequence for the construction of these necessary physical improvements. Enlargement of a treatment plant may be needed before new sewers can be fed into the disposal system. A bottleneck intersection may prevent free-flowing traffic on a new street to be built some distance away. Many of the physical facilities of a city are so interrelated that an addition to one part of a system may not operate optimally, or function at all, until another capital improvement in another part of the city is completed. The master city plan is the best reference for a capital improvement program scheduling the construction of major public projects.

Unfortunately, politics rather than rational sequence usually determines which projects are built when and where. Since most city councils are composed of members representing districts rather than the city at large, council members believe they should receive their proportionate share of the total money available each year for capital works projects to spend in their district as they see fit—whether or not this conforms to the most sensible programming. Unless council members can point to physical improvements made in their electoral district "for the eye to see and the hand to touch," they will not be able to respond successfully to the most important question posed by voters at reelection time, expressed by former Mayor Fiorello LaGuardia of New York City as: "What have you done for me lately?"

environmental impact report

The most recently established means of effectuating city plans are *environmental impact reports* or statements. These were first required for every project proposed by a federal governmental agency that would affect the environment significantly. They have since been adopted by most states and extended to include projects proposed by private enterprise that must obtain some local governmental approval. Since private construction projects must obtain a building permit and certificate of occupancy, almost all private projects need an environmental impact report unless specifically exempted. Since the total urban environment encompasses every element and aspect of a city and its master plan, theoretically environmental impact reports could be correlated directly or indirectly with anything and everything in a city, and could therefore be required for every kind of effectuation.

As a practical necessity, environmental impact reports are not required for certain categories of development projects. Another means of simplifying environmental reporting is a "mitigated" environmental report. The city planning commission or another municipal body spells out a set of requirements which will compensate for, or "mitigate," what it considers are the adverse effects of the proposed project. This special form of environmental report is emerging as a device for eliminating the preparation of a report, avoiding formal disapproval or prolonged consideration of proposed projects, and a means of imposing a wide range of requirements. When the requirements are met by the developer, the project can proceed subject only to applicable rules and regulations that are not part of the environmental review. Since mitigation requirements may call for features indirectly or remotely related to the proposed project, this represents a considerable expansion of the powers of effectuation available in comprehensive city planning, discussed further in Chapter 11 on Environment.

If comprehensive city planning is to be realized, municipal land use and operating plans must be combined and the process of planning extended. A *city planning center* is needed for information collection and storage, analysis, decision making, and monitoring operations and effectuation.

city planning center

There exists no regular staff procedure for arriving at decisions; instead *ad hoc* groups are formed as the need arises. No staff agency to monitor the carrying out of decisions is available. There is no focal point for long-range planning on an inter-agency basis. Without a central administrative focus, . . . policy turns into a series of unrelated decisions—crisis oriented, *ad hoc* and after-the-fact in nature. We become the prisoners of events. (Rockefeller, 1979).

The city planning center is a mechanism for *planning*, not for operational control. . . . While such planning cen-

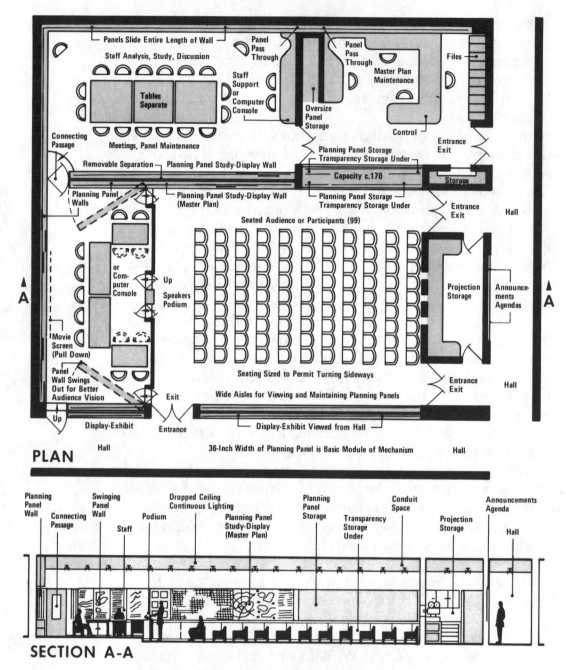

Figure 13
City Planning Center for a Large Municipality

ters must maintain up-to-date information on operations if plans are to reflect current reality, their purpose is to provide staff support for planning ahead. (Figure 13) (Branch, 1981)

The organizational arrangement and procedure for comprehensive city planning that combines operational and land use activities will reflect developments in the theory and practice of public administration and business management. Undoubtedly, the precise form of organization and method of planning will vary with the size of cities and with their political, organizational, and socioeconomic situation. But these different applications will incorporate basic procedural steps required for any comprehensive planning to be analytically valid and procedurally successful.

In small communities, the city center can be maintained on simple displays in a small office. Planning procedures can utilize existing facilities and available services. The critical requirement is to apply the comprehensive planning process of collecting information, conducting analysis, and reaching conclusions.

CITATION
[1] Branch, Melville C., *Continuous City Planning, Integrating Municipal Management and City Planning*, New York (Wiley), 1981, p. 155. [2] Rockefeller, Nelson in Henry Kissinger, *White House Years*, Boston, MA (Little-Brown), 1979, p. 39.

SELECTED REFERENCES
[1] Netzer, Dick, *Economics and Urban Problems*, Diagnosis and Prescriptions, New York (Basic Books), 1970, 213 pp. [2] Pressman, Jeffrey L. and Aaron Wildavsky, *Implementation*, Berkeley, CA (University of California Press), Second Edition, 1973, 209 pp. [3] Robinson, Ira M., *Decision-Making in Urban Planning*, An Introduction to New Methodologies, Beverly Hills, CA (Sage), 1972, 628 pp. [4] Scheidt, Melvin E., *Long-Range Programming of Municipal Public Works*, National Resources Planning Board, Washington, DC (Superintendent of Documents), 1941, 72 pp.

Zoning is alive and well, and is living in every urban and suburban neighborhood. . . . People love zoning! Its the greatest thing since sanitary sewers. Planners tend to forget that zoning is a *political* exercise. People can become involved in the zoning process: they can see it, they can identify with it, and they can show up at meetings. . . .

Zoning in the future will be different—no doubt about that. It will make use of two techniques that are rapidly gaining strength [exactions and special districts]. And a third technique is shaping up in the wings [quantitative zoning].

Richard Babcock, "The Outlook for Zoning," *Urban Land*, 1984.

CHAPTER 10

LAND USE CONTROL

Collectively, the different zones comprise a powerful instrument of land use planning and control. With such an arsenal, failure to attain effective physical planning is because of inadequate support by the public, political, or other power structure rather than because the procedural means of achieving better land use planning are not available.

VARIOUS FORMS of land use control have been exercised since the earliest human settlements. Restrictions on land use in the United States date back to soon after the founding of the original 13 colonies. The basic purpose of these controls has always been to establish limitations on the use and development of land that are believed to be necessary or desirable in the general public interest. In autocratic societies these limitations are imposed by the central authority and enforced by its regulatory apparatus. In the United States today, they are the product of progressive development over many years. During the past 20 years this development has accelerated to the point that there now exists a variety of land use controls that can effectuate a much broader range of city planning objectives than was envisaged not long ago.

In large part the discussion of controls in this chapter reflects the experience in California, which has been a leader in land use legislation and procedures, incorporating precedents from other states whenever feasible. As the most populous state with the second, eighth, and fourteenth largest cities in the United States, the California experience represents a range and degree of land use controls that may not be appropriate for some cities. Sooner or later, however, they are likely to find themselves following the California example if it fits their situation.

Building codes, by establishing requirements for safe and sanitary structures, affect the cost of construction which in

building code

117

turn affects the type and location of new and remodeled buildings. If these standards are too high, housing for people with low incomes cannot be built without subsidy; if they are too low, unsafe and shoddy construction will likely result. The specific requirements for on-site parking spaces affect not only the use of the property itself, but also curbside parking and the traffic flow capacity of adjacent streets. When building codes effectively prevent construction along earthquake faults, in areas subject to landslide, subsidence, or other severely unstable ground conditions, they affect the spatial pattern of develop-

health code ment. Before any building can be occupied, *health codes* require its connection to municipal water and sewer lines when septic tanks are not allowed or private water wells are not practical. The direction and distance utility lines are extended into undeveloped land at the urban periphery determines what building can take place in which areas, and to this extent the spatial shape of the built-up city. Municipal water and sewer systems have been used to direct or restrict the growth of communities. Building and health codes constitute an indirect form of land use control.

subdivision   Transforming farmland and other undeveloped property into an urban area containing more buildings housing more people is controlled by the *subdivision* process, conducted by the city planning commission and department or the engineering unit of the municipality if there is no planning agency. In a well-developed approval process, the plans submitted by the subdivider are examined from many points of view. Property to be graded to create level building sites must conform to the grading regulations of the building code or, in the absence of specific standards and requirements, the change in landform must pose no threat of flooding, landslide, or other physical intrusion on abutting property. In some cities, the new landform proposed must be aesthetically compatible with adjacent development existing or planned. The proposed street system must provide adequate access and egress for the area to be subdivided and developed, and for each of the new parcels of property created. It must also connect efficiently with the surrounding network of streets and highways. The size, shape, and arrangement of the new parcels of property must be suitable for the intended uses and conform to zoning and any other relevant regulations.

The public utility systems to service these properties must *improvements*
meet the engineering standards of the municipality and rights-
of-way may have to be dedicated for future public utility lines.
The *improvements* to be constructed and paid for by the subdivider and those to be installed by the municipality are identified at this point in the approval process. The land uses, population density, and other features of the proposed development
are checked for their compliance with "applicable general or
specific plans" as may be required by a *state map act*, and find-   *state map act*
ings are made concerning the environmental impacts of the
subdivision.

Some of the municipal operating departments have specific
requirements that must be met. For example, there may be
limitations on the length of dead-end streets so that fire engines
entering these streets by mistake will not be long delayed by
turning around and retracing their path to reach the location
of the fire. The dead-ends of streets can be made large enough
to permit fire engines to turn around or can include emergency
driveways to an adjacent street. Police departments may want
the subdivision design to eliminate areas that cannot be observed
by police or security services in motor vehicles. Examples of
good and bad subdivision design are included in Chapter 13
on Urban Design.

Recent trends in subdivision control have had to do with   *off-site*
off-site improvements and a lengthening list of facilities and   *improvement*
installations that are required of the subdivider before his proposed project can proceed. When the subdivision "leapfrogs"
across undeveloped land at the urban periphery, more and
more communities are requiring the subdivider to pay for
extending water and sewer lines from the outer edge of the
built-up city across undeveloped land to the proposed subdivision. In addition, many facilities previously paid for by
municipalities are now being requested of subdividers: parks,
parkways, school sites, construction and continuing maintenance of flood control basins, even bookmobiles in lieu of a
library. Improvements can be paid for by dedication of land
within the subdivision to the municipality, construction and
dedication of the facility or installation to the city, posting a
performance bond, or direct payment of money into a fund
earmarked for the required improvements. As discussed in the
next chapter on Environment, municipalities are passing on to

private land developers more and more costs related only indirectly to proposed projects. Developers, in turn, are passing them to the "consumer."

subdivision
process
    In large cities with active land use planning, proposed subdivisions are first examined by the city planning department to determine if they conform to established requirements. The proposed plan is then circulated to municipal departments that have an interest in its features. For example, the engineering department or its equivalent will check provisions for public utilities and might require an easement for a trunk line planned for the future. The public works, traffic department, or another unit of municipal government will examine the proposed arrangement of streets and their detailed design. A review committee or an individual in the city planning department formulates the final changes, additions, or conditions required for approval of the proposed subdivision plan. The director of the department may or may not be directly involved, depending on the extent to which he can or wants to delegate authority for subdivision examination and decision. Upon appeal, the city planning commission will review the departmental determination and make a final decision, subject to further appeal to the city council. In small communities without a city planning department the city engineer or the commission itself processes proposed subdivision plans. In medium size cities with established land use procedures individuals often perform the role of departments in larger cities. In some places there is no land use planning, zoning, or subdivision control.

official map
    Official maps preceded both zoning and master city planning. They were needed to indicate where future streets would be placed so that structures would not be built where extensions to the existing street system were planned. The approximate locations of future parks were also shown. Official maps have evolved into cartographically exact records of present street locations, public utility easements, flood control installations, and other municipal facilities. Many future locations are not shown exactly, to avoid legal claims by property owners that the value of their land is reduced or eliminated when it is disclosed that all or part of it will be acquired for a public purpose at some indefinite future time; specific locations are shown when the municipality is prepared to condemn and pay for the property.

What is shown on official maps may or may not be also shown on the master city plan. When no such plan exists, municipal operating departments may incorporate their own specific or general projections of streets and utilities on the official map to protect these routes from encroachment.

The first modern *zoning* ordinance in the United States was enacted in New York City in 1916. This early beginning has expanded gradually into an array of many kinds of zoning. Many of these are probably employed in most parts of the country, authorized under the *police power* delegated to counties and municipalities by the states:

zoning

police power

> For the purpose of promoting health, safety, morals, or the general welfare of the community, the legislative body of cities and incorporated villages is hereby empowered to regulate and restrict the height, number of stories, and size of buildings and other structures, the percentage of lot that may be occupied, the size of yards, courts, and other open spaces, the density of population, and the location and use of buildings, structures, and land for trade, industry, residence, or other purposes. . . . The local legislative body may divide the municipality into districts of such number, shape, and area as may be deemed best suited to carry out the purposes of [the] act. . . . Such regulation shall be made in accordance with a comprehensive plan and designed to lessen congestion in the streets; to secure safety from fire, panic, and other dangers; to promote health and the general welfare; to provide adequate light and air; to prevent the overcrowding of land; to avoid undue concentration of population; to facilitate the adequate provision of transportation, water, sewerage, schools, parks, and other public requirements. (Hagman, 1971)

To secure passage of the first zoning ordinance, it was politically necessary to zone larger areas for apartment and commercial use than market demand would justify for a very long time. Many single-family property owners were unwilling to accept a realistic projection of demand and insisted that their properties be zoned for apartments or commercial use as the price for their supporting the introduction of zoning. They reasoned that their properties would be more valuable were they ever used for multiple dwellings or commerce. As a conse-

overzoning

quence, these denser developments were scattered more randomly throughout the city than if zoning matched market demand. This scattered development introduced incompatible land uses in areas consisting entirely of single-family detached houses. It also made it more difficult to forecast where in the city the additional public utilities required for apartments and commercial activities would be installed.

downzoning

For these reasons there have been continuing efforts by city planners to roll back this *overzoning. Downzoning*, as it is also called, has been most successful when master city plans have been adopted by the city council and are supported politically. In the early days after comprehensive zoning was introduced,

zone atlas

zone atlases were immediately prepared showing the zone of every parcel of property. The preparation of master city plans lagged years behind, and rarely were these plans officially adopted by the municipality and supported by the political power structure. Since municipal operating departments needed some land use guide to plan the installation of public utilities, zone atlases were used as master city plans. In recent years, an increasing number of viable city plans have been formulated and more of them have been formally adopted. When state enabling legislation requires that zoning conform with adopted master city plans some cities have corrected overzoning by citing the legal requirement that zoning conform to the master plan. This has been possible practically and politically because property owners are advised individually by mail of zone change requests by other property owners within a given distance, but they are not advised and may not be aware of a proposed change in the master city plan that would roll back the zone on their property.

area classification

Area classification is the oldest and most widely applied type of zoning. It divides the community into areas or districts zoned for a designated category of land use: agricultural, residential, commercial, parking, and industrial. Within each of these categories, subcategories permit different forms of the same land use. For example, the residential category may include single-family detached houses, duplexes, row houses, and several different intensities of multiple dwellings or apartment buildings. The industrial category may include several subcategories of light, medium, and heavy industrial land use. Initially, restrictions within each of the subcategories had to be uniform in order not to discriminate between property owners. Figure 14 reproduces a portion of one page of a two-volume zoning atlas for a large city in the United States with approximately 800,000 separate parcels of property. This area of 8.6 square miles contains 17 different zones each with specific approved uses: A1 (Agricultural); RA (Suburban), R1 (One-Family Dwelling), R2 (Two-Family Dwelling), R3 (Multiple Dwelling), R4 (Multiple Dwelling); C1 (Limited Commercial), C2 (Commercial), C3 (Commercial), C4 (Commercial); CP (Commercial, Parking); P (Parking), P1 (Parking, Limited); O (Oil Extraction); M1 (Limited Industrial), M2 (Light Industrial). In recent years the requirement of uniformity has been relaxed, if not abandoned, in favor of treating each zone change individually and often differently, as discussed later in this chapter.

In area classification zoning the major categories may be *cumulative* or *exclusive*. In the first of these the law provides that all the "lower" zones having the least potentially objectionable impact on adjacent properties are permitted in the "higher" zones. Thus, agriculture can be conducted in any zone since all the others are less restrictive. Residences, the second lowest zone, are allowed in commercial and industrial zones, and commercial activities are permitted in industrial zones. Cumulative zoning is being abandoned because of problems that result when homeowners in commercial and industrial zones protest the construction of commercial and industrial facilities next door—despite the fact that both zones were intended for these facilities and not for homeowners who chose to ignore potential land use incompatibility and built or bought homes in non-residential zones. In contrast, exclusive area classification zoning allows no activity in each subcategory other than the land use for which it was created. This is why the agricultural zone is often employed as a *holding zone* when a rural area with few residents is annexed and municipal authorities do not want to designate the new zoning until a master plan for the area has been formulated.

When area classification zoning was first established there were almost always some activities in the new districts that did not conform to the new restrictions on land use. Since achieving complete uniformity of land use would require dispos-

cumulative
exclusive

holding

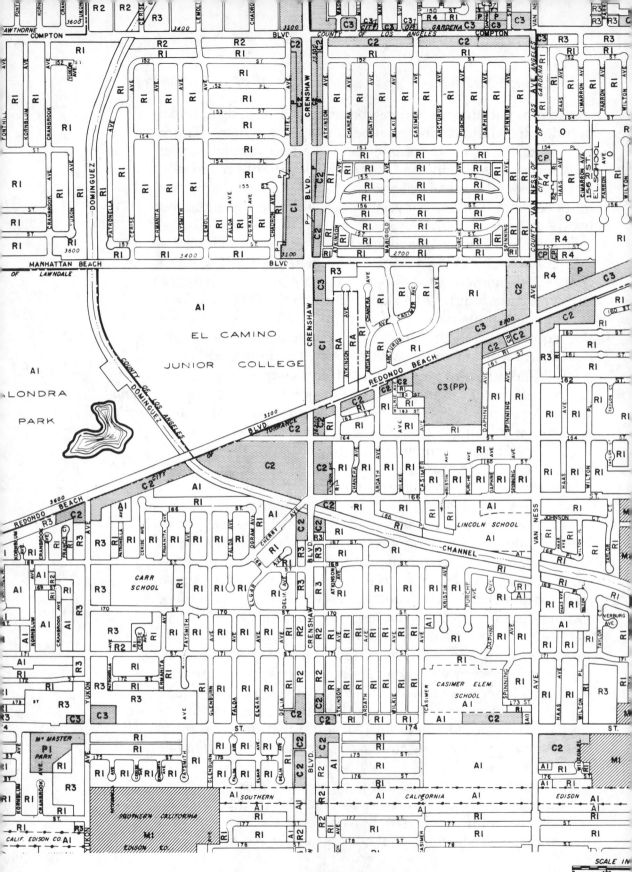

Figure 14
Area Classification Zoning

sessing the owners of the properties that did not conform and compensating them for their loss, the uses have been allowed to remain subject to *nonconforming use* regulations. These reg- *nonconforming* ulations stipulate that the nonconforming activity must be phased out in time by prohibiting expansion of physical facilities, or their replacement unless there is more than 50 percent catastrophic destruction. In most instances, nonconforming uses are not phased out because of political sympathy by city councils, and with few exceptions they continue until economic conditions bring about voluntary change.

An unanticipated consequence of area classification zoning has emerged in recent years. In some communities, districts were zoned for single-family detached houses on not less than five-acre lots, limiting the resident population to those who could afford such large properties. Legal action was instigated claiming that this was *exclusionary zoning* since it excluded all *exclusionary* but the wealthy. Following a series of legal actions and court decisions, exclusionary zoning was declared illegal and *inclu-* *inclusionary* *sionary zoning* upheld. In the latter, new residential developments may be required to include a percentage of properties that are "affordable" by middle and lower income families.

The uniform standards applied in area classification zoning cannot be used for activities and facilities that are few in number and inherently unique, such as colleges and universities, airports and heliports, cemeteries, prisons, waste disposal sites. Each such special use requires a particular plan that details its physical form. Usually the city planning commission and department impose various conditions before approval. No changes can be made in the particular plan without approval by the municipal planning authorities. Since the "planned projects" and "planned unit developments" noted in the previous chapter are also unique in that they are relatively few in number and each is different in some significant way, they are often submitted and approved as *conditional uses*, permitted within *conditional* a designated area within an appropriate underlying area clas- *use* sification zone.

The special conditions originally imposed as part of conditional use zoning are now being applied to area classification zoning in parts of the United States. Although each of the area classification zones prescribes the operational characteristics of the uses permitted in each zone, the applicant for a change in zone can no longer expect automatic approval when the proposed use meets these characteristics. Additional conditions may be imposed before the applicant's request for a zone change is approved. These conditions may involve physical features such as increased setback from adjoining property, provision of a landscaped berm as a spatial separator, prescribed hours of operation for the proposed activity, or fewer dwelling units than allowed under the regular area classification zone. Unless on appeal the courts declare the addition of certain conditions unreasonable and therefore illegal, it appears that linking an increasing variety of conditions to zone change requests is leading to separate and individual treatment of every such application.

overlay

supplemental use

As their name suggests, *overlay zones* are superposed over area classification districts to establish additional restrictions or permissions. *Supplemental use zones* accomplish the same purpose. To illustrate, an overlay zone that establishes a horse-keeping district in a residential area adds to the uniform requirements of the underlying residential zone specific conditions taken from the health code to reduce the possibility of contamination or disease from equine waste and flies. In the same way "aircraft-keeping districts" have been formed where all or most of the property owners have a private aircraft and use a common runway extending down the middle of the sub-division. Supplementary zones permit oil extraction in urban oil drilling districts superposed over residential, commercial, or industrial zones, or allow combined light industrial artcraft studios and dwelling units in exclusively commercial zones. Another set of overlay zones imposes requirements reducing the destructive potentialities of exceptional fire, flood, landslide, or beachfront hazards, or reduces the population density allowed in hazardous areas below the number of people permitted in the underlying area classification zone. *Solar zoning* may be superposed over an area to prevent a new building from obstructing the access to sunlight required for the energy source supplying an existing building.

solar

cluster

Cluster zoning permits larger size properties in area classification zones to concentrate development within a small part of the entire parcel. The remaining area is retained as an inseparable part of the property developed as shown in the application for zone change, providing open space for recreation and enhancing environmental quality. An additional condition requires continued maintenance of the open area by a home-owners association or some other responsible entity. *Hillside zoning* or designation as a mountainous area may alter the lot size requirements or reduce the permitted densities of the underlying residential zone. A *floating zone*

hillside

floating

> . . . . first creates a zone of certain characteristics, for example, a planned unit development, and then provides that land will be or may be designated by a second ordinance as being in such a zone when the property owner applies for it. . . . Upon receipt of an application meeting the criteria, the zone can float down to the surface by enactment of the second ordinance. (Hagman, 1971)

Another form of floating zone allows a land developer to locate a designated land use of given size and shape anywhere within the approved project or zoned area, or according to more specific conditions related to the final design of the installation.

An innovative mechanism emanating from area classification zoning is the *transfer of development rights* (TRD). This originated as a way of preserving a historically important office building in the downtown area of a large city in the United States. Under area classification zoning, the owner of the office building was entitled to tear it down and replace it with a larger, taller, and more profitable building. If the building were declared a "historical landmark" and its demolition prohibited, the value of the property would be reduced because it could not be sold for the most intensive use. A solution was devised that takes into account historical preservation and the owner's vested rights by transferring these rights to another property in the city. The additional unused cubic footage of building bulk to which the owner was entitled downtown would be transferred and added to the spatial volume of building permitted by the existing zoning on a different parcel of property, in accordance with the master city plan or as specifically approved by the planning authorities.

development rights

Transferring development rights has since been expanded to preserve prime agricultural land close to cities. Because of this proximity, tax assessments on agricultural land are based on the possibility of zoning for more intensive land use in the future, rather than on the current use; the farmer is hard pressed to pay these higher presumptive taxes. This situation induces offers by land developers to acquire the property for a more intensive use. The construction industry advocates premature subdivision to provide employment, and real estate and other special interests favor the additional dwelling units that would be provided. In some states owners can donate farmland or development rights to charities set up to promote conservation; the value is deductible for tax purposes. Cities and counties can purchase the development rights for the difference between the value of the land for farming and its market value.

The concept has advanced to the point that in one state a municipality can use a TRD ordinance to preserve not only landmarks, historical sites, open spaces, and farmland but also residential, commercial, and industrial real property of "economic significance." The local planning board places an economically significant activity to be retained in a preservation zone and designates a potentially profitable parcel as a transfer site, appropriately located with relation to present and future patterns of urban land use. When the development rights obtained in creating the preservation zone are utilized at the transfer site, construction at this replacement location can begin. Some municipalities are authorized to issue certificates signifying the ownership of development rights, and to establish municipal land banks for their acquisition and sale.

height   *Height* restrictions are part of area classification zoning. Usually absolute limits are part of some residential zones; buildings may not exceed stipulated heights. In commercial, industrial, and dense residential zones, height depends on the maximum size of the building permitted on the parcel of property, the product of the ground area it covers times its height. The developer can choose a low structure covering the entire "buildable area" of the lot, or a tall thin structure covering only a portion of the property. Height limits are implicit in solar zoning which prohibits one building casting a shadow on the solar panels of another for more than a certain number of hours per day. And as shown in the Profile portion of Figure 4c

(Chapter 5, page 44), *airport* or *flight plane zoning* is required around airports by federal aviation authorities to prevent high-rise buildings, radio and television towers, or any other physical structure from obstructing aircraft take-off and landing pathways in the airspace. There are also *height zones* that cover sections of the community or the entire city. Ordinarily taller buildings are permitted in the downtown area. The master plan or development policy may call for areas of more intense activity at designated subcenters or "growth centers" where commercial establishments and apartment buildings are encouraged to concentrate. The height zone will allow taller structures at these locations while the areas in between may be retained in low density, low height development as long as feasible. *airport flight plane*

Many special zones have been conceived and applied for a wide variety of particular purposes. *Historical zones* preserve such areas by limiting the size of redevelopment to that which is consistent with the historical character of the designated district, requiring that the façades of existing buildings be retained in any reconstruction, and permitting any uses within the historical buildings that enhance their economic viability but do not threaten their preservation. Tax relief may be provided or the transfer of development rights may be applied. *historical*

For years, various forms of zoning directed toward controlling *outdoor billboard advertising* have been attempted, with limited success because of the opposition of powerful special interests and judicial determination that compensation for lost revenues is due if current use is restricted. Not even the millions of dollars spent by the federal highway beautification program has succeeded in reducing the number of billboards along the national highways. The most recent attempts at local control have been directed toward preventing the use of property for large size displays advertising "off-site" products or services that are not produced on the property itself. *outdoor advertising*

The "mobile homes" that occupied "trailer parks" years ago have been reconstituted as buses, vans, or large campers. They have been replaced in "mobile home parks" by "mobile manufactured homes" which are much in demand because they are now the lowest priced "single-family detached house." Since moving them to a new location is no longer feasible, mobile home parks have become places of permanent residence, comparable to the traditional subdivision, except for the size and layout of lots and, with few exceptions, their being leased rather than owned. In this transition, the resident of a mobile home park has become the owner of a permanent home on a rented site, subject to eviction at the pleasure of the manager or owner of the mobile park.

mobile park   This situation and the rapid increase in the number of mobile home parks has produced state legislation protecting the resident of a park from unjustified actions by his landlord. *Residential mobile park* zones have also been enacted by local governments, establishing design requirements consistent with their new function as a form of residential subdivision. State legislation has also been passed allowing mobile manufactured homes in any residential zone permitting single-family homes, provided the mobile manufactured homes are aesthetically "compatible" with surrounding buildings.

In recent years, a set of special zones has been proposed and enacted in some cities aimed at lessening social problems by controlling the spatial location of certain land uses. These

video   have had to do with *video game* and *movie arcades* near public
pornography   schools, concentrations of stores specializing in *pornographic*
prostitution   *materials*, motels used as places of *prostitution*, and *liquor stores*
liquor   that sell alcoholic beverages but also operate as places to "hang out," and deal in illicit drugs. To deny such land uses entirely would be challenged on constitutional grounds; by limiting their number and preventing their concentration within small areas, proponents of this zoning believe that the social problems caused or aggravated by these businesses will be reduced.

performance   *Performance zoning* was first proposed as a way of permitting any activity to locate anywhere in a community, provided it could meet a set of performance standards that would ensure it would not adversely affect adjacent property.

Performance standards are zoning controls that regulate the effects or impacts of an activity on the surrounding neighborhood, instead of separating uses into separate zones. In other words, single-family residential, multi-family residential, stores, and offices may be permitted in the

same neighborhood if *certain standards of performance are met*
. . . designed to regulate traffic, visual impact, noise, lights,
or other emissions, overall density, water run-off and other
environmental concerns. (Oregon State University, 1979)

Standards are required that set absolute limits on noise,
vibration, odor, glare, smoke and other exhaust, effluents, fire
and explosion hazards, traffic generation, operational requirements, aesthetic impact, and other potentially adverse environmental effects on the surrounding neighborhood (Figure
15A, Chapter 11, page 146). This is next to impossible because
of the difficulty and cost of measuring the separate and combined environmental effects of the many different human activities taking place in a wide range of spatial situations. Certain
selected performance standards can be incorporated as part of
conditional use zoning, and an increasing number of performance standards are being imposed as conditions for the
approval of ordinary zone changes.

A form of performance zoning could be established as a
simple set of rules applying to an entire community. It might
be employed in connection with an area classification zone to
regulate certain land uses; or zones that allow different intensities of development may be established, each permitting various uses with different performance standards.

Managed growth zoning involves a community's master plan, *managed*
capital improvement program, zoning ordinance, and a special *growth*
means of implementation. The adopted master plan designates
the sequence of development for residential areas best suited
to maintain or attain their desirable character, and avoid overloading existing and planned public facilities and services. The
sequence of development is coordinated with the capital budget and programs scheduling new construction. The zoning
ordinance is amended to require a special permit that relates
the approval of new development to the availability of supportive infrastructure. A system is devised to evaluate individual project proposals with the community situation as the basis
for choosing among prospective developers. Provision may be
made to reduce increases in the assessed value of properties
made by the tax assessor based on his appraisal of their potential value with more intensive uses likely to be approved. If a

request for a more intensive use had been submitted, but not acted on before enactment of the managed growth ordinance, the property owner is entitled to relief from subsequent disapproval of the requested zone change.

variance   Zoning designed to apply to broad categories of land use and large areas of a city invariably involves exceptional situations that "prove the rule" but justify *zoning variances*. Since zoning ordinances, like most laws, cannot anticipate or allow for all unusual circumstances, reasonable requests for special review and relief are justified. When first introduced, variances were to be granted only if "hardship" would result from strict enforcement of the law. In recent years, especially in larger cities where there is great diversity of activities and land use situations, the "desirability" of proposed development has been added as another justification for variances from the "area" and "use" regulations incorporated in zoning ordinances.

Justification for an area variance would exist in the following situation. A residential city block is almost completely built up with single-family detached houses, built years ago in accordance with zoning regulations that required houses be set back 10 feet from the property line along the street to provide space for front yards. Subsequently, the area classification zone was changed to require a minimum front yard setback of 15 feet to provide more open space along new and underdeveloped streets and to provide for street widening if properties with existing houses were replaced by more intense land use in the future. The purchaser of one of the several remaining empty lots in the block should be entitled to an area variance permitting him to match his front yard with those of his neighbors and almost all the other houses on the block, rather than set his house back 15 feet to conform to the most recent area classification zone requirements.

An example of a use variance is a request by an existing enterprise in a light industrial zone to exceed a 2.5 horsepower limit by installing new machinery needed to remain competitive that uses 3.5 horsepower electric motors. The more powerful motors are safer to operate, quieter, and vibrate less than the motors currently installed, and involve no intensification of the total production process.

Both these examples of variances are hardship cases. The owner of one of the last undeveloped lots on the block would be harmed economically if he were denied the same "buildable area" as almost all his neighbors. The ability of the business-man to compete and stay in business depends on his being able to operate efficiently.

The parking requirements of an underlying zone occupy space that could be used more profitably for productive activity within a building. But requests for relief from parking require-ments are seldom hardship cases. They involve variances jus-tified in the interest of desirable, reasonable, and continuing best use of property affected by unexpected changes in the site situation or in the nature of the activity on the property. Specific examples are the reduced need for resident parking places at convalescent homes, in addition to those required for staff and visitors, or the reduced need for employee parking as tele-phone exchanges are automated and employ fewer people. In both of these examples, approval of the variances on the basis of desirable development should stipulate that any change of zone in the future will involve reexamination of reduced park-ing requirements.

In small communities engaged in land use planning, the *appeal* city planning commission or the city council handle variances as part of their regular activities. Some larger cities have estab-lished *boards of zoning appeal* separate from the city planning commission. In a well-developed procedure "zoning adminis-trators" or other officials investigate requests for variances, hold public hearings where proponents and opponents are heard, and render their decisions—which are final unless appealed to the board of zoning appeal and, in some municipalities, there-after to the city council. As in all land use planning and zoning matters, final recourse is to the courts on those issues they accept for judgment.

An exemplary procedure for *processing* zone changes has *processing* been developed over the years by a large municipality in the United States. Hearing examiners investigate every zone change proposal by personally surveying the site and later holding one or more public hearings at which proponents and opponents present their facts, figures, and opinions under rules of pre-sentation and procedure determined by the hearing examiner. The hearing examiner then prepares a written report of his on-site investigation, summarizes the information and opinions expressed at the public hearing, and makes a recommendation.

This report is reviewed by a chief hearing examiner who appends his concurrence or disagreement, explains any disagreement and makes an alternate recommendation. The written report of the hearing examiner and the appended comments and conclusions of the chief hearing examiner are distributed to the members of the city planning commission at least a week before the official meeting when they make the final recommendation to the city council. The council receives the case file and accepts, rejects, or modifies the recommendation of the commission. Occasionally, the director of the city planning department may comment on the case or make a different recommendation to the commission. This thorough procedure is feasible only in larger cities where there are many requests for zone changes and the budget supports such a process.

special conditions   Zoning in the United States is changing. More and more *special conditions* are being attached to zone change approvals that once were granted subject only to physical improvements needed at the site, such as the dedication and improvement of streets, installation of storm drainage, street trees, street lights, and fire hydrants. Today, some cities may add to these required improvements: off-site installations; monetary contributions for a neighborhood park, local school, or sewer treatment plant; an increase or decrease in the population density allowed on the property by the uniform provisions of the underlying area classification zone; a density bonus for providing some special feature such as a plaza or an arcade within the building; affordable housing on or off the site; a day care nursery for employees; art works displayed in public spaces; even a municipal request that fair employment practices be assured on the new land development.

Many of the growing list of conditions imposed before zone change requests are approved are based on environmental legislation discussed in the next chapter. Land use planners are also changing their attitude toward the area classification zoning prevalent in the United States for so many years. Rather than favoring the same land use category throughout large areas of the city, different land uses in close proximity are advocated today for certain locations. The loss in property value, increased susceptibility to property deterioration, and functional conflict presumed to result if different categories of land use are located next to each other, is giving way to the concept of *mixed* residential, commercial, and even light industrial *land uses*—a concept long accepted abroad.

*mixed
land use*

Different land uses located close together are now regarded as desirable. They support each other economically and are responsive to the diverse land use market in cities. They enable people to live near where they work and close to some of the commercial activities they patronize regularly, shortening the average length of the trip to work and for shopping, and reducing urban traffic congestion. Mixed land uses are also believed to promote desirable social contact between different income groups and types of people. And if properly planned, it is believed that they do not produce a more stressful or deteriorated environment.

This change in concept has led to the modification of some master city plans to incorporate concentrations of mixed land uses at selected locations in the city. It has encouraged the requirement that more land development proposals be submitted as *project plans, planned unit developments, specific,* or *precise plans,* since these permit the most extensive shaping of proposed projects and the attachment of a wide range of construction and operating conditions.

special plans

The role of the private land developer in building and shaping cities also is changing. New kinds of zoning have been introduced. Conditions of local governmental approval have proliferated. Environmental impact reports have been added as a new form of land use control. For years, land developers have complained that the time required for project approval is excessive. They must invest considerable money in planning and presenting project proposals, and pay interest on construction loans which are deferred until the project is authorized to proceed. The rising cost of improvements and special conditions required to obtain approval also adds to the cost of the project and is almost always passed on to the consumer. In larger cities, costs incident to a zone change are often greater than the cost of the land for the project. They increase the cost of housing appreciably.

Even when it is doubtful that some of the requirements imposed in the land use planning process would be upheld by the courts if appealed, few land developers can afford the attorneys' fees and long delay typical of litigation in the United States today, with interest costs on loans continuing unabated during the period awaiting trial. City planning commissions and departments can impose legally questionable requirements knowing that appeal of their decisions to the courts is rare. And appeals are likely to be so drawn out that a favorable decision would be of little practical value to the private land developer making the appeal, because almost always he has long since abandoned the project. Also, courts are reluctant to render decisions that invalidate practices that have been employed for some time.

Zoning and other restrictions on the use of land under the "police power" have accumulated during the many centuries such constraints have existed. At the same time many societies established limits on these constraints, beyond which purchase of the real property or compensation was required. The prevailing legal view in the United States has been if zoning eliminates "all or most of the beneficial use" of real property, a *taking* of the owner's *vested rights* has occurred and compensation is due for the value of the right taken. What constitutes a taking and the nature and extent of an owner's vested rights are undergoing reevaluation in the courts. Fundamental questions are involved and are being asked.

taking
vested rights

Are owners of land constitutionally assured the use of their land only in its natural or original state, or its "highest and best use" determined in the marketplace? Can legislative and administrative bodies decide the extent to which the public interest should be paramount? What combination of market mechanisms of private enterprise and actions by government will determine the growth, socioeconomic and physical development, and planning of cities?

If a taking occurs, what is the appropriate remedy: monetary compensation, or nullification of the restriction that constituted the taking? If compensation is due, will it be based on the value of the ownership, or the value of the use of the land foregone while the offending restriction was under appeal?

These are difficult questions indeed. Clarification will emerge gradually from a progression of court decisions at different levels of the judicial system in different parts of the nation. Ultimately, the reality of urban needs and the financial condition of municipalities will determine how vested interests and taking are construed.

In the legal conflict between private rights and the public interest inherent in city planning, private developers have recently employed *antitrust law* providing triple damages to challenge such local government decisions as disapproving additional hotel and condominium projects in a resort community, not allowing private enterprise to compete for municipal trash collection, or refusing to rezone for a new shopping center near the city boundary because it would compete with certain downtown businesses. On balance, however, land use planning in the United States now enjoys stronger directive control than ever before, closer to the almost total land use control exercised in Europe and other parts of the world.

Another significant change is the growing involvement of the judiciary in zoning. After many years of regarding zoning as the prerogative of local legislatures, the Supreme Court of the United States has acted on a number of zoning cases. State supreme courts have become even more active, establishing various precedents: such as forbidding "exclusionary" zoning and mandating the procedures local governments must follow with respect to "affordable housing"; allowing local governments to set up "land banks" for the acquisition and retention of land for many more municipal purposes than were permitted in the past; and extending the transfer of development rights to a wider range of urban situations than originally contemplated.

State legislatures are also becoming directly active in local land use control. For example, an additional category of indus- *mineral* trial *mineral resources zones* has been established for the mining *resources* of rock, sand, and gravel. The state geologist identifies deposits of rock and gravel that have a dollar value above an amount designated in the zoning ordinance, and a "life expectancy" of excavation longer than a designated minimum. Local governments must then take these sites into account in their zoning plans and actions. New excavations may not be conducted without a permit and a reclamation plan approved by the local government; existing operations must have an approved reclamation plan within a "reasonable time." Another example of state legislative intervention is requiring municipalities to allow "mobile manufactured homes" in less restrictive residential zones, provided they are environmentally compatible with surrounding land uses.

It is important to note that zoning practices, court decisions, and land development situations vary tremendously between different sections of the country, different states, and among municipalities. Court decisions may even be contradictory. Generalizations applying equally throughout the United States are few and far between. There are, however, trends that produce more and more common aspects of diverse procedures and practices.

The thorough procedures of zoning described in this chapter are found in larger cities having a planning commission and department with adequate budgetary support. Smaller communities will have more informal and less extensive zoning procedures with individuals, rather than departments, performing one or more of the steps involved. Many small towns and villages in parts of the United States have no land use planning, zoning, or subdivision control at all.Gradually, sad experiences resulting from the absence of land use controls are causing communities without them to inaugurate planning and zoning.

nuisance   *Nuisance law* can also be used to control land uses that
law   adversely affect the community at large or individual property owners. However:

> The spread of comprehensive zoning has decreased the use of nuisance law to prevent discordant land uses. But zoning has raised expectations, and if the local legislature fails to deal with incompatible development through zoning, persons still turn to the courts for protection through the application of nuisance law. (Hagman, 1981) The state's supreme court held . . . that shading someone's solar collector can constitute a private "nuisance" and construction of a home can be stopped . . . the first time a state's highest court has recognized access to sunlight. (The court did hedge its ruling slightly, saying solar access rights cannot be used to block "reasonable" development of adjacent property.) (Guenther, 1983)

State legislatures can modify the activities or environmental situations that constitute a common law nuisance, or delegate this authority to local governments.

Real property taxation affects land use and may be employed to restrain or stimulate development. A low tax on vacant land favors its being held for future appreciation in value, or continuing in its current use if developed. A tax assessor can literally force a change to a higher zone and more intense land use by increasing the appraised value of the property because denser development has been constructed nearby. This can eliminate desirable open spaces in cities since agriculture, landscape nursery, and other uses of open land with few buildings on the site can rarely afford the higher real property taxes imposed by the tax assessor's judgment of potential development. Paradoxically, for a brief period in the past the federal government was making grants to some cities to enable them to acquire more open space at the same time municipal tax assessment policy was reducing the supply. Few communities have accomplished the integration of local tax policy and city planning that would be more likely if comprehensive planning were practiced. *taxation*

Coastlines have always been important, geographically, politically, and economically. Frequently they are jurisdictional boundaries and throughout history they have served as lines of defense. They are the end points for land and water transportation where goods and people are transshipped. They are places of dynamic physical forces and unique environmental features at the interface of land and water. For different reasons and in different ways coastal areas attract recreational, residential, commercial, and industrial activities. And certain facilities and installations must be located at the coastline.

It is not surprising therefore that the most recent addition to land use control in the United States are the *coastal commissions* that have been established as independent "non-political" agencies in one-half of the coastal states. The objective is to produce or encourage unified comprehensive land use planning of the entire coastal zone of a state as a special area requiring separate treatment, rather than uncoordinated or even conflictive planning by the local governments along the coast. *coastal commission*

Coastal situations and programs vary widely among the states. One coastal zone includes an entire state, one extends up to 40 miles inland; another covering one and one-third million acres extends from several hundred feet from the coastline in some places to more than five miles in others. The most rigorous state coastal planning program established a set of policies and formulated a master plan of coastal land use; when local governments resume responsibility for land use planning along their portion of the coast, their policies and plans must conform with the state coastal master plan.

Conditions of approval can range from a prescribed residential density, required public access to the beach, disapproval of people building a house on their property if it would be visible within a scenic prospect designated on a master plan, the amount a hotel in the coastal zone can charge for a weekend room, or the exterior color of a single-family house. Other states, by contrast, seek to persuade, rather than require or pressure, local governments to follow state guidelines in their planning and actions relating to land development proposals in coastal areas.

In effect, state programs of coastal planning preempt or influence land use control in coastal areas located within counties and municipalities. Whether the same logic of directive treatment will be applied by states to other geographically distinct areas—such as deserts, high mountain areas, everglades, tundra, and prime agricultural land—remains to be seen. It has been done by the federal government for a large area of desert land it owns, and states appear to be gradually assuming a more directive role in local land use planning.

Collectively, the different zones noted in this chapter comprise a powerful instrument of land use planning and control. There are additional zones that cannot be covered here for lack of space. There will be new zones created in the future. Some may be discarded. Not only can the physical-spatial elements of urban development be shaped in the United States as never before, but increasingly economic and social objectives related to proposed development can be attained by conditions imposed as a requirement for project approval. With such an arsenal of land use planning controls, failure to attain effective physical planning is because of inadequate support by the public, political, or other power structure, rather than because the procedural means of achieving better city planning are not available.

CITATIONS

[1] Guenther, Robert, "Legal Trends in Solar Power, Zoning Rules, Condemnation," *The Wall Street Journal*, 3 March 1983, p. 31. [2] Hagman, Donald C., *Urban Planning and Land Development Control Law*, St. Paul, MI (West), 1971, pp. 80-81, 117, 289. [3] Oregon State University, "Community Growth Management, Performance Zoning, An Option for a Small Oregon City," Corvallis, OR (Oregon State University Extension Service), Circular 963, March 1979, p. 1.

SELECTED REFERENCES

[1] Ditton, Robert B.; John L. Seymour; Gerald C. Swanson, *Coastal Resources Management, Beyond Bureaucracy and the Market*, Lexington, MA (Lexington), 1977, 196 pp. [2] Federal Housing Administration, *Planned Unit Development*, With a Homes Association, Washington, D.C. (Federal Housing Administration), Land Planning Bulletin No.6, December 1963, 64 pp. [3] Hagman, Donald G., *Public Planning and Control of Urban & Land Development*, Cases and Materials, St. Paul, MI (West), 1973, 1208 pp. [4] Harriss, C. Lowell (Editor), *The Good Earth of America, Planning our Land Use*, Englewood Cliffs, NJ (Prentice-Hall), 1974, 179 pp. [5] Jaffe, Martin and Duncan Erley, *Protecting Solar Access for Residential Development*: A Guidebook for Planning Officials, Washington, DC (Department of Housing and Urban Development), HUD-PDR-445, May 1979, 154 pp. [6] Lynch, Kevin and Gary Hack, *Site Planning*, Boston, MA (M.I.T.), Third Edition, 1984, 450 pp. [7] Reilly, William K. (Editor), *The Use of Land: A Citizen's Policy Guide to Urban Growth*, New York (Thomas Y. Crowell), 1973, 318 pp. [8] Steiner, Frederick R. and John E. Theilacker, *Protecting Farmlands*, Westport, CT (AVI), 1984, 312 pp.

A nationwide survey of 263 top business executives indicates two-thirds of them want to protect the environment even if it means slowing economic growth. . . . roughly 60% of the general public polled on the same issue said they would be willing to pay more for products and services in order to clean up the environment. More than 55% of these respondents said they want to maintain current antipollution standards even if that forces some factories to close.

"Survey Indicates Support For Antipollution Rules," *The Wall Street Journal*, 10 November, 1982.

CHAPTER 11
ENVIRONMENT

In the hands of municipalities and their city planning commissions, the environmental impact report constitutes a powerful instrument for meeting many local needs and desires.

S INCE ENVIRONMENT is by definition "the aggregate of all external conditions and influences," it has always been an inescapable consideration in city planning. No activity or project can exist without numerous relationships with its surroundings. People have always been aware of the positive and negative aspects of the environment: a geographically favorable site or an economically sound location, a convenient street pattern, a pleasing visual prospect; or conversely, dirt, noise, unpleasant odor, or physical ugliness as environmental pollution. Almost 2,000 years ago, the Roman poet Horace complained:

> The hot tempered contractor is hurrying about
> with his carrier and mules;
> A mighty machine turns here a stone, lifts there
> a wooden beam.
> Mournful funerals contend with heavy wagons
> (to see which makes the most noise). . . .

Since the Industrial Revolution began in England some 200 years ago, manufacturing and transportation activities have multiplied many times. They have produced gaseous emissions, liquid effluents, and solid waste largely disregarded or unknown not so long ago. Science has created new chemicals, biologicals, and forms of radiation. The loudest noise to which people are subjected increased sixfold during the second quarter of this century, an average of one decibel per year.

Advances in scientific and medical knowledge have revealed *pollution* the actual and potential range of environmental pollutants and their damaging effects on people. Air pollution is found in many places around the world. In some cities dirt and noise

143

have reached the level of pollutants. Water pollution exists in many rivers and streams and underground aquifers are being degraded by various contaminants seeping down from the ground surface. Concentrations of pesticides are found in ocean waters, plants, and animals far from where they were used originally. The upper atmosphere is being affected by chemicals introduced into the air by increasing industrial activities on the ground. Toxic waste is becoming a more widespread environmental hazard. Radioactive waste is being produced in increasing amounts, some of it with a half-life of many centuries.

Milder forms of environmental pollution can have an aggregate effect on cities that is cumulatively harmful to urban populations. Dense concentrations of people can produce expanses of concrete, metal, and other hard materials that are spatially constricted with few open areas, little vegetation, and lots of shade and shadow. This environment is likely to have above average contamination of the air, more noise, dirt, glare, odor, waste, and visual ugliness. While no one or several of these may constitute an immediate health hazard, the combined effect over time is psychologically depressing and physically debilitating.

A growing awareness of what was happening and could become progressively worse led to passage of the National Environmental Protection Act (NEPA) in 1969. This was followed within several years by federal legislation concerning the most important considerations of environmental protection: refuse, clean air, noise control, coastal zone management, and safe drinking water. NEPA and subsequent presidential *environmental* executive orders direct federal agencies to prepare an *environ-* *impact* *mental impact statement* (EIS) for any activity on their part that *statement* affects the environment "significantly."

The purpose of EISs is to ensure that federal agencies are aware of the environmental consequences of their proposed actions and projects, and that these consequences are considered as an integral part of federal decisions and approvals. Each statement must indicate the purpose and need for the proposed activity, its environmental effect, and the environmental consequences if it is effectuated.

The initial requirements established for federal agencies have been extended by most states to their own governmental units and to municipalities, and subsequently to private develop-

ment projects subject to any one of the many kinds of governmental approval needed for most private activities. The *envi-* *environmental*
ronmental impact reports (EIRs) of states and municipalities are *impact*
called reports rather than statements. They describe the pro- *report*
posed project or activity and its environmental setting, indicate
its *impact* and *adverse effects*, relate its *short-term uses* of environmental resources to the maintenance or enhancement of *long-*
term productivity, and identify any *irreversible* or *irretrievable com-*
mitments of resources involved.

These last two requirements are best explained by examples. Clear cutting the timber on forest land removes its long-
term productivity until seedlings are planted and reach maturity many years later. Selective cutting would leave the remaining timber as a long-term productive resource. A project
extracting oil is expending an irreplaceable resource, as is the
removal of topsoil without providing for its return or replacement. Nature requires hundreds of years to create new humus.
An example in city planning would be allowing most of a large
gravel deposit to be permanently committed to residential
development with only a small part available for excavation.
When gravel from this portion of the site is exhausted in a short
time, the remainder of the gravel resource is no longer available
for the concrete mix needed for local construction over the long
term; gravel must be imported at greater cost from farther away.

Two additional responses in environmental impact reports
are required in one state: measures to *mitigate* any adverse environmental effects of the proposed development, and an indication of any urban *growth inducing* effects.

The legislative provisions for EISs and EIRs cover almost
every proposed activity of consequence affecting the physical
environment in the United States. However, reports for legislative, managerial, financial, and other actions indirectly related
to the spatial environment are rarely required. In city planning,
environmental impacts are considered in land use planning but
infrequently in connection with the activities of municipal
operating departments. EIRs treat only the more important
issues involved in the project proposal. Were all conceivable
environmental effects studied in detail, the length of the report
and the time needed to prepare it would be excessive, impractical, and cost prohibitive. Furthermore, existing analytical
knowledge cannot measure precisely and compare conclu-

sively the diversity of environmental considerations. The range of possible effects is shown schematically in Figure 15, which is arbitrarily divided for easier exposition into Physical (A) and Social, Economic, Political, and Other (B). In reality, these two views are inextricably interrelated.

EIRs are prepared by the organization proposing the project or activity, on its own or with consultant help. As noted in

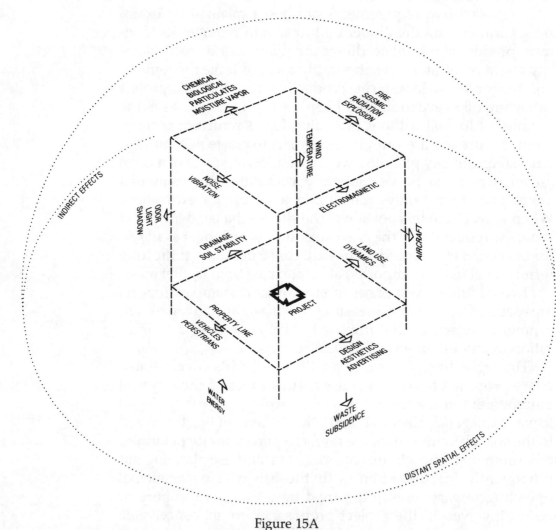

Figure 15A
Environmental Impacts
Physical
("Environmental Impact Statements: Boon or Bane?" *Facets*, May 1977, p. 4)

Chapter 16 on Professional Practice and Education, approximately one-half of urban and regional planning consulting firms are engaged in preparing environmental impact reports. EIRs are submitted to the governmental unit whose approval is required before the proposed development can proceed. Four kinds of procedural action have been established for handling environmental approvals. *EIR has been prepared* signifies that a   *preparation*

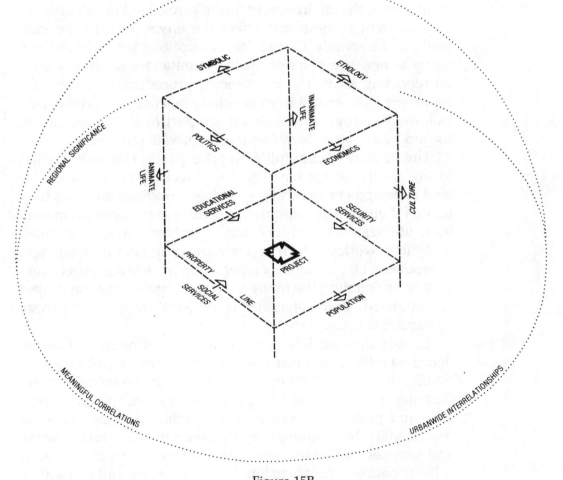

Figure 15B
Environmental Impacts
Social, Economic, Political, Other
("Environmental Impact Statements: Boon or Bane?" *Facets*, May 1977, p. 6)

report was required because the proposed project would affect
negative the environment significantly. *Negative declaration* indicates that
declaration there are no adverse effects and therefore no legal requirement
for an environmental impact report: for example, a change of
zone or height limit that does not alter the environmental sit-
categorically uation. *Categorically exempt* indicates classes of comparable pro-
exempt posals or actions affecting land use that do not have an impact
on the environment significant enough to require an EIR: emergency repairs, replacement, or reconstruction; new construction of small structures or minor alterations to land and acces-
sory structures; actions by regulatory agencies to protect natural
resources or the environment; ordinances, land dedications, or
management matters that affect the environment only indirectly and remotely. Categorical exemptions are reviewed regularly as new situations or practical limitations to environmental reporting arise. The most recent procedural classifications
represent a departure from previous practice in land use control and a changing attitude on the part of local government
toward urban land development by private enterprise.

Unlike many communities in other parts of the world, cities
in the United States have left the direct profits of most new
land development to private enterprise. Traditionally cities have
limited their own development activities to transportation facilities, utilities, water supply, and other projects long accepted
as "public works." Much of the remaining land development
is produced by private developers with an average expectation
of at least doubling the money invested by the time the project
is completed. Both categories of projects are built by private
construction companies.

changing Greatly increased fiscal difficulties are bringing a *change of*
attitude *municipal attitude* and introducing a new element into the economic city. As noted previously in a different connection, communities are reasoning that private land development is possible and profitable because over a period of many years the
municipality has supplied its inhabitants with public works
and services that enable people to congregate in cities, and it
is these people who as customers, proprietors, and employees
enable new developments to succeed. It is argued, therefore,
that the past practice of limiting the "improvements" required

of land developers to physical installations next to and directly related to the proposed project is no longer justified.

City planning departments and commissions are imposing more requirements on individuals and organizations requesting approval of a zone change, subdivision design, or environmental impact report. The range and extent of these conditions varies with the local political and financial situation, the size and nature of the proposed development, the resources of the applicant, and the needs and desires of the community. A *bargaining* situation is developing in which each side seeks to optimize its gains without forcing one side to withdraw or the other to disapprove the proposed development. *bargaining*

This change in attitude has necessarily involved reconsideration of what constitutes a *windfall* and a *wipeout* for the property owner. The two terms were coined to describe undue increases and decreases in land value resulting from changes in land use. Windfall designates an increase in land value and potential profit resulting from a change in land use permitting a much more profitable utilization of the property. A wipeout signifies a large loss in value and potential profit when property is restricted to a less intensive use, or when the ways it can be developed are eliminated or curtailed. As indicated in the previous chapter on Land Use Control, when city planning action deprives "all or most of the beneficial use" of a parcel of real property, this constitutes a *taking* under applicable law and compensation must be paid the owner. Although the improvements or conditions proposed in an EIR do not constitute legal requirements, in most cases they affect whether the proposed project is approved or disapproved. And they may lead to modification of the zoning ordinance to reflect changing attitudes toward the respective rights of the municipality and the obligations of the private land developer. *windfall* *wipeout* *taking*

In a *mitigated* or *conditional negative declaration*, the city planning commission and department compile a set of actions and installations by the private developer that will eliminate or "mitigate" what the commission concludes are the adverse effects of the proposed development on the municipal environment; ipso facto, an EIR is not needed. With the new attitudes toward the responsibilities of the private developer, conditions of *mitigated* *negative* *declaration* approval may be only remotely related to the particular adverse impacts of the project on its immediate surroundings since all elements of a city are interrelated in one way or another, directly or indirectly.

The range of mitigating requirements or requests that are being imposed by some communities on developers is indicated by two examples from the western United States. Original conditions for mitigated environmental approval of a large commercial development required the developer to: provide 100 "affordable" rental units somewhere in the municipality, a three-acre park, a day care center; ensure traffic abatement, energy management, and an affirmative action program directed to the benefit of surrounding neighborhoods; and promote art and social activity on the site by paying a substantial fee to the municipality or by incorporating acceptable features in the project for this purpose.

In another city, developers of highrise office buildings downtown are required to build or rehabilitate dwelling units in residential zones anywhere in the municipality at a rate of 400 square feet for each 250 square feet of office space in the proposed project. The developer may cancel one residential unit for each $6,000 contributed to the city's mortgage revenue bond fund or to one of its low- or moderate-income housing programs. These are examples of the far-reaching requirements that are being imposed in some places on private development as part of environmental impact control. They are in addition to those imposed when a change of zone is involved.

variations   The cost of environmental impact reports, the time required to prepare them, and their length varies depending on the nature and size of the proposed project, the extent of the reporting requested by the approving authority, and the difficulty of investigating the environmental effects to be considered. The cost may range from several hundred dollars for a routine zone change request, to more than $500,000 for doubling the passenger capacity of an international municipal airport, or $9 million, more than a decade ago, for a major pipeline extending several hundred miles over unusually sensitive terrain.

Report length varies from a few pages for the routine zone change to 950 pages for the EIR submitted for the approval of two new dormitories at a large state university, six volumes for the municipal airport, and a stack of material ten feet high for the pipeline. The time needed to prepare environmental impact reports is roughly proportional to their comparative cost. As a single example of the excessive time that may be required, it took a public utility company four and one-half years to obtain environmental approval from the state regulatory agency for a high voltage overhead transmission line traversing urban areas for only a small portion of its 85-mile length.

There are ambiguities in the basic terminology of environ-   *ambiguities*
mental legislation, differences in state environmental protec-
tive laws, and different opinions concerning appropriate requirements for approval. The word "environment" itself can be interpreted to include almost any activity anywhere, or it can be narrowed by further definition. There is no accepted standard, useful description, or even general agreement on what constitutes a "significant" impact, the basic criterion for determining when EIRs are required. There is no accepted method for deciding which are the most important impacts that should be incorporated in the environmental analysis, and which of lesser importance can be treated briefly or disregarded. There is no consensus concerning what requirements and conditions are justified in order to eliminate or mitigate environmental impacts. Legal guidelines provided by the courts are few and far between; and the attitudes of different states, municipalities, and planning commissions vary widely concerning the appropriate use of EIRs to secure municipal improvements indirectly related to the project proposal.

Experience since the federal enabling act in 1969 has produced advances in concept and practice. At first, EIRs were often used as tactical devices. By insisting that all possible environmental effects be thoroughly studied and conclusions verified beyond challenge, opponents could cause such delay that most private developers could not afford the time and cost of continuing with their project. This led to approving agencies limiting the number of potential effects that must be studied and incorporated in environmental impact reports to those that are of primary importance; some states suggest such a limitation in the guidelines they issue for local governmental bodies carrying out the state environmental protection act. Also, the vast number of proposals that could be interpreted strictly as affecting the environment in some way has been reduced by exempting single proposals and classes of projects that do not have a significant impact on the environment. Unfortunately these procedural improvements do not reduce the years of delay when regulatory agencies engage in a vain political attempt to obtain peaceful agreement by all concerned and interested. The consumer pays for the money spent while public utilities, obligated to extend their services and other organizations obliged to meet market demand, repeatedly revise their environmental impact statements to obtain approval.

The basic ambiguities and the wide range of interpretation that remain provide a powerful instrument of city planning that can be used to secure municipal participation in profits, new sources of revenue, installations of many kinds, desired activities, and land use control. The scope and application of federal legislation has extended to many more forms of environmental pollution than was probably intended in the first place. In the hands of municipalities and their city planning commissions, the EIR constitutes a powerful instrument for meeting many local needs and desires. The shortage of municipal revenue, together with court decisions on appeal, will determine how widely EIRs are employed to impose a new set of requirements on private land development as well as to protect the environment from pollution.

SELECTED REFERENCES

[1] Bannister, Robert D., *Environmental Controls: A Handbook for Realtors*, Chicago, IL (National Association of Realtors), April 1977, 90 pp. [2] Branch, Melville C., "Environmental Impact Statements: Boon or Bane?," *Facets*, 1977, pp. 1-12. [3] _____, *Outdoor Noise and the Metropolitan Environment*, Case Study of Los Angeles with Special Reference to Aircraft, Los Angeles, CA (Department of City Planning), 1970, 60 pp. [4] Dubos, René, *Man Adapting*, New Haven, CT (Yale University), 1965, 527 pp. [5] Erley, Duncan and Martin Jaffe, *Site Planning for Solar Access*: A Guidebook for Residential Developers and Site Planners, Washington, DC (Department of Housing and Urban Development), HUD-PDR-481, September 1979, 148 pp. [6] Hagman, Donald G., *Urban Planning and Land Development Control Law*, Chapters 20 and 21, St. Paul, MN (West), 1975, pp. 525-673. [7] Kirlin, John J. and Anne M. Kerlin, *Public Choices—Private Resources*, Financing Capital Infrastructure for California's Growth Through Public-Private Bargaining, Sacramento, CA (California Tax Foundation), 1982, 101 pp. [8]

Marsh, William M., *Environmental Analysis for Land Use and Site Planning*, New York (McGraw-Hill), 1978, 292 pp. [9] Smith, Fred, *Man and His Urban Environment*, A Manual of Specific Considerations for the Seventies and Beyond, New York (Man and His Urban Environment Project), 1973, 57 pp. [10] Thomas, William L. (Editor), *Man's Role in Changing the Face of the Earth*, Chicago, IL (University of Chicago), 1956, 1193 pp. [11] Warden, Richard E. and W. Tim Dagodag, A Guide to the Preparation and Review of *Environmental Impact Reports*, Los Angeles, CA (Security World), 1976, 138 pp.

In broad terms, urban redevelopment is an attempt to reconstruct those portions of our great cities that have deteriorated into slum conditions, and that are urgently in need of rehabilitation. In almost every city of the United States areas can be found, usually surrounding the central business and wholesale districts, which have fallen into a state of physical disrepair. These are also areas of "social disrepair" characterized by crime and delinquency, high rates of disease, family disorganization and poverty. On the one hand, these areas exhibit a very high density of population—at least in number of persons per room—while on the other hand, large parts of the areas are often in vacant land or in commercial and industrial use. These "blighted" areas constitute a heavy drain upon the community in terms of public services and tax delinquency, and their reconstruction has become one of the fundamental . . . municipal problems.

Herbert A. Simon, "What Is Urban Redevelopment?," *Illinois Tech Engineer*, December, 1946.

CHAPTER 12
REDEVELOPMENT, REHABILITATION

As yet, no best and most effective method of urban redevelopment and rehabilitation has emerged in the United States, but subsidy in one form or another seems to be the most essential ingredient for the short-term, and significant reduction in the number of the poor a long-term aspiration requiring an increase in their monetary income.

REDEVELOPMENT IN city planning is concerned with improving in one of two ways the blighted and deteriorated residential areas that have existed in larger cities throughout history. *Urban renewal* has to do with removing the dilapidated buildings that characterize blighted neighborhoods and replacing them with new structures. It also includes efforts to revitalize economic activities within the blighted area which will increase family incomes sufficiently to enable the inhabitants to renew their own places of residence. *Urban rehabilitation* refers to the physical improvement, remodeling, or partial reconstruction of existing houses and apartments in deteriorating neighborhoods rather than their demolition and replacement.

renewal

rehabilitation

First among the causes of urban blight is poverty. Many of the undesirable social conditions of the blighted area are simply a reflection of the general economic condition of the people who live in the area. . . .

A second factor that must be considered is land speculation. The blighted area usually surrounds a commercial district. . . .

A third major cause of blight is the blight itself. . . .

The first symptoms of deterioration spread rapidly and ultimately bring about a deterioration of the neighborhood as a whole. (Simon, 1946)

The spontaneous redevelopment of blighted neighborhoods would require a desire, or at least a willingness, on the
part of many property owners to bring about change. Enough
of them would have to join forces to assemble a contiguous
land area large enough to resist the destabilizing effects of surrounding properties that are probably also depressed. Money
must be found to pay for purchasing and clearing the land of
existing structures and constructing new buildings. The people
living in the area must relocate. Experience has shown that
these essential requirements for urban renewal cannot be met
without governmental intervention and assistance because of
the conflicting interests and limited financial resources of the
many different individuals and organizations owning real
property in the blighted neighborhood.

Years ago, federal and state legislation was enacted in the
United States to enable the essential conditions of redevelopment to be met. *Urban renewal* or *urban redevelopment agencies*
were formed to initiate, manage, and provide the organizational continuity required for urban renewal projects. These
eminent agencies were given the power of *eminent domain* which enables
domain them to assemble and acquire real property by condemnation
for the public purpose of rebuilding areas shown by survey to
be blighted. Blight exists when most of the buildings have
structural weaknesses or inadequate sanitary facilities or utility
connections, or the area is subject to environmental deterioration because of poor subdivision or some other depressive
condition. If justified for the public purpose, there is precedent
for delegating the power of eminent domain to individuals or
private organizations acting under redevelopment law, and for
local governments to acquire land for later sale or lease to private developers.

The city planning commission and department may be designated as the urban redevelopment agency. But the analytical,
coordinative, and longer range capabilities involved in comprehensive city planning do not normally include the shorter
range, operational, and entrepreneurial competences needed
for urban renewal—not to mention time enough to do both.
When a city planning commission is inappropriate or does not
exist, the city council or another municipal body can serve as
the urban redevelopment agency, although ordinarily they are

too busy to take on this additional task, one that would almost certainly involve public controversy and confrontation. Since federal programs of assistance were introduced 35 years ago, urban redevelopment has usually been conducted by a separate agency as shown in Figure 8 (Chapter 6, page 80).

The current "fair market value" that must be paid for blighted land and buildings is almost always high, reflecting the intensity of use and speculative anticipation of commercial expansion into the residential area. This inflated cost of land and blighted buildings in downtown areas of cities must be reduced or "written down" by the redevelopment agency to a price a private developer is willing to pay. This is the major *financial subsidy* required to induce private enterprise to provide new *subsidy* low-cost housing at rents that poorer people can pay. Even with governmental subsidies, the financial facts have caused many urban renewal projects in the downtown area of cities—originally intended to provide housing—to end up mainly commercial because the greater income from business supports higher costs of land acquisition and construction. The alternative to the special forms of renewal subsidy is providing the necessary financial support by a general increase in local taxes, a solution considered by elected officials in the United States as politically undesirable, if not fatal, to their reelection.

Many methods of promoting urban renewal have been tried over the years. All of them involve different ways of inducing or enabling private land developers to rebuild the poorest residential neighborhoods; or small businesses and new industries to revitalize these areas economically by employing people living in the neighborhood and raising their income to the point they can support better housing. Over the years, governmental subsidies and incentives have taken many forms. In urban renewal they have included cash grants-in-aid, low-interest loans, reduced taxes, tax-exempt bonds, rent supplements, and resale of the land acquired through condemnation to the private developer for substantially less than the price paid for it. Efforts to revitalize blighted areas by increasing business activity within them may include some of the subsidies provided for the replacement of dilapidated buildings, and reductions in real property, business, capital gains, or social security payroll taxes, and employee training programs supported by local government.

Most states have empowered municipalities to engage directly in urban renewal by buying land, selling bonds, reducing taxes, and arranging construction and eventual transfer of ownership. A number of states have authorized the establishment of *enterprise zones* to encourage greater business activity within areas of widespread poverty, high unemployment, and low income. The specific procedures of designating and administering these zones vary among the states. In one of them, local governments identify distressed areas within their jurisdiction that meet criteria set by the state, which must approve them as enterprise zones in order for business moving into or expanding within the depressed area to qualify for financial subsidy. This assistance may take many forms: reduced state sales or income taxes; reduced motor vehicle use, equipment, or inventory taxes; exemption from the costs of various licenses and approvals required in business operations, or from water or sewer hookup fees; modification of the zoning code; or eliminating some other restriction that discourages business.

enterprise zones

Tax increment financing is another method of underwriting redevelopment established in recent years. The tax base within the renewal area is "frozen" at the assessed value existing when the project is officially established. Additional real property taxes generated as new buildings are constructed are not added to the general revenue of the municipality as is normally done, but are "fed back" into a special fund for the renewal area to be used for public improvements and neighborhood purposes that make the area more attractive for private investment and further renewal. Usually a number of years or a limit on the total amount of taxes committed to the renewal area are specified at the beginning of the project. Initial start-up costs are met by the sale of municipal bonds to be repaid from the tax increment funds. Requirements and provisions for revenue financing differ among states, but they have been used more often for commercial than low-cost residential redevelopment. Some enabling legislation permits such liberal definitions of "blight" and "public purpose" that tax revenue financing is used for projects that are very different from the original legislative purpose of low-income residential renewal.

tax increment financing

The essential requirement in both urban renewal and revitalization is sufficient subsidy to make up the difference between what it costs to produce "minimum acceptable" dwelling units and the rents or interest low-income people can pay, or between profitable and unprofitable revitalized business. In urban renewal this has been made more difficult in the United States by the lingering belief that somehow private enterprise can meet the low-income housing need without assistance through the market mechanism of supply and demand. Federal subsidies are provided for such broad and continuing applications as transportation and public utility systems, agricultural products and farm programs, flood control, maritime shipbuilding, and a thousand and one other programs and specific projects—but rarely by comparison for housing projects for the urban poor.

In the two decades from 1950 to 1970 some 3.6 million substandard dwelling units were renewed within metropolitan areas, 2.1 million in central cities and 1.5 million in the suburbs; this left 2.5 million substandard units within metropolitan areas (Downs, 1970). The average yearly renewal of 180,000 substandard dwelling units in metropolitan areas during the 20-year period has been reduced in subsequent years by smaller governmental appropriations for urban renewal, and a federal policy of transferring responsibility for low-income housing to local governments. By some estimates the total number of low-cost dwelling units available anywhere in the United States is being reduced at a rate of a half million units every year.

Successful urban renewal also requires skillful *planning and design* to minimize those conditions in the physical environment that contributed to deterioration in the first place. Most redevelopment legislation requires approval of the initial plan and subsequent amendments by the city planning commission, city council, or another municipal body. Buildings, streets, and open spaces can be designed to form a visually attractive physical environment, with a community center containing commercial establishments and municipal facilities serving the project area. Urban design can also reduce any adverse environmental effects from surrounding districts and facilitate access by residents to other sections of the city. If needed, provision for adequate maintenance of dwelling units, outdoor spaces, and public places can be incorporated as part of the project approval. As indicated in the previous chapters on Environment and Land Use Control, a wider range of continuing

planning and design

requirements are being imposed on land developers than was the case not long ago. Sound planning, skillful design, and the option of special operating conditions can serve neighborhood needs and contribute to lasting stability.

displacement of people   Another primary problem in urban residential renewal springs from the *displacement of people* with low incomes who live in the buildings that will be torn down and replaced with new structures. During the six to nine years it takes on the average to complete a renewal project, these residents must live somewhere else. It is never easy and often impossible for them to find comparable living quarters because the low rents characteristic of blighted areas do not exist in other parts of the city. There are also the expenses of physically moving the household. Besides being poor, many of those living in blighted areas are blacks and members of other minorities that are not welcome in most sections of the city. The modest compensation given in recent years to displaced residents of renewal areas and the assistance provided them in moving have not matched the costs and personal strains of eviction. Only a very small percentage of those "temporarily" displaced can afford or choose to return years later to the completed renewal project, which at best will have only a few dwelling units "affordable" for previous tenants.

In view of the difficulties, it is not surprising that urban renewal is the most difficult problem confronting comprehensive city planning. Blighted areas and slums are a characteristic of most larger cities. In the United States the problem has been intensified by unprecedented immigration in recent years, mostly people of low income who have settled initially in blighted or deteriorating urban neighborhoods. In many other parts of the world, the spread of slums and squatter settlements in cities has been so widespread and severe that their elimination appears impossible until sometime in the future when the number of poor people decreases. Basically, urban renewal replaces the decay that is inevitable in living organisms including cities. The urban renewal process of physical surgery and reconstruction is the only known treatment for this urban disease and the most challenging task in city planning.

urban rehabilitation   As the term itself indicates, *urban rehabilitation* seeks to make deteriorated single-family or apartment housing more habitable and safer by improving the physical structures, rather than tearing them down and replacing them with new buildings. Rehabilitation can involve a single building in need of improvement to meet minimum municipal standards for habitable dwelling units. It can involve an abandoned and gutted building that will disintegrate beyond saving unless reconstruction is undertaken immediately. And it can be applied to an entire neighborhood composed of hundreds of homes that require physical improvement to prevent further deterioration until the area becomes so blighted it can be restored only by clearance and reconstruction.

There are various approaches to urban rehabilitation that involve subsidy to the property owner or long-term lessee. One of these underwrites part of the loan normally needed to pay the costs of construction, obtained from a local bank, savings and loan association, or other financial institution. Another reduces the total cost of reconstruction through tax relief or by subsidizing part of the mortgage payments or the rent that provides the income to pay off the loan for reconstruction. If the building is historically significant, it is eligible to receive a rehabilitation grant under federal legislation enacted for this particular purpose. And by purchasing blocks of loans made to individuals by municipalities for rehabilitation, the federal government enables additional loans to be made locally.

In *homesteading*, the federal government transfers title to *homesteading* properties it has acquired through foreclosure for nonpayment of taxes to the municipal government for a nominal payment; this enables the city to make these properties available at a minimum purchase price for self-help reconstruction by the new owners. Federal grants are also made to local governments and nonprofit organizations to enable them to start a revolving fund for local rehabilitation by private financing; municipalities assist by making public improvements in the neighborhoods being improved. Approximately 16 percent of federal subsidies for lower income housing are directed to urban rehabilitation. A majority of the states have some type of rehabilitation program providing grants, loans, or tax incentives.

Rather than creating a redevelopment agency to replace or *revitalization* rehabilitate blighted sections of cities, programs of *economic revitalization* seek to stimulate existing businesses in deteriorating areas and encourage other enterprises to locate in these districts. It is reasoned that increased business activity will gradually reduce local unemployment and increase incomes sufficiently to enable owners to borrow money to rehabilitate their own homes. This endeavor is defeated at the outset if private lending institutions "redline" depressed areas within which they refuse to consider making the mortgage loans essential to success, and government supported mortgages are not available. Local development corporations have been established to encourage business expansion in deteriorating areas. The approvals and actions required by government agencies are expedited by joint action. Obstructive land use regulations are modified by the municipality. Businesses in deteriorated neighborhoods may be favored in bidding for municipal contracts. Or special zones have been created to prevent new commercial development from threatening the socioeconomic stability of vulnerable areas, and to discourage the displacement of shop owners and residential tenants by different land uses.

Several companies have located production plants in depressed neighborhoods as a corporate policy to provide local employment, stimulate small businesses in the area, and engender constructive optimism within the community. Several large private corporations have attempted to rehabilitate single buildings with limited success. The deteriorated single-family houses rebuilt by private land developers at high cost on high priced land near city centers can be afforded only by *gentrification* upper income people; this *gentrification* of small segments of the inner city does not address the low-cost housing shortage which is the generally recognized objective of rehabilitation.

Urban redevelopment is being pursued in the United States with limited success by a frequently changing variety of programs with different degrees of involvement by federal, state, and local government agencies and private enterprises, and with different means of accomplishment. As yet no best and most effective method has emerged but subsidy in one form or another seems to be the most essential ingredient for the short term, and significant reduction in the number of the poor is a long term aspiration requiring an increase in their monetary income.

CITATIONS

[1] Downs, Anthony, *Urban Problems and Prospects*, Chicago, IL (Markham), 1970, pp. 117, 119. [2] Simon, Herbert A., *Illinois Tech Engineer*, December 1946.

SELECTED REFERENCES

[1] Abrams, Charles, *Man's Struggle for Shelter*, Cambridge, MA (M.I.T.), 1964, 307 pp. [2] Goetz, Rolf, *Building Neighborhood Confidence*, The Humanist's Strategy for Urban Housing, Cambridge, MA (Ballinger), 1976, 176 pp. [3] Greer, Scott, *Urban Renewal and American Cities*, The Dilemma of Democratic Intervention, Indianapolis, IN (Bobbs-Merrill), 1965, 195 pp. [4] Listokin, David (Editor), *Housing Rehabilitation, Economics, Social, and Policy Perspectives*, New Brunswick, NJ (Rutgers), 1983, 370 pp. [5] Niebanck, Paul L., *Relocation in urban planning: from obstacle to opportunity*, Philadelphia, PA (University of Pennsylvania), 1968, 123 pp. [6] Wilson, James Q., *Urban Renewal: The Record and the Controversy*, Cambridge, MA (M.I.T.), 1967, 683 pp.

Community design is the process and the product of organizing and integrating all the environmental components (manmade and natural), in a manner that will enhance local image and sense of place, as well as functional adequacy, and also instill civic pride and desirability as a place of residence. It can be applied to a variety of settings and physical densities ranging from very urban to suburban to rural. It is also applicable at a range of scales from individual neighborhoods to entire regions, and it may focus on community-wide issues or special components such as residential neighborhoods, business centers, open space systems or major roadway character.

Robert F. Dannenbrink, Jr., "The Community Design Element—Blueprint for Local Form and Image," *Orange County Architect*, October/November, 1980.

CHAPTER 13
URBAN DESIGN

Urban design requirements may be imposed on projects involving zone changes, those that are subject to an environmental impact report, or those submitted as a planned unit development, specific plan, or conditional use that requires submission of a detailed project plan.

T HE WORD design is used in different ways with different meanings by different fields of interest. In everyday conversation it can be employed as a universal term referring to almost any activity. In comprehensive city planning, urban design has a specific meaning, differentiating it from other aspects of the urban planning process. It has to do with the sensory response of people to the environment of the physical city: its *visual appearance, aesthetic quality*, and *spatial character*. It is concerned with how these affect people's sense of well-being, their awareness of different places within the city, and their behavior to the extent it is directly or indirectly responsive to the physical-spatial "envelope" within which people reside, work, and play.

At the neighborhood scale, urban design involves the prospect and environmental situation of a single building or group of structures, a park or plaza, boulevard or pedestrian path, lamp post or bus bench, or any element of the physical community with which its residents are in frequent contact. Architects, landscape architects, and industrial product designers are most directly involved with this aspect of planning cities, since their education and professional practice equip them with the required visual, spatial, and aesthetic sensitivities.

At a citywide scale, urban design considers the primary *visual elements* of a community which consist of landmarks, nodes, districts, paths, and edges (Lynch, 1960). (Figure 16) This concept of a leading theorist and practitioner has been incorporated in a number of land use city plans. (Figure 17) Whatever particular concept is adopted, there is general agreement that urban design should identify and enhance the key

visual elements

165

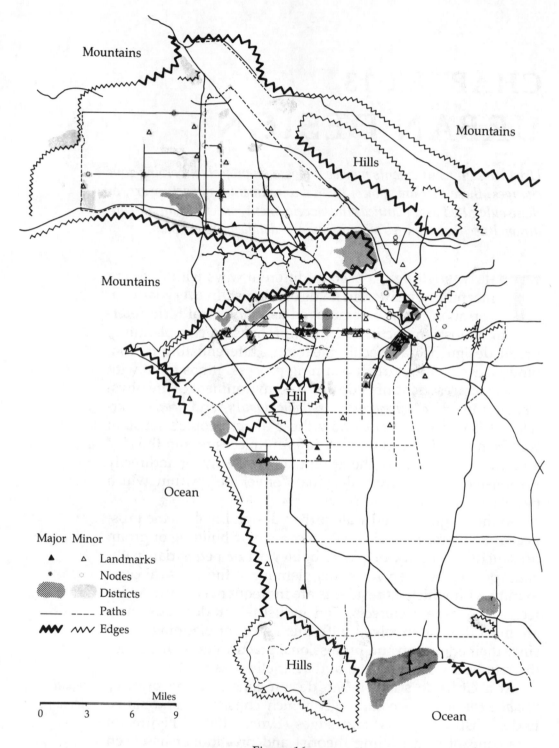

Major Minor

▲ △ Landmarks
⬤ ○ Nodes
Districts
—— ---- Paths
〰 〜 Edges

Miles
0   3   6   9

Figure 16
Visual Form of a Large City
(*The Visual Environment of Los Angeles,*
Department of City Planning, April 1971, p. 6)

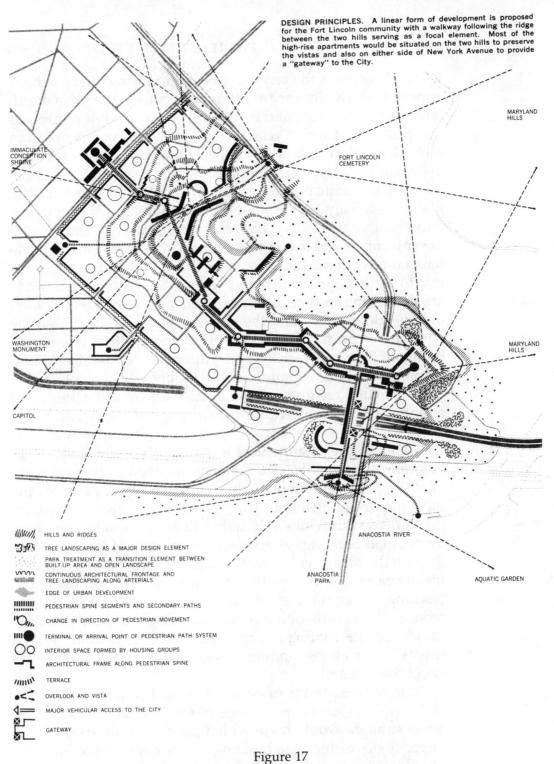

DESIGN PRINCIPLES. A linear form of development is proposed for the Fort Lincoln community with a walkway following the ridge between the two hills serving as a focal element. Most of the high-rise apartments would be situated on the two hills to preserve the vistas and also on either side of New York Avenue to provide a "gateway" to the City.

MARYLAND HILLS

IMMACULATE CONCEPTION SHRINE

FORT LINCOLN CEMETERY

WASHINGTON MONUMENT

MARYLAND HILLS

CAPITOL

ANACOSTIA RIVER

ANACOSTIA PARK

AQUATIC GARDEN

HILLS AND RIDGES	
TREE LANDSCAPING AS A MAJOR DESIGN ELEMENT	
PARK TREATMENT AS A TRANSITION ELEMENT BETWEEN BUILT-UP AREA AND OPEN LANDSCAPE	
CONTINUOUS ARCHITECTURAL FRONTAGE AND TREE LANDSCAPING ALONG ARTERIALS	
EDGE OF URBAN DEVELOPMENT	
PEDESTRIAN SPINE SEGMENTS AND SECONDARY PATHS	
CHANGE IN DIRECTION OF PEDESTRIAN MOVEMENT	
TERMINAL OR ARRIVAL POINT OF PEDESTRIAN PATH SYSTEM	
INTERIOR SPACE FORMED BY HOUSING GROUPS	
ARCHITECTURAL FRAME ALONG PEDESTRIAN SPINE	
TERRACE	
OVERLOOK AND VISTA	
MAJOR VEHICULAR ACCESS TO THE CITY	
GATEWAY	

Figure 17
Urban Design Element in a Land Use City Plan
(*The Proposed Comprehensive Plan for the National Capital,*
National Capital Planning Commission, February 1967, p. 168)

167

visual elements of the physical city by increasing their aesthetic appeal, their significance as reference points in the often undifferentiated cityscape, and their contribution to civic awareness and pride. That such a relationship exists between people and their physical environment has been demonstrated by research in "cognitive mapping." People are asked to recall from visual memory the principal places and outstanding features in cities that are spatially and aesthetically meaningful for them. Various groups have widely different views of the city. People with lower incomes and less education have the most restricted spatial and environmental awareness, but most people are sensitive to a city's appearance and want to see it improved. They are discerning in their likes and dislikes with respect to their own neighborhoods and the city as a whole. They dislike the environmental characteristics that adversely affect their neighborhood. They appreciate spatial openness, cleanliness, landscaping, new buildings and cultural facilities. In general, people have difficulty relating parts of a city to its overall pattern and orienting themselves within urban space. (City of Los Angeles, 1971)

multiple considerations   Planning the treatment of a major urban trafficway is an example of the *multiple considerations* involved in urban design. The form and placement of abutting buildings is probably the most important element of the street design. For example, if the trafficway provides a desirable view to one side, the placement of tall buildings alternately on one side of the street and then on the other, with lowrise buildings in between, prevents the development of a continuous "wall" of tall buildings from blocking the scenic view from one side of the street. It also reduces the reverberative noise and intensified air pollution caused by the confined space that is formed within "walled streets" by an almost uninterrupted line of tall buildings rising along the sidewalk.

Both of these forms of pollution would be reduced further, and a wider view of the "dome of the sky" above and more direct sunlight would be provided people on the street, if the upper floors of highrise buildings are stepped back from the front lot line rather than rising vertically for their entire height. When the first floors of abutting buildings have no openings to the street other than their entrances, the use and character of the street are different than when the ground floors are occupied by shops and commercial enterprises opening on to the street. And if there are no plazas, setbacks, or other open spaces extending back from the street, the sense of confinement and congestion within a narrow "canyon" of space is increased for commuters, residents, and shoppers alike.

In severe climates, arcades along major thoroughfares may be desirable to protect pedestrians from sun or snow, providing at the same time an element of urban design that "ties together" and visually unifies at street level the disparate and sometimes discordant structures located along a major thoroughfare (Figure 18). If the street is intended for vehicular use only, pedestrian pathways and shopping concourses are provided at the second-story level with connecting overpasses above the trafficway. Installation of the same type of street trees and compatible landscaping also provides a unifying effect. Selection of well-designed matching "street furniture"—street and traffic lights, bus benches, telephone booths, mail boxes, newspaper dispensing stands, trash receptacles—enhances the appearance of the shopping street, and careful placement of the installations optimizes their use.

Superior urban design that makes a city more attractive and creates better urban environments is appreciated by most people. Research indicates that beauty is not "in the eye of each idiosyncratic beholder"; to the contrary, "people generally agree on what is pleasing and what is not" (Langdon, 1984). The means of effectuating urban design exist in the land use and environmental controls discussed in Chapters 10 and 11. However, with regard to the design treatment of planned trafficways, political pressure in the United States for equal development rights on adjacent properties has favored continuous

Figure 18
An Arcade as an Element of Urban Design

"strip development" along both sides of the street and precluded the diversity of land use and building form needed for the best urban design.

cleanliness Although the visual scene of cities as a whole ranges from the ugly to the beautiful, there are two ways urban attractiveness can be enhanced. One is to keep cities *clean*. The other is *advertising* to eliminate the massive *billboard advertising* that characterizes most American municipalities.

Waste removal and disposal can be accomplished in one of several ways, at a cost, despite the increasing difficulty of finding disposal sites near cities. But adequate laws, penalties, and enforcement ensuring that individual dwelling units and neighborhoods are kept clean have not been enacted, because enforcement may be socially as well as politically impractical.

Outdoor advertising in cities is of two types. One identifies and promotes the use or activity that is taking place on the property where the sign is located. Urban designers have suggested limiting this advertising to a maximum size, eliminating the progressive enlargement of signs that often results from seeking competitive advantage or meeting competitive challenge. The second type of outdoor advertising involves large billboards placed where they will attract sufficient attention to justify their cost. As a consequence, they represent a hazard for the motorist as well as an aesthetic blight. Urban designers recommend that if these billboards cannot be eliminated entirely, they be restricted to properties whose products or activities they advertise. With regard to billboards along state and federal highways, it is proposed that they be eliminated except at designated locations where signs not to exceed a certain size may be concentrated.

None of these restraints has been enacted. Advertising interests exert great political power. Those who are paid to allow billboards on their property resist relinquishing this income. And when existing billboards are eliminated, court decisions require costly compensation or deny their restraint as an unconstitutional limitation of free speech.

competitions In Europe, design *competitions* are recognized as an excellent way of tapping a wider range of creative ideas and urban design talent than is normally available within a single municipality. A competition may seek the best designs for projects already funded, proposed land developments, urban installations

duplicated in many parts of the community, or particular provisions of the urban design element of the master city plan.
The United States is finally acknowledging the value of design
competitions; legislation has been introduced in Congress
mandating design competitions for all federal projects costing
more than $5 million.

In contrast with these largely unrealized opportunities for   *subdivision*
urban design in the United States, its application to the *subdivision* of land is recognized and procedures are well established. To illustrate the nature of this design in the simplest
way, Figure 19 shows eight ways a single city block can be
arranged for single-family houses of the same size; comparative costs are not taken into account. At a larger scale involving
additional considerations, Figures 20 and 21 show medium-
and large-size subdivisions of land for single-family detached
homes submitted for review to a mortgage lending agency (A),
and the superior arrangements proposed by the agency to
incorporate one or more of the following subdivision design
principles (B):

Discourage heavy through traffic.
Plan for extension of major streets.
Traffic should flow toward thoroughfares.
Minor streets should enter major streets at right angles.
Avoid planning of dead-end streets.
Streets should fit contours of irregular land.
Short blocks are not economical.
Long blocks require crosswalks near center.
Plan commercial sites where needed.
Provide school and church sites.
Parks are a definite community asset.
Preserve natural features of site for better appearance.
Deep lots are wasteful.
Plan lots of adequate width.
Avoid sharp-angled lots.
Plan wider corner lots.
Make lot lines perpendicular to street.
Plan lots to face desirable views.
Protect lots against adjacent nonconforming uses.
Protect residential lots against major street traffic.
(Federal Housing Administration, 1938)

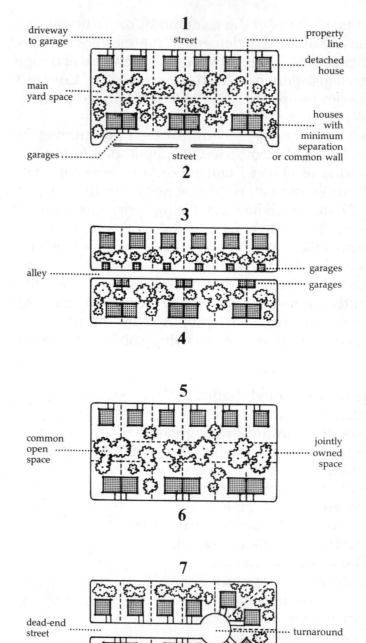

Figure 19
Different Designs for a Small City Block

In addition to determining if the proposed layout of the land is satisfactory, there have been many specific requirements imposed as part of the subdivision process: compatible roofing materials or exterior color, enclosure of rooftop air-conditioning equipment, closed garages rather than carports, standard directional signing, or the use of plants in landscaping that prevent erosion or resist the spread of brush fires.

People often associate historic preservation with urban design because the design arts are usually required in the actual physical conservation or reconstruction. But other elements of comprehensive city planning are involved. The structures or areas to be preserved must be officially designated as culturally or symbolically significant. Land use controls and the transfer of development rights must be effected, and economic provision must be made for any restoration needed and continued compatible use of the building or area.

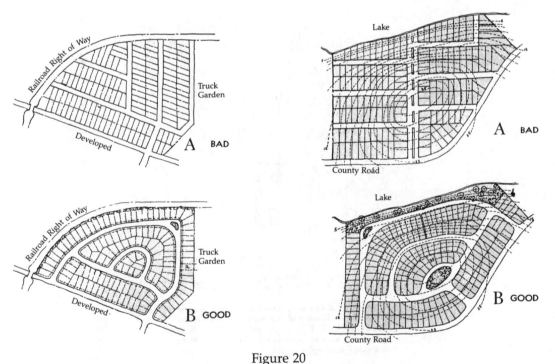

Figure 20
Residential Subdivision Design
(*Planning Profitable Neighborhoods*, Federal Housing Administration,
Technical Bulletin No. 7, 1938, p. 9)

ORIGINAL PLAN

Contours of the land were not considered in the original plan of this subdivision. Neither the streets nor the lots were located so as to take the best advantage of the terrain. The plan also failed to provide a comprehensive neighborhood.

SUGGESTED REVISED PLAN

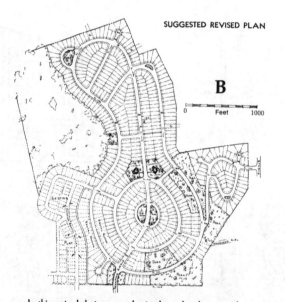

In this revised design every lot is planned to be a good building site. Roads and lots are arranged to follow natural conditions of the subdivision thus reducing street grades and cost of improvement construction. Parks and public building sites are included in the new plan.

Figure 21
Residential Neighborhood Design
(*Planning Profitable Neighborhoods*, Federal Housing Administration,
Technical Bulletin No. 7, 1938, p. 33)

Urban design requirements may be imposed on projects involving zone changes, those that are subject to an environmental impact report, or those submitted as a planned unit development, specific plan, or conditional use that requires submission of a detailed project plan. Under these circumstances, there are no legal limitations to the requirements that can be imposed as part of the approval of the proposed project; they are subject only to reversal by the courts on appeal as "unreasonable."

Works of art have been required occasionally in the United *works of art* States as part of the approval of project plans. But recognition of the importance of this strictly aesthetic element of urban design has been stronger in other parts of the world where there is a longer history of incorporating sculpture, frescoes, murals, or mosaics in plazas, religious and civic buildings, palaces, and more modest dwellings.

During the last 10 or 12 years, however, a number of American artists in different parts of the country have devoted themselves primarily to working in public spaces, in highly original ways. Their projects include playgrounds, gardens, fountains, pedestrian paths, viewing platforms, traffic islands, bridges, outdoor and indoor rooms, and even public utilities. . . .

The Arts Commission [of an American city] has initiated a process of getting artists involved at the ground level of urban design. More than a dozen artist "design teams" have been put together to collaborate with architects and engineers on specific projects for community centers, electric power substations, police headquarters, streets and sidewalks, and other city-owned real estate.

In casting about for ways to rebuild confidence and civic pride,. . .the mayor at the time gave his enthusiastic assent to an ordinance that set aside 1 percent of the city's capital-improvement funds for spending on the arts. (Tompkins, 1984)

CITATIONS

[1] City of Los Angeles, *The Visual Environment of Los Angeles*, Los Angeles, CA (Department of City Planning), 1971, p. 8-11, 6. [2] Federal Housing Administration, *Planning Profitable Neighborhoods*, Technical Bulletin No. 7,

Washington, DC (Government Printing Office) 1938, pp. 8-17. [3] Langdon, Philip, "The Legacy of Kevin Lynch," *Planning*, October 1984, p. 12. [4] Lynch, Kevin, *The Image of the City*, Cambridge, MA (M.I.T., Harvard), 1960, 194 pp. [5] National Capital Planning Commission, *The Proposed Comprehensive Plan* for the National Capital, Washington, DC (Superintendent of Documents), February 1967, p. 168. [6] Tompkins, Calvin, "Perception at All Levels," *The New Yorker*, 3 December 1984, pp. 176, 179.

SELECTED REFERENCES

[1] Appleyard, Donald, Kevin Lynch, John R. Myer, *The View from the Road*, Cambridge, MA (M.I.T.), 1964, 64 pp. [2] City and County of San Francisco, *The Urban Design Plan*, for the Comprehensive Plan of San Francisco, San Francisco, CA (Department of City Planning), 1971, 155 pp. [3] *Journal of the American Institute of Architects*, Special Issue on Urban Design, March 1961, pp. 29-99. [4] Lynch, Kevin and Gary Hack, *Site Planning*, Boston, MA (M.I.T.), Third Edition, 1984, 506 pp. [5] Rudofsky, Bernard, *Streets for People*, A Primer for Americans, New York (Doubleday), 1969, 351 pp. [6] Sixta, Gerhard J., *Urban Structure*, A Study of Long Range Policies Which Affect the Physical Structure of an Urban Area, Burnaby B.C., Canada (Planning Department of the District of Burnaby), 1971, 144 pp. [7] U.S. Department of Housing and Urban Development, *1968 HUD Awards for Design Excellence*, Washington, DC (S/NP-70), October 1968, 68 pp.

CHAPTER 14
NEW TOWNS

Existing cities in industrialized countries can adopt as desirable objectives, in whole or in part, the common characteristics that have emerged from experience with new towns, to be attained gradually step by step as opportunities arise over a period of many years.

ALL CITIES existing today were once new towns. In the long history of human evolution extending over several million years they are a very recent development. The oldest "permanent" settlement excavated to date is only some 8,000 years old. In their number, size, and diversity, cities as we know them now are a new phenomenon. Many of them have come and gone as archaeological ruins or the ghost towns of the western United States attest.

Settlements have been established for many reasons. The earliest represented the transition from primitive nomadism to the next stage of socioeconomic organization, production, and culture. New towns were an essential feature of extensive colonization by the ancient Greeks and Romans. Renaissance bastides were established for defensive purposes at territorial borders; 30 of these were laid out in France under King Edward I of England during the period when the British controlled part of France. In 1298, he wrote from his royal court in London for

> four persons competent to lay out a new town, the most clever and able, who best know how to divide, order, and arrange a new town in the manner that will be most beneficial for us and the merchants . . . and who shall be ready and willing to go for that purpose wherever we may send them. (Adams, 1935)

Some cities sprang up around religious shrines, and "Utopian" communities have been founded as the physical manifestation of a religious or communal movement. A large project in the undeveloped countryside requires a new town first for construction workers and later for the operating work force. New

177

towns are built as national or provincial capitals, regional centers, retirement communities, or recreational resorts, as science and research centers, or to house missile crews manning underground emplacements in the remote countryside. In a number of countries, new towns are part of their national policy with respect to the distribution of population, national defense, and regional development.

A *new town* as defined today is a community of prescribed size, master planned as a whole in advance, and normally completed as planned with few modifications in a period of 10 to 15 years. It may be intended for a single purpose such as supporting a production plant or recreational activity. A *single-function* new town differs from a large residential subdivision by having an economic base within the community. The *diversified* new town incorporates a number of basic economic activities providing local employment, all of the major categories of land use, and the features and facilities found in most older established cities. The U.S. Department of Housing and Urban Development (HUD) has attempted unsuccessfully to enable private enterprise to create such diversified communities by guaranteeing the mortgages obtained for the purchase of land and making grants supporting advance planning.

single-function diversified

> The HUD new towns are only one kind of new community representing only a portion of the new towns established by other governmental agencies and by private enterprises in the United States. Hundreds of new towns are founded in many countries around the world. For developing nations particularly new towns are important in connection with the extraction and processing of natural resources, and planned national and regional economic development. Furthermore, new towns are as relevant as ever as places where new and experimental urban developments can be tested. (Branch, April 1980)

organization

New towns are planned, constructed, and operated until completed by *one organization*. Otherwise it would be impossible to achieve the coordination, perseverance of purpose, and timely effectuation required to plan and construct an entire new town in a short period of 10 to 15 years compared to the more usual rate of urban growth. New *company* towns are built by the business enterprise that will provide the main economic base for the community at least during the early years of the town's existence. Formally or informally, this primary industry will be a dominant voice in the conduct of the community. Diversified new towns are planned, built, and operated by a unit of local government or by a special governmental agency established for the purpose. The power of *eminent domain* is needed to acquire square miles of land at fair market value without the excessive cost that results when a large area must be acquired on the open market at whatever price individual property owners will accept. Without eminent domain, hold-out parcels whose owners are unwilling to sell at any price can force radical revision of the proposed project or cause its abandonment.

eminent domain

In both single-function and diversified new towns a large part of the funds required to complete the project must be available in the first years, for this *front end money* is needed to pay for the "infrastructure" of transportation, utility, flood control, and service systems and facilities, which must be installed immediately if the city is to function. Income from the sale and lease of land and buildings is not forthcoming until later years. Usually, as the majority of properties are sold, the property owners are given an increasing voice in directing the community until, as it nears completion, it is established as a municipality with an elected city council as the controlling governmental body.

front end money

There are significant *differences* between planning new towns and existing cities. Planning a new town is far easier. A comprehensive city plan is formulated at the start by the single organization that will control development until the new town is complete. Engineering can be conceived and carried out in an orderly manner, taking into account the multiple interrelationships that affect installation costs and efficient operations. The community is built on a large expanse of open land sufficient to accommodate a planned population within a prescribed area. Construction can be scheduled in an orderly sequence.

difference

An existing municipality consists of hundreds or thousands of separate parcels with different owners and vested interests.

These multiple ownerships must be coordinated somehow over time to achieve some of the purposes of city planning. The legal rights, ingrained interests, and political and cultural customs established over many years constitute spatial and operational rigidities that are redirected only very gradually and with difficulty. Very few decisions can be made and carried out in a short time; they are thrashed out and implemented by a prolonged political and bureaucratic process at city hall and at non-governmental power centers within the community.

The master plans of new towns are realized in their entirety in the completed city except for adjustments brought about by unforeseen site conditions, changes in the market demand or housing preference of those who will populate the new town, or by unexpected political or economic developments nearby. The planning process involves fewer variables and imponder-

models ables. Mathematical *models* can be formulated, programmed for the computer, and maintained for use at any time to improve the quality and coverage of comprehensive planning. This integrated analytical representation of the new community can include the financial and cash flow situation, the schedule and progress of construction, and the market demand for housing, commercial, and industrial properties. A physical model of the new town can be made showing at a glance existing and proposed structures, physical systems, and other features. Experimentation is possible. New urban forms, types and arrangements of housing, commercial development, and utility installations can be tested in a section of the new town before they are applied elsewhere in the community.

New towns around the world take many spatial forms and incorporate various features depending on the circumstances discussed in Chapter 4. One type exhibits certain characteristics derived from the British experience which introduced the

greenbelt term *greenbelt towns* to the city planning vocabulary. During a
towns 50-year period, the British produced more than 30 of these new towns surrounded by a greenbelt of open land committed to agriculture, recreation, or other uses requiring few structures. Originally intended to house 30,000 people, their planned population has since been increased to 150,000 or more inhabitants, needed to support a community that is better balanced economically and culturally. The greenbelt types of new towns

exhibit many of the common characteristics noted in Figures 22A and B.

Sometimes, rather than a surrounding belt of open land, comparable space is provided within the town as landscaped parkways along major thoroughfares and waterways, public parks, private golf courses, recreational areas, and other less intensive land uses. This is the case in the new town developed by private enterprise depicted in Figures 23A and B. Only in the United States have several such diversified new towns been completed by private enterprise. When public policy allows such sponsorship, the private developer must control the large block of land required. Rarely will a prospective developer own enough acreage at a location suitable for a new community. Contiguous parcels of land under different ownership could be purchased on the open market; however, unless the intent can be kept secret until all the properties have been acquired, the cost of such assembly is prohibitive. For private development to be feasible financially, the local government may have to delegate to private enterprise the power to condemn land for the sole purpose of creating a new town; or acquire the land itself and transfer control to the private developer for long enough to build the new community under specified conditions. Countries other than the United States form a special public authority that acquires the land under eminent domain, plans, and manages the construction of the new town; as is the case with private development, it is replaced by a municipal government when the new community is completed.

New towns in town and squatter settlements are two special forms of new communities. The first of these refers to urban renewal or redevelopment in the downtown area of existing cities that includes industrial activities as well as residential and commercial uses. When industries committed to employing local people are included in the renewal area, redevelopment is economically stronger and the taxable income from these industries is preserved for the municipality. Since all three primary categories of land use are included in the downtown development it is referred to as a new town in town. There are few such redevelopments in the United States. It has been difficult to persuade industries—even with various financial incentives—to remain in the blighted sections of central cities

New towns in town

Overall Spatial Form/Design

• Prior designation of population size, total urban area and the densities of different land uses and areas.

• If feasible, sufficient size to support the range of social and cultural activities, facilities and services required for a well-balanced urban life.

• A radial-concentric pattern of primary highways/streets (sometimes arranged in a generally rectangular layout which retains the basic radial-concentric design).

• 'Cellular' pattern of neighbourhoods and villages formed by the secondary street system and an 'interior' system of interconnected open-space corridors containing pedestrian and bicycle pathways separated from roads by differences in grade level.

• Each of these spatially defined residential 'cells' designed for a designated population housed in areas with different types of housing and densities.

• An 'external' green belt of agricultural/recreational open land encompassing the built-up area of the new town (or substitution of an approximately equivalent area in narrower 'internal' green belts separating neighbourhoods/villages).

• A centrally located town centre containing the primary governmental, civic, commercial and cultural activities/facilities.

• Neighbourhood and village shopping centres with facilities selected and sized to fit the population in the immediate vicinity.

• Extensive use of landscaping in open spaces and throughout the town.

• Preservation of scenic and other natural resources existing at the site.

• Compatible architectural/engineering design of different areas, facilities and street furniture.

• Incorporation of art in public places (sculpture, mosaics, murals).

Transportation

• Situation: located along a railroad, at a regional 'growth pole,' at or close to a juncture of major highways, or accessible to a natural resource if this will be a major economic activity during the formative years of the new community.

• Major and secondary street systems clearly defined and differentiated.

• Deliberate elimination of through streets other than those that are part of the primary and secondary street systems.

• Widespread use of 'superblock' designs and 'dead-end' and 'semi-circular' streets of limited length in residential areas; no primary or secondary traffic circulation through residential neighbourhoods.

• Moderately curvilinear primary street pattern, avoiding the sameness of a strictly rectilinear pattern but retaining a sufficiently rectangular shape to facilitate driver orientation.

• A city-wide system of bicycle pathways.

• Grade separation of automobiles and other forms of transport and pedestrian circulation.

• Free-flowing traffic system with minimum traffic lights and signs.

• Provision of a public bus system serving all sections of the town.

• Use of traffic arteries to spatially define 'neighbourhoods', and 'villages' when they are part of the town plan.

• 'Interior' pedestrian/bicycle pathways within residential areas (separated from the secondary street system) connecting them with town, village, and neighbourhood shopping centres, and with other local facilities.

• Adequate vehicular/bicycle parking at all commercial facilities requiring such parking.

• Clustered residential parking places rather than separate provision at each dwelling unit (this is not a common characteristic of US new towns).

• 'By-pass' route for traffic wanting to pass by rather than through the new town.

• Use of international traffic signs and symbols which do not require an understanding of the local language.

• Selection of well-designed, compatible traffic equipment and 'street furniture' (traffic lights, signs, street dividers, street lights, benches, trash receptacles, etc.).

Figure 22A
Common Characteristics of Many New Towns
Overall Spatial Form/Design, Transportation
Courtesy of *Cities* (Butterworths, Guilford)

Land Use

• Designation of the number of people, population density, and ground coverage for the major categories of land use (residential, commercial, industrial, governmental, transportation, agriculture, recreation, open space) and/or for neighbourhoods and other spatially defined areas.

• Allocation of land to each primary use category based on past experience, trends and the proportionate area and spatial disposition desired in the completed new town.

• Land zoned for industry concentrated in one or two areas to the leeward (occasionally in three or four smaller areas in different parts of the new town).

• Commercial land concentrated in 'centres' (rather than 'strip development' along primary streets).

• Concentration of higher density, multiple residential land use around the town centre, and to a lesser extent around village and neighbourhood subcentres.

• Mixture in close proximity of low-rise and higher-rise residential apartment buildings, row houses, atrium houses, detached single-family dwellings, and other residential housing (rather than separate areas each zoned for a single type of residential use as in the USA).

• Vertical 'zoning' in certain areas permitting residential, commercial and other uses in the same building usually on different floors.

• Lower building coverage and density of population than in long-established cities; generous setback of structure from the property line and open space between multistorey buildings (except when deliberately eliminated by area or project design).

• Generous provision of public recreation centres and recreational land use.

Residential Neighbourhoods/Villages

• Population usually between 1,200 and 5,000 people (375 and 1,563 families at 3.2 persons/family; 286 and 1,190 at 4.2 persons/family).

• Internally located convenience shopping centre accessible by car and 'interior' pedestrian/bicycle pathways.

• Elementary, grammar, and secondary schools centrally located adjacent to or near a local shopping centre and/or interior greenways or parks available for adult use after school hours.

• Community facility for recreation, social and other meetings, located centrally, sometimes associated with a school.

• Mixture of different types of dwelling units and residential structures for different income, ethnic, age, and/or other population groups (some publicly subsidized if necessary or desirable).

• Small neighbourhood parks, maintained by municipal government and/or home owners' association.

• Clustering of several neighbourhoods to form a larger residential unit or 'village' with a shopping centre.

Development Provisions/Controls

• Initial acquisition or control of total land required for the completed new town by a public authority.

• Establishment of a single office or unit to plan, programme, and generally supervise realization of the new town.

• Preparation of a master plan indicating the physical characteristics of the completed town, together with plans and programmes for its financing and construction.

• Financial provision for delayed return on the large 'front-end' costs required to install the primary street and utility systems.

• As far as possible, conformity with the original master plan for 10–15 years or until the new town is completed.

• Construction by private enterprise in accordance with the master plan and development specifications (except in countries where private enterprise does not exist).

• Accommodating continued demand for urban settlement in the area by building another new town nearby, rather than by increasing building coverages on the land and population densities within the existing new town.

• Retention of control by development authority of at least the major revenue producing land uses and facilities, and all or part of the value added by construction of the new town.

• Incentives promoting the location of 'clean' (non-polluting) industry in the new town to provide an economic base.

• Attraction of one or more non-commercial, non-industrial institution/enterprise (such as a university or government agency) to provide relatively stable employment, strengthen the municipal tax base, and increase local consumer demand for commercial products and services.

• Employment of design competitions in planning certain sections or elements of the new town.

• Restriction of outdoor advertising during and after construction, in accordance with provisions in the master plan.

• In the USA, a gradually greater voice in the operation and management of development and progressive assumption of directive control by a designated group of inhabitants until a municipal government is established upon the completion of the new town.

Figure 22B
Common Characteristics of Many New Towns
Land Use, Residential Neighborhoods/Villages, Development Provisions/Controls
Courtesy of *Cities* (Butterworths, Guilford)

Figure 23A
A New Town
(Valencia, California)
Aerial photographic view: showing area of new town 25 percent
complete, internal agricultural and vacant land to be developed, and surrounding land
use. Photo insert: showing parallel cul-de-sac (dead-end) residential streets, ending
in a pedestrian walkway (paseo) leading to a local shopping center, elementary
school, and apartments.
Courtesy of Valencia Company

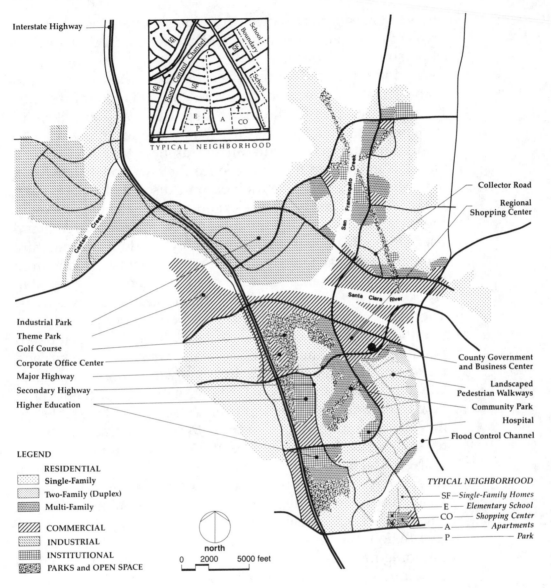

Interstate Highway

Collector Road

Regional
Shopping Center

TYPICAL NEIGHBORHOOD

Industrial Park
Theme Park
Golf Course
Corporate Office Center
Major Highway
Secondary Highway
Higher Education

County Government
and Business Center

Landscaped
Pedestrian Walkways

Community Park

Hospital

Flood Control Channel

LEGEND

RESIDENTIAL
Single-Family
Two-Family (Duplex)
Multi-Family

COMMERCIAL
INDUSTRIAL
INSTITUTIONAL
PARKS and OPEN SPACE

TYPICAL NEIGHBORHOOD
SF —Single-Family Homes
E —— Elementary School
CO —— Shopping Center
A ——————— Apartments
P ———————— Park

north
0   2000   5000 feet

Figure 23B
A New Town
(Valencia, California)
Master land use plan of present development, 17,000 people, and planned future
development to 61,000 population. Insert: enlargement of street system and land use in
Typical Neighborhood.
Courtesy of Valencia Company

and even harder to attract new productive enterprises to these areas of physical deterioration and greater threat to the safety of persons and property.

squatter
settlements

As indicated in Chapter 3, *squatter settlements* are found in many large cities around the world. In some countries they house a large part of the urban population and are likely to remain an endemic part of the urban scene for many years to come. Squatter settlements qualify as new towns in several ways. They are certainly new, since they are constructed in a very short time out of purloined and discarded materials, at the most over a period of weeks and occasionally literally overnight. They contain all of the different categories of urban land use, although usually in a thoroughly random intermixture compared with the more organized arrangements resulting from municipal planning. Small-scale productive enterprises exist in shacks devoted to "industry" or in the home as a family activity. They are also new towns in that they become permanent communities as illegal occupation of land, irregular and indeterminate property lines, indiscriminate circulation routes, and makeshift utility lines are finally acknowledged and legalized. Obviously, the common characteristics of this special form of new community are different from those of legally established new towns; and planning for the future development of squatter settlements is a special case of new town planning.

New town planning relates to planning existing cities in several ways. New towns may be part of planning metropolitan areas, discussed in the next chapter. Several areas in Europe have carried out a deliberate spatial structuring of the urbanized region into an existing central city and a number of surrounding new towns. These elements are separated from each other and contained within a prescribed ground area by open spaces preventing the uninterrupted expansion or "urban sprawl" typical of most metropolitan regions. Further population growth is restricted in the central city and encouraged in the new towns until they reach their planned capacity.

Existing cities in industrialized countries can adopt as desirable objectives, in whole or in part, the common characteristics listed in Figure 22 that have emerged from experience with new towns, to be attained gradually step by step as opportunities arise during a period of many years. Existing cities can also employ new designs, types of dwelling units, methods of construction and of delivering municipal services, or new equipment first used and tested in new towns.

CITATIONS

[1] Adams, Thomas, *Outline of Town and City Planning*, New York (Russell Sage), 1935, p. 88. [2] Branch, Melville C., "Common Characteristics of New Towns," *Cities* (Butterworths, Guilford), November 1983, pp. 148-149. [3] _____and Eliane Guedes Mazza, *Selected Annotated Bibliography on New Town Planning and Development*, Monticello, IL (Vance Bibliographies), April 1980, p. 2 (133 pp.).

SELECTED REFERENCES

[1] Abrams, Charles, *Squatter Settlements*, The Problem and the Opportunity, Washington, DC (Department of Housing and Urban Development), April 1966, 48 pp. [2] Burby, Raymond J., III and Shirley F. Weiss, *New Communities U.S.A.*, Lexington, MA (Heath), 1976, 593 pp. [3] Golany, Gideon, *New Town Planning, Principles and Practice*, New York (Wiley), 1976, 389 pp. [4] _____, *Strategy for New Community Development in the United States*, New York (Halsted), 1975, 293 pp. [5] Greater London Council, *The Planning of a New Town* (Hook), London (Greater London Council), 1961, 182 pp. [6] Hertzen, Heikki von and Paul D. Spreiregen, *Building of a New Town* (Tapiola), Cambridge, MA (M.I.T.), 1971, 232 pp. [7] Llewelyn-Davies Weeks and Partners, *Washington New Town Master Plan and Report*, Washington, UK (Washington Development Corporation), December 1966, 135 pp. [8] McKeever, J. Ross (Editor), *The Community Building Handbook*, Washington, DC (Urban Land Institute), 1968, 526 pp. [9] National Resources Committee, *Urban Planning and Land Policies*, Part I, Planned Communities, Washington, DC (Superintendent of Documents), 1939, pp. 1-161. [10] Spiegel, Erika, *New Towns in Israel*, New York (Frederick A. Praeger), 1967, 192 pp. [11] Underhill, Jack A., *French National Urban Policy and the Paris Region New Towns*, Washington, DC (U.S. Department of Housing and Urban Development), April 1980, 131 pp. [12] United Nations, *Planning of Metropolitan Areas and New Towns*, New York (United Nations), 1969, 255 pp. [13] U.S./U.S.S.R. New Towns Working Group, *Planning New Towns, National Reports of the U.S. and the U.S.S.R.*, Washington, DC (U.S. Department of Housing and Urban Development), September 1981, 162 pp.

For several centuries a trend toward concentration of activity and population in relatively few urban centers has been observed. This trend has been generally accelerating and spreading from the "developed" to the "developing" countries. For at least a century this centripetal trend has been supplemented by a centrifugal trend from urban centers to their [surroundings]. The resulting new form of human settlement has been recognized as a "Metropolitan Area" by the Census of the U.S.A., and under the same or another name, by many other countries. The Metropolitan Area is essentially defined as a commuter watershed, constituting a common labor and housing market. It has long been recognized that such a concentration leads to a substantial increase of activities and population well beyond its boundaries, up to a travel distance of about two hours from its center.

Hans Blumenfeld, "Where Did All the Metropolitanites Go?" *Personal Communication*, March, 1982.

CHAPTER 15
METROPOLITAN URBAN PLANNING

Municipalities and counties in the United States remain unwilling to delegate comprehensive planning to the next higher level of government. But they are willing to pass on planning and operational management of certain public services involving all or a substantial part of the urbanized area to a special authority established for each one.

S MALLER COMMUNITIES are usually found around a large dynamic city which sustains them in part by providing employment and business opportunities, certain commercial and professional services, and forms of recreation available only in the larger central city. Before the urban population explosion that has occurred in most parts of the world during the past century, open fields or countryside separated these smaller communities from the center city and from each other. As urban populations have increased, each community *situation* has built up to its borders. In so doing, as many as 30 or more municipalities have coalesced into one continuous built-up expanse stretching for miles in the larger metropolitan regions in the United States. Each of these municipalities retains its legal identity and independence, but its geographical boundaries are indistinguishable on the ground unless they are identified by territorial signs. In the example shown in Figure 24, there are 80 different municipalities side by side, together with unincorporated areas that are urban but remain under the jurisdiction of the county in which the conurbation is located. Although it may not appear so graphically, the entire southern two-thirds of the area shown in Figure 24 is urbanized, comprising a metropolitan urban area of some 2,500 square miles. In addition, the urbanized area extends into two adjacent counties not shown in the illustration.

At the same time that this population increase and spatial *changing* expansion and coalescence have occurred, the nature of urban *conditions* problems and requirements has changed accordingly. Almost

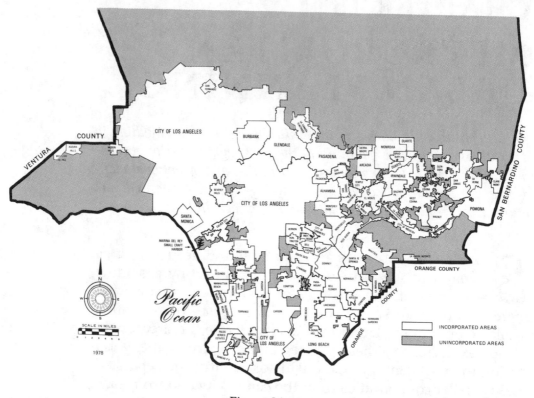

Figure 24
Municipalities Within a Metropolitan Urban Area
(County of Los Angeles, "Its People and Their Government," 1978)

all municipal facilities and services now involve geographical areas larger than the space within city limits. At least part of the water supply is imported. Storm water drainage, flood control, and the disposal of liquid and solid wastes can seldom be accomplished within a single city's jurisdiction. Air pollution is likely to involve a large geographical airshed. Electrical and electronic networks are designed and scaled with regard to the entire urbanized area and only to the extent necessary to fit separate legal jurisdictions. Wholesale markets and major financial institutions located in the center city serve the entire metropolitan area, which has become the spatial habitat rather than individual municipalities as was once the case.

home rule   These developments have not eliminated the desire of municipalities to preserve *"home rule,"* a separate identity, and self-determination—all the more as they recognize their increasing dependence on economic, political, and social forces beyond their boundaries, and reliance on utility services they cannot provide for themselves. They are distrustful of higher levels of government. As a consequence, there was a time in the United States when inherent conflicts between jurisdictional independence and operational dependence produced serious and sometimes tragic consequences. For example, cities with excess capacity in some facility or service operated without regard for a municipal neighbor suffering from a severe shortage; immediate response to nearby emergencies was sometimes refused because they were across the boundary line in an adjoining municipality. Gradually, a degree of coordination between municipalities within metropolitan urban areas has been brought about by a combination of common sense, necessity, self-interest, and various actions by federal and state governments.

There is *professional cooperation* on many operational matters because it is essential or sensible for the street and utility systems of adjoining municipalities to be compatible. As an extreme example, it would be disadvantageous for all concerned if the number of traffic lanes in a major thoroughfare extending for many miles was reduced and increased by the different city engineers as it progressed through adjoining municipalities. The advantages of cooperation between fire and police departments is achieved by *joint powers agreements* which specify when and how different municipalities will cooperate. This may require operational adjustment, such as technical modification of communication or other equipment to allow direct interconnection, or some adjustment in procedures to avoid conflicting actions during emergencies. Joint powers agreements are easier to effectuate in some states than in others.

cooperation

joint powers

Some public services become too extensive and expensive for individual municipalities and are taken over by special districts, the county government, or an agency of the state with their larger areal coverage, broader tax base, and economies of scale. Otherwise, for example, separate cities must each maintain facilities and equipment used only occasionally but needed to provide adequate public health services. Welfare costs cannot be borne by the central city alone since the needy from the

contract services

entire metropolitan area congregate in the blighted areas often found around its downtown district. Municipalities pay their proportionate share of the services provided by a higher level of government, usually the county. In some metropolitan areas, municipalities that are too small to provide adequate fire and police protection or some other essential public service arrange with the county in which they are located to provide these essential services *under contract*.

In some states, small urban areas have been able to achieve a transient or special purpose by incorporating as a munici- pality, although it may not have a sufficient tax base to support itself financially or be able to function effectively in other respects as a separate governmental entity. Because this also adds to the number of municipalities that already exist and creates problems of coordination in most metropolitan areas in the United States, special commissions have been established to review and approve applications for incorporation. Urban planners hope that such reviewing bodies will limit additional incorporations to those that are justified with respect to their surroundings and do not add another small jurisdiction to an already politically oversubdivided metropolitan area. The more than 80 separate municipalities depicted in Figure 24 range in population from about 600 to more than three million.

special
districts
As shown in Figure 6B (Chapter 5, page 61), *special districts* are a common means of providing a single public service to many of the municipalities constituting a metropolitan region. Water supply and storm drainage, for example, often require systems that are designed and engineered for the entire urban- ized area rather than one or several of many adjacent munici- palities. Other public services such as firefighting, cemeteries, and sanitation are supplied more efficiently on a large scale to the benefit of all concerned. Some functions, such as air pol- lution control and the provision of larger "regional" recrea- tional areas and facilities, cannot be effected in the first instance and financed in the second case by single cities. Special districts are also formed for a political purpose: to obtain the revenues necessary for a particular service without the increase in gen- eral taxes municipal voters resist and politicians want to avoid. Special districts may involve various combinations of munici-

palities and counties or townships, and include several states. They are functional organizations well suited to providing single public services throughout a contiguous built-up urban area.

Integrating comprehensive planning by municipalities in a *integration* metropolitan area is much more difficult than administering districts and municipal departments that provide single services. It involves a large number of crucial elements and considerations, some of which are controversial, others indefinite or unquantifiable. The multiple functions that must be correlated in comprehensive planning, each related to the others, are difficult to express and evaluate analytically. Additionally, comprehensive planning is the responsibility of elected representatives, mayors, and city managers who are more vulnerable to political constraints than agency and department heads.

For some people, the concept of comprehensive metropolitan urban planning represents the final step in the abrogation of political independence or "home rule." It also requires resolving many practical problems. For example, what is to be done about the top executives or officials in the departments and agencies of different municipalities? Only a few of the fire and police chiefs, chief engineers and inspectors, city attorneys and other officials of high rank would be needed in top management if their operations were integrated into a single metropolitan organization. Unless this personnel problem is resolved in some way acceptable to high level administrative officials, they can generate strong opposition to integrated metropolitan urban planning.

Various ways of attaining different degrees of metropolitan *proposals* planning have been advanced over the years. One of these proposes a *single government* for urbanized metropolitan areas, achieved by the central city annexing surrounding territory or merging with adjacent municipalities or the surrounding county. Another approach calls for municipalities to continue to plan and operate those public activities of immediate interest and direct concern to their constituents, but to *delegate* to the county or to a new *federated local government* those functions involving the metropolitan area as a whole. A third approach relies on formal or informal *cooperation*, according to various arrangements between local governments.

Except for a few cities that have acquired jurisdiction over the entire urban area by annexation or *city-county consolidation,* only voluntary cooperative planning is practiced in metropolitan areas in the United States today. This is largely the result of federal encouragement and financial support of planning activities by state and federal governments, begun by the U.S. National Resources Planning Board in 1934. Besides promoting local planning generally, the federal government has influenced the practice of city planning by supporting various programs requiring more comprehensive consideration of components, greater citizen participation, and more attention to environmental quality. Most recently, it has instigated and supported *councils of government* (COGs), which have been established in many metropolitan areas throughout the nation.

councils of government   Councils of government are permanent organizations with a voluntary membership composed of local governments interested in achieving a degree of metropolitan planning and coordinated operations. They are supported by grants from various federal departments and agencies in connection with programs they are sponsoring at the local level, and by dues collected from participating local governments. Their major influence results from their designation by various federal agencies as the organization that reviews and evaluates the applications of local governments for federal funding of a wide variety of projects within the metropolitan area. They may also be designated as the "area wide planning agency," "metropolitan planning organization," or "lead agency" to prepare plans covering the particular activity of a federal or state agency within the metropolitan area. The councils correlate local requests for federal funding with existing commitments within the metropolitan area, the plans of constituent governments, and the COGs' own formulation of desirable area wide development.

Ordinarily, councils of government are composed of one representative from each participating government, usually meeting once a year in general assembly to approve policies, adopt a budget, and elect an executive committee and appoint standing committees concerned with such major elements of metropolitan analysis and planning as growth policy, the allocation of facilities or services mandated by higher levels of government, transportation, land use, building codes, waste disposal, or environmental quality. Most decisions are by unanimous vote.

COGs can effect only that planning which is voluntarily delegated to them. This may be because their members find the broader scope of council planning to their advantage, or because it prevents adverse recommendation by the council on certain of their project applications for federal assistance. COGs cannot formulate metropolitan plans that are binding on their members. They cannot collect taxes, enact ordinances, or require implementing legislation or other actions by local governments within the metropolitan region. Besides their function of generating voluntary coordinated planning and reviewing requests for federal aid, they serve as a center of regional information and analysis, provide a means of pooling local resources, and act as a focus for the discussion and resolution of metropolitan issues and prospects.

Municipalities and counties in the United States remain *trends* unwilling to delegate comprehensive planning to the next higher level of government. They are willing, however, to pass on planning and operational management of certain public services that involve all or a substantial part of the urbanized area to a special authority established for each public service. Also, as noted previously in this chapter, special districts are being used by elected representatives to avoid association with an increase in general taxes. As technical developments bring about further delegation of functional planning to special agencies, fewer elements of comprehensive planning remain under the control of each municipality. What appears to be occurring is a gradual transfer of key local government functions to higher authorities. If special districts were combined at some future time, they would constitute in effect a form of metropolitan government responsible for many of the most critical elements of comprehensive planning for the urbanized area. Although the municipalities within the metropolitan area would probably retain their legal independence, they would become more like urban districts than self-governing cities, because each would retain control of only those activities with the most direct and noticeable impact within their jurisdictions—subject to the constraints imposed by the functional systems planned and operated at the next higher level.

SELECTED REFERENCES

[1] Bollens, John C. and Henry J. Schmandt, *The Metropolis*, Its People, Politics, and Economic Life, New York (Harper & Row), Fourth Edition, 1982, 461 pp. [2] Hoover, Edgar M. and Raymond Vernon, *Anatomy of a Metropolis*, Cambridge, MA (Harvard University), 1959, 345 pp. [3] Research and Policy Committee, *Reshaping Government in Metropolitan Areas*, New York (Committee for Economic Development), February 1970, 83 pp.

"City planning is an emerging field, in both traditional and nontraditional areas". . . .

The issues might involve traditional problems such as real estate, as well as the impact of nontraditional areas such as economics and pollution. . . .

The emergence of the field comes as ordinary citizens are becoming more vocal in civic planning. Commercial ventures are expanding further into residential areas, condominium living has become popular, more people worry about water and air pollution, and fights about the location of dumps for waste material have been increasing.

Even the air has become the cynosure of community interest.

Elizabeth M. Fowler, "Careers: Emergence of City Planning," *The New York Times*, 10 April, 1985.

CHAPTER 16

PROFESSIONAL PRACTICE AND EDUCATION

It is an axiom of planning that its scope is determined by the organizational jurisdiction of the person applying the process as part of his or her managerial control. In cities this means that comprehensive planning must be directed by someone organizationally and jurisdictionally concerned with the municipality as a whole.

T HEORETICALLY, COMPREHENSIVE city planning is concerned with every aspect of urban life and activity. It can be argued that all knowledge and every field of professional practice are involved in some way, directly or indirectly, at one time or another, intermittently or continually.

Since such universal participation is unrealistic, the professional fields actually involved are those that have to do with the conduct of planning for the municipality as a whole, and those that are concerned with the substantive content and planning of one of the elements taken into account in comprehensive planning in practice. Public administration and urban and regional planning are the two professional fields associated with the process of overall municipal management and comprehensive city planning. Engineering, economics, law, architecture, landscape architecture, and medicine are professional fields closely involved with its components.

The primary focus of *public administration* is on governments and their effective functioning. In its early years the field emphasized the managerial and administrative aspects of executing public policy, primarily within the context of specific government organizations. While retaining this emphasis as one of its concerns, public administration now

public administration

197

addresses broader matters including: the formulation of public policy in the three branches and numerous agencies of government; special non-bureaucratic and not-for-profit means of delivering public services; and the efforts of private enterprise to resolve societal problems. (Clayton, 1985)

Accordingly, public administration has to do with all directive positions and personnel in municipal government. Although the elected members of city councils and an elected mayor may be more politically than managerially concerned, they exert a pervasive influence on the administrative organization and conduct of municipal affairs. But the diversity of their backgrounds precludes a particular professional classification. The most influential of the officials in larger municipalities in the United States—normally appointed rather than elected—are the City:

Manager/Chief Administrative Officer
Clerk
Finance Director
Controller
Auditor
Treasurer
Engineer
Director of Public Works
Superintendent of Streets
Fire Chief
Police Chief
Planning Director
Chief Personnel Officer
Attorney
Health Officer
Director of Parks and Recreation
Superintendent of Parks
Director of Recreation
Librarian
Superintendent of Schools
Director of Data Processing
Director of Budget and Research
Assistant Manager/Assistant Chief Administrative Officer
Chief Building Inspector

It is an axiom of planning that its scope is determined by the organizational jurisdiction of the person applying the process as part of his or her managerial control. In cities, this means that comprehensive planning must be directed by someone organizationally and jurisdictionally concerned with the municipality as a whole: the city council or one of its standing committees, the city manager or chief administrative officer, or the mayor when he or she exercises managerial authority as well as political influence.

The city manager, chief administrative officer, or the mayor in a strong-mayor form of municipal government is the operational focal point for comprehensive city planning, responsible for implementing the policies, operational decisions, and laws enacted by the governing body organizationally above. At the same time, he or she is responsible for coordinating the planning and activities of the operating departments administratively below.

City managers act as *staff* to municipal governing bodies which make the final decisions: providing its members with the information, analysis, and recommendation they request or need, and carrying out their policies, decisions, and directives.   *staff*

City managers, chief administrative officers, and mayors also formulate and propose policies and legislation to the city council. They are in a particularly favorable position to implement those of their proposals that are accepted and formalized as council directives or municipal legislation. One of these officials also acts in a *line* capacity as chief executive of the municipal operating departments and agencies, overseeing their planning and performance. The degree to which these units are responsive to this executive authority depends on whether provisions of the legislation governing their operations give them a degree of independence, or the extent to which they maintain direct contact with the city council and thereby circumvent the chief executive officer.   *line*

In 1983, there were more than 45,000 *municipal officials* in some 7,000 cities in the United States of over 2,500 population, including a number of smaller communities with recognized council–manager forms of government. Almost 11,000 of these officials are mayors or municipal administrators potentially capable of conducting comprehensive city planning. An additional 3,300 planning directors act as staff to the chief executive officer of the city or its governing body. If municipal governing bodies are assumed to have an average of six members, there are also 35,000 elected representatives who could take the lead in establishing or improving comprehensive planning by municipalities. (International City Management Association, 1983)   *municipal officials*

salary   In 1984, the average *salary* of municipal officials closely
involved with the comprehensive planning process was
approximately:

> City Manager, $42,000
> Director of Budget and Research, $40,000
> City Engineer, $35,700
> Assistant City Manager, $35,600
> Planning Director, $35,300
> Director of Data Processing, $34,300

The average salary of the remaining 18 municipal officials listed
in the Baseline Data Report of the International City Management Association was $30,250, ranging from a high of $46,700
for Superintendent of Schools to $22,500 for City Clerks. (Inter-
national City Management Association, 1984)

education   These public officials possess a wide range of *educational
backgrounds*. Elected representatives are probably the most
diverse in this respect. The education of appointed officials
varies with different departments. As would be expected, engineering is the educational background of most city engineers,
public works directors, chief building inspectors, and other
positions requiring technical knowledge. A law degree and
certification to practice law are required for city attorneys. Health
officers are usually physicians. Public administration is the most
common educational background for municipal directors of
personnel, purchasing, civil service, and other operating
departments that require general managerial competence more
than technical knowledge. It is also the background of most
city managers and chief administrative officers who are in the
best position to exercise primary responsibility for comprehensive city planning. In addition, many professional specialists
such as fire and police officials, engineers, or school supervisors undertake postgraduate adult education in public administration to broaden their knowledge, improve their managerial
competence, and otherwise prepare for higher executive
positions.

More than 6,350 graduate degrees in public administration
were awarded in 1984 by 186 accredited programs of graduate
education: 70 of these within departments of political science,
64 in separate departments within larger educational units, 36

in professional schools, and 16 in departments combining public administration and another professional discipline. More
than three-quarters of these were master's degrees in public
administration, 12 percent were masters of art or science with
a major in public administration, the remainder were masters
degrees in urban, public, and international affairs, and urban
and regional planning. In addition, almost 150 doctor of philosophy degrees or professional doctorates were awarded. This
education was acquired by an almost equal number of men and
women; two-thirds of them were employed part-time while
studying, reflecting the close and continuing relationship
between education and practice in public administration.
(National Association of Schools of Public Affairs and Administration, 1984)

Local, state, and federal governments *employed* more than   *employment*
one-half of these graduates with master's degrees. Positions in
quasi-governmental agencies, business, and industry accounted
for an additional one-quarter. Foreign students are well represented because of the great need for capable public administrators and middle managers in developing countries around
the world.

There are almost as many professional *organizations* repre-   *organizations*
senting different public officials as there are different activities
and administrative positions involved in municipal government, ranging from associations of fire and police chiefs to
those of hospital administrators and librarians. The most
important for comprehensive city planning are the International City Management Association, American Planning
Association, Municipal Finance Officers Association, and
American Society for Public Administration. In addition to these
associations of professional practitioners, there are organizations representing different governmental groups, including
municipalities, cities, towns and townships, counties, regional
councils, community affairs agencies, port and airport authorities, states and state legislatures, and school boards.

Practitioners of *urban and regional planning*, the second of the   *urban and*
two fields most directly involved in comprehensive city plan-   *regional*
ning, normally perform as staff to the line executives or the   *planning*
executive bodies that conduct land use planning for the activity
or jurisdiction they control. As staff planners, their line author-

ity is limited to employees within their own office or department who report directly to them.

employment   For the most part, *employment* in urban and regional planning in the United States today is in government or is dependent on it. Usually, these positions include the word planning in a wide range of descriptive titles, such as:

Director of Planning	Economic Development Planner
Chief of Current Planning	Community Planner
Director of Planning Data	Neighborhood Planner
Zoning Administrator	Historic Preservation Planner
Principal Planner	Engineer Planner
Urban Planner	Transportation Planner
Regional Planner	Traffic Planning Specialist
Environmental Planner	Transit Planner
Physical Planner	Planning Analyst
Land Planner	Planning Technician
Project Planner	Planner Landscape Architect
Research Planner	Urban Designer

Like their counterparts in public administration, many urban and regional planners in the United States are employed in local, state, or federal governmental agencies. Approximately one-third are associated with non-governmental regional planning organizations or private consultant firms.

Of those employed by government, the largest group of some 3,500 people work for cities; approximately half this number are associated with city, county, and state governments, and one-quarter with metropolitan and regional organizations. A small group of planners work for agencies of the federal government and joint city–county governmental bodies engaged in some form of metropolitan planning activity.

These public agency planners work in places almost equally divided between cities of 250,000 population and over, communities from 50,000 to 250,000, and those under 50,000 people. They define the jurisdictions of the agencies for which they work as 58 percent urban, 26 percent suburban, 16 percent rural, and 4 percent mixed; 84 percent are therefore engaged in city planning as considered in this book. Nearly 41 percent of these hold the position of director of planning.

Most urban and regional planners not employed in government are associated with private planning consulting firms, but a large share of their work is producing special studies for governmental planning bodies. Some 750 planners are working for business, colleges and universities, and non-profit and other organizations.

The median *salary* of all respondents to a 1983 American *salary* Planning Association national survey of practicing urban and regional planners was $30,000. As would be expected, the median salary varied with experience: $21,250 for the 18 percent or so with four years or less in practice, $29,500 for the 44 percent with between five and ten years experience, and $40,000 for those with more than eleven years experience. One-fifth of urban and regional planners are women, whose salary levels and employment positions have not yet caught up with those of their male counterparts. (Hecimovich, Butler, 1984)

Of the colleges and universities offering undergraduate and *education* graduate *education in urban and regional planning* in the United States, 109 are members of the Association of Collegiate Schools of Planning. Some 70 of these offer professional two-year master's degrees "recognized" by the American Planning Association after review of faculty, curriculum, and facilities. By the end of 1980, a total of 20,833 master's degrees and 932 Ph.D.s had been awarded. Two-thirds of these master's were awarded by 25 of the 59 recognized graduate programs in the United States, and almost the same percentage of the Ph.D.s by 6 of the 21 universities offering this advanced degree. Based on the academic year 1982–1983, almost 2,000 newly graduated urban and regional planners with master's degrees in this field and 80 with Ph.D.s are introduced into the labor market each year. (Sawicki, 1983)

Some graduate programs offer dual degrees with related fields of study closely involved in urban and regional planning. The fields include public administration, business administration, economics, social work, gerontology, urban design, landscape architecture. Since several basic courses apply equally to urban and regional planning and each of these associated disciplines, the dual professional master's degrees can be obtained with only one more semester than is required for each separately.

Years ago, the educational background of graduate students in urban and regional planning was almost exclusively architecture and landscape architecture. Today these graduate students come from a wide variety of educational backgrounds: including engineering, economics, political science, sociology, geography, law, mathematics, and history. Although both educational background and curriculum reflect a broadening scope in recent years, most graduate programs in urban and regional planning are concerned with physical land use planning rather than truly comprehensive planning. Also, despite the inclusion of the word "regional" in the name of almost all programs and academic degrees, curricula emphasize urban planning more than the subject matter, analysis, and planning of regions.

association   Most urban and regional planners belong to their own *professional association*: the American Planning Association (APA) with over 20,000 members. The American Institute of Certified Planners (AICP) is part of APA and is composed of some 5,000 members whose professional competence has been established by a written examination and review of education and experience. Urban and regional planners are likely to belong also to the professional association corresponding to their initial educational background or continuing major interest or emphasis within the field of planning. Such associations exist for just about every area of special interest.

The salary range for public administrators and urban and regional planners is still below that for comparable positions in private enterprise, although this difference is being reduced gradually by personnel policies calling for equal compensation for comparable positions in government and in business and industry. This equalization is likely to continue as the complexity of government increases.

Some public administrators and urban and regional planners are employed by private enterprise in the same functional positions they would be qualified to hold in government. They may be the ablest of those seeking the position. If they have studied government as part of their graduate education and perhaps worked in government, this knowledge and experience may be useful to private enterprises doing business with public bodies. A steady stream of higher ranking public officials transfer to business on or before retirement for precisely these reasons. Some business organizations utilize the same information and knowledge for certain of their operations that are required for certain aspects of city planning. For example, utility companies need demographic, land use, and local planning information to forecast future demand and determine precisely where utility lines and facilities will be located. The socioeconomic data on urban areas needed by banks for investment decisions is much the same as that required by municipalities for land development and redevelopemnt policies, proposals, and action programs.

There are some limitations particular to professional planning as now practiced in government. As noted at the beginning of this chapter, public administrators are subject to the decisions and directives of the city council when they are city managers, or to the instructions of the city manager when they are subordinate municipal department heads. But they exercise managerial authority over any organizational units they direct.

Urban and regional planners are employed for the most part *staff* as *staff* personnel, conducting studies and making recommendations for the municipal officials or executives for whom they work. When they are directors of planning staffs or departments, they act as staff to their superiors, and as line executives for the employees within their organization. For most urban and regional planners, this important supportive role fulfills most closely and immediately their professional education. For those planners who are not content functioning as staff and have the necessary motivation and capabilities, there are many positions in municipal government that involve executive or supervisory responsibilities and authority. In a high enough position, the urban and regional planner as a *line* executive in *line* charge of an operational activity may be supported by another professional planner as staff to provide the background information and analysis needed. In city planning, as well as in other activities, optimum performance results from matching personal motivation and capabilities with organizational position.

Staff positions are not "inferior" because it is line executives who accept, reject, modify, and act upon staff recommendations. Staff personnel in government

. . . . are not elected, but their views, many in government say, often carry more weight than the views of those who are. They negotiate bills, are sought out eagerly by lob-

byists and, on occasion, float proposals on behalf of the
leadership . . .

It is widely recognized that with the growth of larger,
full-time staffs over the last two decades, senior staff members are often in a far better position to know the depth
and breadth of a vast range of issues than many of the
lawmakers. . . .

It is not the budget alone over which the staff exerts
influence. Indeed, over vast areas of state policy key staff
people are often the driving force behind new legislation. . . .

States and cities [have been required] to administer things
they never administered before. State and local governments became the fastest growing sector of the economy.
(Gargan, 1985)

Employment in the public sector appeals to those who derive
greater satisfaction from association with the general public
interest than maximizing profits in private enterprise. Management competence is required in both instances, but the
underlying motivation and objective of the two types of endeavor
and organization are different. Also, the personalities of those
who choose each of these areas of endeavor tend to be different.

Comprehensive city planning is inherently stimulating. It
incorporates more of the myriad aspects of individual human
existence and societal activity than any other application of
planning. No private enterprise or single project of any kind
involves equal diversity. Planning at the higher levels of government does not require the same specificity needed at the
local level, where actions have a direct impact on the individual
and details must therefore be thought through. Developing an
analytical construct or "model" that represents or "simulates"
this complexity, diversity, and detail is one of the most difficult
intellectual tasks confronting human society. Progress in developing such an analytical construct will be intellectually significant, far beyond its use in comprehensive city planning.

Regardless of the particular political system in power or the
role of private enterprise, recent societal developments
throughout the world confirm that enlightened government is
the most critical requirement for the survival of the human

species. Fortunately, the intellectual challenge and operational importance of comprehensive city planning are sufficiently stimulating and personally rewarding to attract capable candidates to this field as a career. To fulfill completely its promise, comprehensive city planning will require the brightest and best balanced educational candidates.

CITATIONS

[1] Clayton, Ross, Personal Communication, February 1985. [2] Gargan, Edward A., "Staffs in Albany Wield Strong Unelected Power," *The New York Times*, 2 February 1985, p. Y 13. [3] Hecimovich, James and JoAnn C. Butler, *Planners' Salaries and Employment Trends, 1983*, Chicago, IL (American Planning Association), Planning Advisory Service Report Number 382, February 1984, 18 pp. [4] International City Management Association, *Baseline Data Report*, Washington, DC, March 1984, p. 2. [5] International City Management Association, *The Municipal Year Book, 1983*, Washington, DC, 1983, p. 297. [6] National Association of Schools of Public Affairs and Administration, *Programs in Public Affairs and Administration, 1984 Directory*, Washington, DC, 1984, 261 pp. [7] Sawicki, David (Editor), *Guide to Graduate Education in Urban and Regional Planning*, Atlanta, GA (Association of Collegiate Schools of Planning), 1984, pp. 1-81.

SELECTED REFERENCES

[1] Caiden, Gerald E., *Public Administration*, Pacific Palisades, CA (Palisades Publishers), 1982, 321 pp. [2] Eddy, William B. (Editor), *Handbook of Organization Management*, New York (Marcel Dekker), Chapters 2, 3, 5 and 6, 1983, 548 pp. [3] Harlow, LeRoy F. (Editor), *Servants of All*, Professional Management of City Government, Provo, UT (Brigham Young University), 1981, 362 pp. [4] Krueckeberg, Donald A. (Editor), *The American Planner, Biographies and Recollections*, New York (Methuen), 1983, 433 pp. [5] Mosher, Frederick C. (Editor), *American Public Administration: Past, Present, Future*, University, AL (University of Alabama), 1977, 298 pp. [6] Municipal Management Assistants of Southern California, *A Guide to Public Management Careers for the 1980s*, Pasadena, CA (Center for Public Resources), April 1983, 59 pp. mimeo. [7] Perloff, Harvey S., *Education for Planning: City, State, & Regional*, Baltimore, MD (Johns Hopkins), 1957, 189 pp. [8] Ries, John C. , *Executives in the American Political System*, Belmont, CA (Dickenson), 1969, 151 pp.

Chief executives of 141 companies polled . . . say they want to spend more time on planning and development but less on administrative duties.

Joann S. Lublin, *The Wall Street Journal*, 12 July, 1983.

From the earliest days we saw that our assignment [The USAF Ballistic Missile Program] would demand a new kind of specialized planning to coordinate the myriad elements involved in our program. This specialized planning provided us with the foundation of our newer management concept, the concept of concurrency . . . moving ahead with everything and everybody, all together and all at once, toward a specific goal.

Major General Bernard A. Schriever, USAF, *The United States Air Force Report on the Ballistic Missile, 1958.*

CHAPTER 17
RELATED PLANNING

Because of its emphasis on planning, the breadth of its activities, the diversity of subject matter with which it is concerned, and the monetary support it receives for research and development, the military establishment will continue to advance means and methods of comprehensive planning that can be applied to municipalities. Business planning can be expected to affect comprehensive city planning in similar ways.

SINCE PLANNING is a universal process inherent in all human activity ranging from simple household tasks to large complex projects, advances in one type of planning activity can usually be employed in another area of application. Such dissemination of general knowledge among different uses has been going on since earliest times. Over the years city planning has benefitted from military planning, corporate business planning, and project planning.

Far more in the past than today, the overall form of cities was shaped by the need for defense against land attack. Primitive settlements were encircled by a ring of thorn bushes or a palisade and ditch. Such rudimentary defenses are still found in parts of the world today. Most medieval cities were protected by a rampart or wall. During Renaissance times, peripheral defenses in Europe became so extensive and elaborate that in at least one instance they covered more ground area than the area occupied by the built-up city they protected. *defense*

Except for a few outposts during the opening up of the West, the form of cities in the United States was never determined by peripheral protection. Also, aircraft and missiles have made such defensive features irrelevant in the overall form of cities today, including those in Europe and Asia with extensive civil defense facilities underground. However, "hardening" critical urban communication centers against the destructive *effects*

military planning

effects of nearby explosions and shielding electronic devices against electromagnetic radiation from nuclear explosions high overhead are being effected. New communities in the United States have been built for military purposes, such as those housing support personnel for isolated intercontinental ballistic missile and early-warning radar detection sites. *Military planning* and the national defense budget have a direct impact on the municipal economy of many American cities because of the vast number of facilities required to arm, house, feed, clothe, transport, and entertain the many military forces.

Besides the procurement planning required to obtain this array of products and services, the military are engaged at all times in many kinds and levels of planning relative to possible conflicts. Since war can come suddenly with potentially catastrophic consequences, time is of the essence. Plans must be prepared well in advance of hostilities to make possible the accumulation and organization of people, machines, and supplies involved in military operations. They range from broad strategic plans to detailed operational plans.

strategic plans

The U.S. Joint Chiefs of Staff are responsible for numerous *strategic plans*, concerning joint objectives, logistics, and integrated mobilization plans, combined plans for joint military action with other nations, and general policies and doctrines for the preparation of plans by the individual departments of the military establishment. The strategic directive of the Joint Chiefs to General Dwight Eisenhower during World War II

> to enter the continent of Europe and, in conjunction with other Allied Nations, undertake operations aimed at the heart of Germany and the destruction of her forces

created a military organism that ultimately integrated the largest number of component military plans ever welded into a single comprehensive operational plan for the biggest military operation undertaken up to that time: the invasion of Normandy (Branch, 1983). The planning, programming, and budgeting process noted later in this chapter

> . . .starts with the Joint Strategic Objectives Plan prepared by the Joint Chiefs of Staff organization with the help of the military planners in the services (Hitch, 1965).

Military strategic plans are generally comparable to the policies portion of comprehensive city plans.

Military *operations plans* are directed toward fixed objectives set by a higher command, such as the capture of a particular place on a certain day, or at a designated time set by weather, past or potential enemy actions, or other known circumstances. *operations plans*

> Once an execution order is approved, ground and air components are alerted, plans for overseas are raised to the action level and standing plans are modified into operations orders. Men, tanks, guns and planes are part of a joint operations planning system that prescribes standardized terms and procedures for development and execution of operations plans. (Middleton, 1977)

Military operations plans are comparable to the operating plans of municipal departments discussed in Chapter 9 and to project plans described later in this chapter. Both strategic and operations plans are revised as existing conditions change and new considerations must be taken into account.

The evolution of military planning over the years has contributed to comprehensive city planning in specific ways, as well as demonstrating the importance of the planning process in general. But usually military achievements cannot be applied with equal effectiveness in civil government. The absolute command and control exercised in the military services is not possible in municipal affairs, and the funds available to the military far exceed municipal budgets that do not meet even the most pressing local needs.

Although supportive and directive roles for people have long been differentiated, *staff* and *line* positions were formalized by the military. They also introduced the concept of a *general staff* to prepare joint strategic plans and provide analyses that neither the separate military services nor commanding officers in the field have the information or the time to produce. Both of these developments contributed to the establishment of urban and regional planning and corporate business planning as staff activities supporting line officials. This was accompanied by greater recognition of the importance of strategic plans setting long-range goals and ways of gradually achieving them, together with operational plans directing short- *staff and line positions* and medium-range activities. Military planning has also emphasized the need to revise or reformulate plans completely when they are no longer applicable.

operations
research
Examination of intractable problems by *operations research* teams was initiated by the military during World War II. When the lifeline of supplies across the Atlantic Ocean from the United States to England was threatened by an intolerable loss rate from German submarines, it became imperative to determine what combination of convoy size and timing, disposition of available destroyer escorts and air cover, arming of merchant vessels, and selection of navigation routes would most likely reduce the disastrous loss rate. Expert knowledge was required concerning merchant ship, naval, and aircraft operations, submarine warfare, meteorology, statistical evaluation, and determination of probabilities. Equally essential members of the team were "generalists" who could perceive the problem as a whole, evaluate and integrate the most critical factors involved, and apply objective perceptions and creative thinking. Reducing the penetration of German bombers over England and maximizing the destructive effects of the strategic bombing of German installations on the Continent were examined in the same way. The team approach has been recommended as the best method of determining what comprehensive city planning can do to resolve some of the most serious urban problems.

control
centers
For years public and private utilities have used *control centers* to monitor and adjust the supply and demand for electricity within the distribution network. Oil refineries, chemical plants, and other continuous production systems have comparable control rooms. Beginning with the naval aircraft carrier, the military services have developed sophisticated command and control centers for strategic bomber, intercontinental ballistic missile, nuclear submarine, and other modern weapons systems. All of these are centers of *operations control*, but they can be designed for *planning* purposes, as was done 30 years ago for the research, development, and construction of the U.S. intercontinental ballistic missile system in a "control room" described as "an information center organized to promote the coordination, planning, and analysis of effort for top management." (Air Research and Development Commands, circa 1959)

The type of information and planning center for cities portrayed in Figure 13 (Chapter 9, page 114) will become in time an essential mechanism of top management. This is because most students of the conduct of government and business believe that what has been termed "seat of the pants" management is no longer feasible for the complex activities characteristic of large organizations today. Top officials need background information they do not have time to collect, and analyses of many kinds they have neither the time nor the inclination to conduct.

Aerial photography, radar imagery, and other forms of electromagnetic *remote sensing* were first developed by the military services. More cartographic, geographic, land use, environmental, and other information concerning physical features and systems on the earth's surface can be obtained for comprehensive city planning by this means than in any other way. Much socioeconomic data can also be collected in this way, but certain personal, economic, and financial information must be gathered by ground survey or census. Remote sensing was made possible by the large expenditures by the military services from funds available to them for research and development. This expenditure has reduced the cost of remote sensing for civilian purposes because commercial companies do not have to increase their charges to recover the costs of research and development. *remote sensing*

The military services have also contributed to management methods. One of these—*planning, programming, and budgeting* (PPB)—was described some years ago by a U.S. Secretary of Defense. *planning programming budgeting*

> [The] intellectual foundation for determining the military forces we should build and support.... is laid out first in the form of an analysis of the potential contingency war plans for a variety of situations and, then, a translation of those war plans into military forces. And finally, that structure must be translated into programs and budgets. (McNamara, 1966)

The military establishment will continue to contribute to the advancement of the means and methods of planning. Planning is an integral part of every military activity—activities so diverse that just about every aspect and type of planning is involved.

Funds are available for research and development. Preliminary results can be tested in actual operations under "field" conditions. Security restrictions delay the transfer of knowledge developed by the military services to the civilian world, but it becomes available eventually.

business planning *Business planning* can be expected to contribute to comprehensive city planning in similar ways. Business has always had to plan its operations to the extent necessary to function, make a profit, and survive. Until some 20 years ago, comprehensive planning was applied to projects, departments, divisions, or other components of a company. But chief executives continued to believe that they could plan for the company as a whole with minimum staff assistance; "seat of the pants" management was considered desirable and possible.

Business organizations have become larger, more complicated, more interdependent and sensitive to developments and events elsewhere in the nation and the world. Self-assurance has given way to recognition that the demands on chief executives are ever more numerous and critical. Too little time is left for planning, which chief executives consider their most important responsibility. As a consequence, most larger organizations in the United States have established planning positions, staffs, or departments reporting directly to the chief operating executive or board. These planning units provide the information and analysis top managers indicate they need to plan comprehensively for the company as a whole. Notices appear frequently in *The Wall Street Journal* and *The New York Times* announcing positions available as vice president, director, or manager of the corporate planning unit of well-known companies.

corporate planning Corporate planning has led to the adoption by many organizations of a planning cycle of seven years: the first year with every operation precisely budgeted, the next year with expected budget expenditures and programs of activity, and the following five years with projections of operational data and expected accomplishments. Some particular plans and operations are projected much further into the future, 60 years for tree farming, 10 years or more to complete most large construction projects or to produce new products representing the next state of the art. A strategic component of the plan expresses the general goals or new directions to be taken in the long-range future. The corporate plan composed of these several parts is maintained in a looseleaf notebook, as a series of computer printouts, or in a secure central computer file available on the display screens of designated executives.

> Planning with more distant horizons has become a familiar theme among major American businesses, especially those competing in global markets where foreign competitors, particularly Japanese trading companies, have used the technique to achieve big gains in market share. As a result, the old systems for rewarding American managers have to be adjusted to keep in tune with the new planning. It is critical, executives say, to shift the rewards from quarter-to-quarter profit gains to the achievement of longer term goals. (Hayes, 1981)

Business planning has progressed further than municipal planning in the computerization of operating and related background data. It has developed mathematical models that simulate the functioning of the business within its external environment. This permits calculating, in the dollar terms of the quantitative model, the probable consequences of the cancellation of a major sales contract or the effects of a contemplated decision in one aspect of the business on other elements. This can be done quickly, important for most businesses since they are subject to many unpredictable events that necessitate immediate changes.

Business made the first extensive use of *cost-benefit analysis*, *cost-benefit* in part because the benefits of specific business activities can be measured more accurately than those resulting from many of the public programs provided by municipal governments. Business was first to use the *Delphi* method of eliciting and *Delphi* cross-analyzing the judgment of experts evaluating subjects that cannot be measured by numbers and compared mathematically, or forecasting developments that cannot be extrapolated scientifically. Business has also devised methods of sampling people's reactions to products, designs, and concepts; these methods could be used as a form of "citizen participation" in city planning, employing a carefully selected sample of the population rather than the unrepresentative group which results from the open invitation usually extended.

Although certain basic differences exist between corporate business and comprehensive city planning, they are reduced as businesses take into greater account considerations once discounted by private enterprise: community relations, environmental impacts, occupational safety, fair employment practices, product liability, housing assistance for essential personnel, stricter accounting disclosure.

project planning   Both the military services and business undertake very large *project planning* involving hundreds of millions or several billion dollars, and hundreds of thousands of people directly or indirectly. During the 1960s,

> The United States Air Force ballistic missile program was the largest military development program ever undertaken in peacetime. Compared to previous programs, it involved many simultaneous technical advances. . . . (Schriever, 1958)

Since then, the nuclear submarine force operating around the world, the landing on the moon, and the space shuttle have been realized. The business sector in the United States and governments in other nations have produced a worldwide network of hundreds of millions of interconnected telephones. A global system of air transportation has been created with reliable aircraft, uniform or compatible flight rules, operating procedures, maintenance, intercommunication, scheduling, flight reservation, and a common language for flight control. There are noteworthy examples of the many thousands of impressive projects undertaken and completed.

systems engineering   *Systems engineering* was required to plan and realize these projects. The term was first applied to large military projects such as the intercontinental ballistic missile system. Like operations research, it uses the special knowledge of a wide range of experts. Quantification is the main method of analysis, and mathematical models are used extensively to correlate and project these numerical data. The systems engineering procedure commences with an exploratory phase during which the project or problem is defined or "structured." Next, all available data bearing on the matter at hand are collected and correlated.

All known options for resolving the problem or completing the project are investigated and reduced to the relatively few solutions that are most likely to succeed. This group of possible solutions is studied in detail and the best one selected for completion by executive management. This best solution is tested by means of a prototype or pilot project. Finally, production is monitored closely and modified as needed. The entire process may take 10 years or more, with planning and execution closely coordinated throughout the process.

> Systems engineering is not merely a technique for producing exotic hardware, it is a new way of approaching complex problems and organizing their solution.... Urban maladies are not isolated problems to be treated one by one but are seen to be bound up in the interwoven context of an environment steadily becoming more unmanageable and unlivable. (Lessing, 1968)

One of the particular management methodologies emerging from this experience is *critical path scheduling*. It identifies those steps or paths in the progressive sequence of operations that are "critical" because a number of previous and subsequent steps depend absolutely on them. An error in execution or delay at these crucial points will halt the entire project because they cannot be bypassed. Special attention is therefore given to these particular points or paths to avoid interrupting progress on the project. *critical path*

Besides its use in large construction projects and other complex production activities, critical path scheduling can be applied in comprehensive city planning to municipal capital works programming. This application is particularly important now that there is a backlog of necessary reconstruction of deteriorated municipal utility systems in the United States requiring the expenditure of billions of dollars over the next 10 to 20 years.

CITATIONS

[1] Air Research and Development Command, Western Division, *Control Room Presentation*, Los Angeles, CA (Air Material Command, The Ramo-Wooldridge Corporation), undated, circa 1959, p.1. [2] Branch, Melville C., *Comprehensive Planning, General Theory and Principles*, Pacific Palisades, CA (Palisades Publishers), 1983, p. 7. [3] Hayes, Thomas C., "Managers Adopt-

ing Long-Term Outlook," *The New York Times*, 1 November 1981, XII, 40. [4] Hitch, Charles J., "Development and Salient Features of the Programming System," in: Tucker, Samuel A. (Editor), *A Modern Design for Defense Decision*, A McNamara-Hitch-Enthoven Anthology, Washington, DC (Industrial College of the Armed Forces), 1966, p. 74. [5] Lessing, Lawrence, "Systems Engineering Invades the City," *Fortune*, January 1968, p. 155. [6] McNamara, Robert S., "The Foundation for Defense Planning and Budgeting," in: Tucker, Samuel A. (Editor), *supra*, pp. 34, 35. [7] Middleton, Drew, "Readiness Command Keeping Low Profile," *The New York Times*, 27 March 1977, p. 15. [8] Schriever, Major General Bernard, USAF, "The USAF Ballistic Missile Program," in: Gantz, Lt. Col. Kenneth F., *The United States Air Force Report on the Ballistic Missile*, Its Technology, Logistics and Strategy, Garden City, NY (Doubleday), 1958, p. 25.

SELECTED REFERENCES

[1] Argenti, John, *Corporate Planning*, A Practical Guide, London (George Allen & Unwin), 1968, 272 pp. [2] Branch, Melville C., *The Corporate Planning Process*, New York (American Management Association), 1962, 253 pp. [3] Churchman, C. West, *The Systems Approach*, New York (Delacourt), 1968, 243 pp. [4] Lockyer, K. G., *An Introduction to Critical Path Analysis*, London (Pittman & Sons), 1964, 111 pp. [5] Lyden, Fremont J. and Ernest G. Miller, *Planning Programming Budgeting*: a systems approach to management, Chicago (Markham), 1968, 443 pp. [6] Optner, Stanford L., *Systems Analysis for Business and Industrial Problem Solving*, Englewood Cliffs, NJ (Prentice-Hall), 1965, 116 pp. [7] Quattromani, Anthony F. (Editor), *Catalogue of Wargaming and Military Simulation Models*, Washington, D.C. (Organization of the Joint Chiefs of Staff), SAGAM 120-82, May 1982, 838 pp. [8] Ramo, Simon, *Cure for Chaos*, Fresh Solutions to Social Problems Through the Systems Approach, New York (McKay), 1969, 116 pp. [9] Steiner, George A., *Strategic Planning: What Every Manager Must Know*, New York (Free Press), 1979, 383 pp.

CHAPTER 18

CONCERNING THE FUTURE

It is clear that comprehensive city planning is a difficult managerial undertaking and a complex analytical task. But it must be effected if cities in the United States are to avoid operational stalemate, environmental impairment, and socioeconomic deterioration.

RAPID URBANIZATION and an increase in the number of large cities continues throughout most parts of the world. In Africa as a whole, according to the World Bank, the number of people living in cities has doubled in the last 20 years, and the cities have grown twice as fast as overall populations. In 1960. . . . Africa had three cities of more than 500,000 inhabitants. Now there are 28. (*The New York Times*, 1984)

While such explosive growth is not occurring in the United States, metropolitan areas are expanding and increasing their populations. At the same time, most of their central cities are losing population.

During the past 20 years, central cities have been losing population steadily to their suburbs, and this phenomenon has been especially marked in the largest central cities, e.g. between 1970 and 1975, 39 of the country's 56 largest cities (over 250,000 population) lost population.

central cities

Another evidence of the decline of central cities in socioeconomic influence as well as population is the emergence of the polynucleated metropolitan area. In contrast to older metropolitan areas, consisting of a large or very large and dominant central city surrounded by a number of smaller dependent satellites, many metropolitan areas today feature a central city much less dominant and a number of other important socioeconomic centers outside the central city (but still within the metropolitan area).

As a result of these developments, central cities have become in large part repositories of populations "left behind," i.e. older persons, ethnic minorities, unemployed and underemployed persons, and others who could not for one reason or another make the preferred move to the suburbs. At the same time, central cities continue to be the preferred location for some other groups: older persons with grown children, smaller households, persons seeking cultural opportunities, etc. (Mars, 1981)

density and transportation   A measure of the effectiveness of comprehensive city planning will be whether it is possible to control the cycle of overbuilding that is characteristic of so many central cities in the United States today. A few private developers identify a market demand for more office buildings downtown; other developers "follow the leader" until the central area of the city is greatly overbuilt. There follows a period of years during which severe transportation congestion sets in. "Gridlock" may become a common occurrence: when automobile traffic becomes so tightly packed that it comes to a prolonged halt until enough space for movement can be found to clear blocked street intersections and gradually restore controlled movement. Comprehensive planning will not be successful until a balance is maintained— not only downtown but in other parts of the municipality— between the density of building permitted on the ground and the capacity of transportation systems to handle the traffic created by those working and shopping in the central city.

Business functions now conducted downtown may be decentralized to the suburbs where operating costs are lower, but also maintain immediate and constant electronic communication with the main offices of the organization remaining in the central city. Some people believe the computer is creating new "cottage industries" in the United States which will further decentralize business activity.

These urban developments underscore the need for effective city planning, especially for metropolitan urban concentrations. Without it, the severe problems now confronting larger cities can worsen to the point of economic collapse, social disintegration, even civil disorder. More and more urban problems and operating activities require planning and action at a metropolitan level, as discussed in Chapter 15. This applies to smaller communities with smaller surrounding tributary areas as well as to larger urban agglomerations.

The people who are both the reason for and ultimate polit- *demographic*
ical power determining the extent of city planning are changing *changes*
in several ways. The population of the United States is aging. At the turn of the century there will be 10 million more people over 65 than there were 30 years earlier. Ten years after the turn of the century the median age will also have risen to 35, an increase of six years in a quarter of a century. The population is also becoming more diverse. The black portion of the population will increase moderately, but Hispanics will become the largest minority in the country. Continuation of the present rate of immigration will increase the number and size of ethnic minorities, many of them living in larger cities.

The number of dwelling units needed to house the population has increased as single-parent households multiply and more people live alone. More elderly parents and grandparents will be expected to live separately and fend for themselves. Unless average income is reduced, families are expected to change their place of residence within and between municipalities as frequently as they have in the recent past.

These demographic changes affect municipalities and city planning in many ways. Public facilities and services are designed and operated with regard to the age and other characteristics of the people for whom they are intended. The number and size of the dwelling units needed to house people relates to the composition of the family and the number of individuals living alone. The political attitudes of people and the political power of organizations representing age groups vary with the age and size of the membership. Social satisfaction also varies with age. The elderly are most concerned with housing, social services, and medical care. Adolescent contentment relates primarily to recreation, athletics, diversion, and social contacts.

Neighborhood satisfactions, dissatisfactions, political attitudes, and voting can change rapidly since city dwellers in the United States move their place of residence approximately every five years. By the time the municipality responds to the expressed needs and wants of a particular section of the city, they may have changed because the residents of the area are no longer the same. Longer range planning for transient areas cannot be based on the judgments and desires of their residents if they are being replaced by another demographic group that will respond differently.

federal
impact The federal government, which has provided up to 30 percent of the annual expenditures of some cities, is reducing its direct monetary support. But the influence it has exerted on municipalities and their planning over the past half century will not disappear. Federal promotion of more effective planning at the local level will continue in one way or another, and specific federal programs relating to highways, sanitation, waste disposal, medical care, social security, and many other activities will continue to affect the local scene. Broader mandates such as those imposed by environmental protection legislation will shape the content and means of city planning.

More revenue sharing by the federal government is being channeled through the state government. As almost always is the case: "He who pays the piper calls the tune." States are exercising greater direction and control of local government, deliberately as a matter of policy and planning, or as a consequence of many incidental requirements casually imposed without consideration of their cumulative effect. A state may not only require that every municipality maintain a master plan, but that it include certain elements and be reviewed for adequacy by a state agency. Also, various operating departments of state governments affect comprehensive city planning in the course of their regular activities. Most recently, as noted in Chapter 10, coastal commissions in a number of states preempt local decisions concerning land use within a given distance from the coast.

State and federal governments establish two environments within which city planning takes place. Private enterprise comprises another, more important in the United States than most other countries. International events may be significant for larger cities with business enterprises linked with foreign lands through sales, raw material or product imports, financial ties, or some other connection.

basic
problems The basic problems of cities have always existed and will not disappear in the future. It will remain as difficult as ever for municipalities to obtain the money needed to function prop-

erly. Increases in taxes, licenses, fees, fines, and other sources of municipal income are always resisted. Nonetheless, the body politic invariably wants new or improved public facilities and services. Urban densities at the center of the larger cities in the United States are destined to increase as they have in cities elsewhere in the world, since there are no restrictions that relate the intensity of building permitted downtown to the capability of existing transportation systems.

"Affordable" housing is a critical urban problem that has existed through the ages. Despite a declining national birth rate, the population of the United States will continue to increase for some time. The birth and survival rates of those with low incomes remain high. Legal and illegal immigration shows no sign of diminishing. More dwelling units are needed for more people living alone and as separate households. The shortage of affordable housing will increase, all the more since there are no policies and programs to reduce the shortage commensurate with the worsening problem. Although "the poor always ye have with you," the proportion of the population in this category is increasing. And to those with incomes below the "poverty line" must be added the "housing poor" who cannot find adequate housing even with their higher incomes. The United States is experiencing the growing disparity between higher and lower income groups—the "haves" and the "have nots"—that is conspicuous in many cities around the world. *affordable housing*

Rising costs of money, urban land, construction, and the requirements imposed on the developer by the municipality as conditions of approval add to the difficulties of improving the situation. Further reduction appears inevitable in the average space and appurtenances in the dwelling unit that middle and lower income groups can afford. Fewer of those who live in cities will be able to afford single-family detached houses. There will be increasing urban economic pressure to convert low-density land uses to the "highest and best" uses, which means higher density development and a higher average height of buildings throughout the community. The proportion of renters and owners of apartment condominiums will be more like that existing in most cities outside the United States.

The necessity of eventually renewing or replacing all of the physical facilities and installations in a city remains a mammoth *infrastructure* economic challenge, but also an opportunity to gradually and progressively reshape the physical city. This can be done only if there is effective and continuing comprehensive city planning over a period of a half century or more with consistent policies and a minimum of contradictory actions—admittedly a difficult if not impossible task when

> . . . the structure and habits of democratic states . . . lack those elements of persistence and conviction which alone give security to humble masses; . . . even in matters of self-preservation, no policy is pursued for even 10 or 15 years at a time (Churchill, 1948).

A considerable period of consistent policy, planning, and action is required to make progress toward resolving many urban problems. All too often this is not available because politics intrude, administrations are replaced, or priorities change.

land use controls   Land use controls by local government will be established where there are none now; they will be made more restrictive where they are unduly permissive, and they will likely be extended or tightened where they exist in full force. This is less a matter of choice than necessity. If the coverage of land with buildings and accompanying population density are not controlled and kept in balance with the public utility systems to which they are connected, either the existing utilities must be enlarged at the high cost of reconstruction, or new installations must be constructed in completely built-up areas.

Controlling incompatible land uses is also required to maintain or improve environmental quality, necessary for public health and desirable for general public satisfaction and enjoyment. Land use and transportation are linked inextricably. Land uses involving dense concentrations of people can quickly overburden adjacent streets unless they were designed for the heavier traffic. From a broader view of the city, the disposition of commercial, industrial, governmental, residential, and other land uses affects the number and length of commuter trips to work and the transportation system required to accommodate them without costly congestion.

municipal activities   Municipal governments will participate increasingly in land development once considered the exclusive province of private enterprise. Attitudes are changing concerning the ways in which municipalities should benefit from land development within their jurisdiction, and the extent to which they should share in the substantial profits derived from such development. Equally compelling is the necessity of finding additional sources of income for municipal operations. An opportunity is also presented for the municipality to attain certain public objectives otherwise difficult to achieve, such as requiring a percentage of lower cost dwelling units in residential developments, the dedication of land for a growing list of public purposes, or the inclusion of specific design features to improve the environmental quality of the project. In time, municipal governments in the United States will probably follow the lead of most other nations and undertake development projects now left to private enterprise, incorporating the development and operating profits in the municipal budget. Project construction will continue to be performed by private contractors.

The conduct of comprehensive city planning should advance in several ways. A more fully developed analytical simulation of the city and its external environment will permit better determination of how a decision or event affects other elements of the community. This simulation should be part of a city center which provides information needed by municipal management, serves as the analytical and procedural focal point for comprehensive city planning, and displays the master city plan and the operating plans of municipal departments and agencies. An extensive use of computers is required in such a center. This may be difficult to achieve if the city chooses to increase the municipal bureaucratic voting block by employing more people, rather than acquiring more electronic equipment to increase the efficiency of personnel and enable them to perform analyses otherwise impossible. *simulation*

A corollary advance will be the adoption by municipalities of a plain coordinate system for all of the cartographic information each maintains relating to public utilities, transportation, property, zoning, and many other physical installations and features which must be located precisely in space. Recording these various locations by geographical coordinates permits their direct correlation. Computerization of the system not only permits this correlation, but facilitates keeping the information up to date and readily available. Before this system can be *cartographic coordination* established, some municipal departments must be persuaded to modify their cartographic methods and relinquish any vested interest in continuing to record locational information in exactly the same way.

multiple
action   City planning would be much more successful if both the government and the public would recognize that no major urban problem can be resolved by a single action or accomplishment. It is surprising how often proponents claim and the public believes that additional traffic lanes on a number of arterial streets will eliminate traffic congestion downtown, a few public housing projects for low-income people will contribute significantly to providing shelter for the poor, or reorganization of one inefficient municipal department will produce efficient municipal management. By their nature, major urban problems are complex and require multiple action.

Consider for example the problem of reducing traffic congestion downtown in a sizable city. Widening several major thoroughfares leading to the central city and staggering work times would help. Imposing a tax forcing an increase in parking fees and charging an access fee to drive a private automobile downtown would also help. Increasing the sales tax and imposing a use tax on private automobiles would reduce the number purchased and their use for commuting. Improving the municipal bus system or building a rapid rail transit network would relieve vehicular congestion on the streets by reducing the use of private automobiles. Restricting construction of additional commercial buildings downtown would ensure that there is no increase in employment in the central city with a corresponding increase in traffic. No one or two of these actions, each producing some relief, would by themselves reduce downtown traffic congestion significantly. Such an achievement would require the application of many of these remedial actions at the same time.

public
management   The two professional fields most directly concerned with city planning have evolved separately in education and practice. Public administration has emphasized shorter range operational management, urban and regional planning the longer range physical development of the city. Except for this difference in emphasis, both are concerned with planning and managing public organisms. It is becoming increasingly appar-

ent that shorter range administrative management, available resources, land use, and longer range spatial planning are primary elements involved in city planning that cannot be considered separately. Public administration and urban and regional planning are part of the theory and practice of public management.

The present separation of the two endeavors within most local governments in the United States is the result of historical circumstance. It is now a managerial anachronism. The city council, mayor, and city manager or chief administrative officer occupy positions signifying their institutional responsibility for the municipality as a whole; they are the organizational focal points for comprehensive city planning. Urban and regional planning as it is now conceived and practiced is one part of planning for the municipality as a whole. As city planning becomes a stronger directive force in municipal management, master city plans that are concerned mainly with land use and are peripheral to the main stream of city government and municipal planning are no longer feasible.

As a primary responsibility of municipal management, comprehensive city planning is concerned with all elements and aspects of urban activity. It is subject to the full range of societal situations and developments. For example, the political climate shapes the policies that can be adopted, the managerial decisions that can be made, and the operational actions that can be taken. The regional, state, national, and international economic and financial situations affect the economic health of the municipality and what it can undertake with available resources of people, time, and money. The increasingly predominant role of the mass media of communication influences city planning as well as every other aspect of government.

To the extent possible, most elected representatives avoid *elective* organized planning in favor of what has been termed "govern- *responsibility* ment by crisis." A considerable proportion of their time and attention is devoted to reelection or to aspiring and working toward higher office. Working full-time or performing well in the present position and the tasks at hand is the exception rather than the rule. Elected officials are reluctant to accept the responsibilities and exposure associated with comprehensive city planning. Their reelection may be jeopardized if voters identify them with planning policies and decisions that later prove mistaken or unpopular.

However, basic urban problems are intensifying and becoming conspicuous. Cities become more functionally and managerially complex. As a consequence, the body politic and special interest groups may begin to evaluate the performance of elected representatives according to their contribution to resolving fundamental urban problems, as well as according to whether their voting record supports a particular interest. Members of the city council and elected mayors may find it necessary to become more active and assume greater responsibility with respect to planning. Or they may limit their actions to broad policies relating to issues that cannot be avoided, and pass specific responsibility for city planning on to the city manager or his executive equivalent. In either event, the role and prospects of comprehensive city planning should be enhanced.

planning
practice
The practice of city planning varies widely among municipalities in the United States. Because urban problems in smaller communities are usually less severe than those confronting larger cities, political attitudes are likely to favor as little government as possible. City planning is an incidental part of municipal operations, limited in scope, informal, often conducted as a corollary duty by a city official with a different primary responsibility. Because minimum funds are allocated in the municipal budget for city planning, consultants are employed for any special studies needed. They may even prepare the master land use plan if one is required or desired. But it is the ongoing interest and continuing activity within the regular municipal government that will determine whether city planning achieves significant results.

To cope with the more serious problems and more dynamic forces associated with larger concentrations of people in limited space, planning in bigger cities considers the broader range of elements and aspects involved in its most highly developed form. The need for greater governmental activity to conduct the more complex operations of the larger municipality, and to identify and represent the general public interest, is recognized and accepted by the public and the political power structure. The city planning staff may consist of a hundred or more professional and clerical personnel requiring a substantial annual budget. City planning is identified as a distinct municipal activity with organized and formalized means and methods of operation.

Comprehensive city planning, as it has been discussed in this book, will be practiced in time first in larger municipalities, and later in smaller communities as technological and institutional development call for comparable sophistication at a smaller scale. As they grow and find that they need to expand their planning, smaller communities will look to the experience of larger cities for guidance.

Certain characteristics of the body politic that affect comprehensive city planning are constant considerations. There are not many people with altruistic motivations and active concern for the public interest. The main motivation of most people is self-interest. This is not the same as selfishness. Self-interest may be impelled by such deep-rooted drives as personal survival or the welfare of one's family. It may be specifically responsive to some proposal relating to one's home, place of work, journey to work, recreation, or any one of the many ways city planning affects the lives of those residing or employed in the community.

constant considerations

Reactions are more likely to be negative than positive. Most people do not have the time or the desire to follow the affairs of the municipal government and take note of those proposals and actions they approve. In industrialized societies today, a person's time is taken up increasingly with the activities and necessary paperwork of daily living. There is a human disinclination to bother to approve, but a ready willingness to disapprove and dissent.

As every elected representative and politically knowledgeable person knows, the strongest reactions of the citizenry occur when the home or another place closely involved in a person's life is threatened by a tax increase, a reduction in city services, a nearby change in zone, a street widening, or some other municipal proposal affecting the individual directly and personally. The threat may be real, imagined, or induced by some event or deliberate provocation by opponents.

Maintaining the monetary value of one's home is particularly vital since usually it is a person's largest investment and major asset. In some situations, avoidance of loss is readily transferred into reactions based on the desire for profit. The pocketbook has become a modern instrument of survival. Matters relating to schools, the safety of children, and public parks are of special concern. Crime has become a major issue in recent years. At any time, in city planning as well as any other activity of government, a random event or unexpected development of the moment can become a cause célèbre with a continuing impact far beyond its relative significance.

Most people are skeptical of new ideas and approaches to recognized problems. They are more comfortable with what is familiar or what they are accustomed to. They are skeptical, if not fearful, of change. Gradual rather than sudden change is most likely to be accepted. Above all, sudden change coming as a surprise is resisted.

Most people are more concerned with the present than the future, in contrast with the consideration of the future that is essential in all planning. People would rather deal with the certainties of today than the uncertainties of tomorrow. There are limits, therefore, to what they will knowingly and willingly forego today in favor of their own or someone else's benefit at some indefinite future time.

By no means are these human traits cause for inaction. They do, however, define the realities of the societal context within which planning operates. If human reactions and behavior are continually borne in mind, the vital contribution of comprehensive city planning can be realized. Plans are formulated and implemented in terms of the real human situation, its pace and its prospects.

It is clear that comprehensive city planning is a difficult managerial undertaking and a complex analytical task. But it must be effected if cities in the United States are to avoid operational stalemate, environmental impairment, and socioeconomic deterioration. Positive accomplishment will not only contribute to attaining the primary objective of city planning by improving the condition of communities and their inhabitants. It will have far-reaching consequences for the advancement of the technique of management and planning because the city is the best place to develop and test comprehensive planning theory and practice.

CITATIONS

[1] Churchill, Winston, The Second World War, *The Gathering Storm*, Boston, MA (Houghton Mifflin), 1948, pp. 17, 18. [2] Cowell, Alan, "An African Menu Tied to a Flight Schedule," *The New York Times*, 25 December 1984, p. 2. [3] Mars, David, "What's Ahead: A Look at Local Government in the Greater Los Angeles Area, 1981-2001," Los Angeles, CA (School of Public Administration, University of Southern California), Working Paper, 1981, 38 pp. mimeo.

ABOUT THE AUTHOR

Since 1966, Melville C. Branch has been Professor of Planning at the School of Urban and Regional Planning, University of Southern California in Los Angeles.

For almost a decade, he served in civil governmental planning as a Los Angeles City Planning Commissioner. For seven years he was Corporate Associate for Planning (West Coast) and a Member of the Senior Staff of TRW Inc., a large automotive, electronics, and aerospace manufacturing company. Early in his career he was on the staff of the U.S. National Resources Planning Board in the Executive Offices of President Franklin D. Roosevelt, and Director of The Bureau of Urban Research at Princeton University. Dr. Branch has been a member of the faculty at the University of Chicago and the University of California, Los Angeles. He has consulted for public and private organizations in the United States and abroad.

His graduate education includes a Doctor of Philosophy in Regional Planning from Harvard University, the first advanced degree in planning awarded in the world. He has received the Distinguished Service Award of both the Los Angeles and California Chapters of the American Planning Association.

At least three of his many publications are considered original contributions important in the development of planning as a field of knowledge and professional practice. *The Corporate Planning Process* (American Management Association, 1962) was the first book on comprehensive planning by business. *City Planning and Aerial Information* (Harvard University Press, 1971) was an expanded statement of an earlier book pioneering the use of remote sensing in city planning. *Comprehensive Planning: General Theory and Principles* (Palisades Publishers, 1983) is the first book in the literature of planning discussing common characteristics of this important directive process and principles of analysis and operation that apply whether it is conducted by civil government, business, or the military services. His *Planning Urban Environment* (Dowden, Hutchinson & Ross, 1974) is believed to be the first book on city planning in English translated into Russian and published in the Soviet Union (Stroyizdat, 1979).

INDEX

This index is designed to serve two purposes. It fulfills the need for page references to specific topics, places, and persons noted, mentioned, or discussed in the book. In addition, it is formulated to serve as a more general indication of the scope of consideration involved in comprehensive city planning. As a consequence, the treatment in the text of some topics referred to specifically in the index is brief: an inevitable consequence of the broad substantive coverage desirable in an introductory volume, together with the limitations on the length of such a book.